ABOUT THE AUTHOR

Lu K'uan Yu was born in C[...] disciple of two famous Ch'an m[...] presenting 'as many Chinese [...] that Buddhism can be preserved

RIDER

By the same author

Ch'an and Zen Teaching Second Series

Ch'an and Zen Teaching Third Series

Taoist Yoga

The Surangama Sutra (translation by Lu K'uan Yu)

Practical Buddhism

CH'AN AND ZEN TEACHING

FIRST SERIES

Lu K'uan Yu
(Charles Luk)

CENTURY
LONDON MELBOURNE AUCKLAND JOHANNESBURG

A Rider Book published in the Century Paperback series by
Century Hutchinson Ltd, Brookmount House, Covent Garden,
London WC2N 4NW

Century Hutchinson Australia (Pty) Ltd
PO Box 496, 16-22 Church Street, Hawthorn, Melbourne, Victoria 3122

Century Hutchinson New Zealand Ltd
32-34 View Road, PO Box 40-086, Glenfield, Auckland 10

Century Hutchinson South Africa (Pty) Ltd.
PO Box 337, Bergvlei 2012, South Africa

First published in 1960
Second impression 1969
Second edition 1970
Fourth impression 1975
Fifth impression 1975
This edition 1987

Printed and bound in Great Britain by
The Guernsey Press Co. Ltd, Guernsey, Channel Islands.

ISBN 0 7126 1711 6

To the Memory of

UPĀSIKĀ MARGUERITE LA FUENTE

of Les Amis du Bouddhisme

whose words of encouragement overcame the translator's hesitation when he began to translate Chinese texts in 1956.

We take refuge in Buddha,
We take refuge in Dharma,
We take refuge in the Saṅgha,
We take refuge in the Triple Gem within ourselves.

CONTENTS

PART IV

A Straight Talk on the Heart Sūtra

by Ch'an Master Han Shan

Foreword

THE Chinese character ch'an (or zen in Japanese) is the equivalent of the Sanskrit word dhyāna which means meditation, one of the six perfections (pāramitās). It has been wrongly used to designate the transmission of mind which the Tathāgata handed down to Mahākāśyapa and was introduced to China by the twenty-eighth Patriarch Bodhidharma. This transmission was outside of the expediences used by the World Honoured One when He expounded sūtras, and aimed at the direct pointing at the mind for the perception of self-nature and attainment of Buddhahood. Therefore, Ch'an is all-embracing whereas dhyāna-pāramitā is only one of the six modes of salvation. The difference between the Ch'an sect and different schools lies in that the former's aim is instantaneous enlightenment whereas the latter's object is gradual achievement of successive stages of sainthood before complete enlightenment. By enlightenment, the Ch'an masters did not mean anything short of actual attainment of the Dharmakāya itself.

Modern commentators have given rise to confusing interpretations of Ch'an or Zen and we have heard of Zen calligraphy, Zen painting, Zen music and Zen archery. If a master was asked to confirm the Zen nature of a piece of calligraphy or a painting, he would reply: 'The sword has gone long ago.' It is appropriate to quote here the following passage from the *Sayings of Chung Feng* (Chung Feng Kuang Lu):

> What is Ch'an? Ch'an is the name of mind,What is mind? Mind is the substance of Ch'an. Bodhidharma came from the West and expounded only the direct pointing at man's mind. At first, the term Ch'an was not used, but the outcome of this direct pointing was the subsequent awakening (of followers of the sect). In their questions and answers, that (which had no name) was referred to as Ch'an (for convenience's sake). However, Ch'an cannot be understood by learning or by a lucky chance. When the self-mind is realized, either speech or silence, and motion or stillness, is unexpectedly Ch'an. At the moment of this unexpected Ch'an, automatically the mind manifests itself. Thus we know that Ch'an does not stray from mind and that mind does not

stray from Ch'an. Ch'an and mind are, therefore, two names of the same substance.'

The aim of the Ch'an sect is to strip the mind of all feelings and passions for the purpose of disentangling it from the phenomenal so that the self-nature can return to its normal state and operate in the normal way without hindrance. With this in view, Ch'an masters rarely used those Buddhist terms found in all sūtras. For men are always prone to cling to the terminology which, in their quest for more learning and wider knowledge, can only stimulate their faculties of thought and intensify their discriminations. The masters taught their disciples to refrain from seeking enlightenment and Buddhahood, for the very idea of enlightenment and Buddhahood gave rise to the twin concept of reality of ego and reality of dharma which split their undivided whole into subject and object, the cause of their illusion and suffering. This is the reason why the usual terms found in sūtras are rarely found in Ch'an texts, which seem very strange and incomprehensible even to Buddhists of the other schools. Those texts are as obscure and incomprehensible as Nostradamus's Prophecies of world events and puzzled readers frequently put them aside for ever, after reading a few pages. No learned masters took the trouble of giving a clear explanation of or comprehensive commentary on the sayings of their enlightened predecessors. Even if they quoted ancient sayings when giving instruction to their own disciples, their commentaries varying from a sentence to an entire gāthā or poem, were equally obscure and confusing to beginners.

A few modern philosophers have been trying to link Ch'an with their own concepts and have even claimed that the ancient masters used totally meaningless words, shouts and other equally meaningless gesticulations, to enlighten their disciples. Obviously these words, shouts, roars of laughter, etc., seem meaningless to a discriminating mind but as soon as it ceases discriminating, it will find that they are full of meaning. For instance, Lin Chi's shouts had four different meanings, each appropriate for a particular case. Likewise, a roar of laughter or the showing of two hands wide open is full of meaning. If one applies one's discriminating mind to commenting on ancient sayings, one will behold only the finger instead of the moon which is actually pointed at.

We cannot, however, blame these masters for their seemingly obscure and abstruse sayings, because as soon as they used the terminology coined by the conditioned human intelligence, their disciples would cling to it, thus straying from the normal course of training. When a monk asked

Yun Men: 'What is Buddha?' the master, knew that the questioner's mind was stirred by the empty word 'Buddha' and, in order to disentangle it from the illusion of Buddha, replied: 'A toilet stick.' In this, there was no disrespect for the Enlightened One, as the reply served only to wash the deluded mind of the disciple from this impure conception, for the Buddha as conceived by a deluded mind could never be the pure Buddha, who is beyond description. This particular case should not, however, be generalized, for the reply was appropriate only for the question at that particular moment. For this reason, Yun Men forbade his disciples to record his sayings. Likewise, we cannot follow master Tan Hsia's example and burn wooden statues of Buddha. Tan Hsia realized that the moment was ripe for enlightening a deluded monk who clung to these statues and disregarded his self-natured Buddha. The monk was first shocked at the sight but when he understood the master's act, his eyebrows dropped and he was instantaneously awakened.

These words, sentences, shouts, roars of laughter, gesticulations and strokes of the staff are known as kung ans (kōan in Japanese), or concurrent causes suitable to provoke the awakening of those disciples whose minds are already disentangled from illusions and whose potentialities are activated to the full, ready to absorb the truth. For instance, when Hui K'o asked Bodhidharma to quiet his disturbed mind but was unable to show it to his master who then declared: 'So have I quieted your mind', the Chinese patriarch was instantaneously enlightened. This was a kung an which concurred with Hui K'o's enlightenment. Literally, kung an means dossier, case-record, public laws and regulations enforced for settling disputes and maintaining law and order. Likewise, all instructions given by the Buddha and Patriarchs to enlighten deluded people, are called the sect's 'Right Commands' or irrevocable guides to reveal the truth, and are known as Ch'an's kung ans. Po Yen said: 'When receiving (men of various) potentialities, the ancients were obliged to give them instructions which were subsequently called kung ans or concurrent causes.'

When men endowed with great potentialities which were responsive to kung ans became rare, the masters devised what we call hua t'ou to strip their disciples' minds of thoughts and discriminations so as to disentangle the same from seeing, hearing, feeling and knowing. Hua t'ou means the moment before a thought or mental word stirs the mind, and its English equivalent is ante-word or ante-thought. Hua t'ou is also a thought of itself, and since all thoughts are wrong, a hua t'ou is also an impure thought used as a device to arrest the thinking process. It is referred to as the precious Vajra king sword, a pointed concentration to cut down all thoughts and eventual visions which assail the meditator during his training. This single thought, fundamentally wrong, will disappear when it falls into disuse after elimination of the last subtle tenet of reality of ego and dharma.

We have pleasure in presenting in this Series One of Ch'an and Zen Teaching:

PART I. *Master Hsu Yun's Discourses and Dharma Words:*
1. Prerequisites of the Ch'an training.
2. The Ch'an training.
3. Daily Lectures at two Ch'an weeks.
4. The Master's arrival at Ts'ao Ch'i.

PART II. *Stories of Six Ch'an masters from The Imperial Selection of Ch'an Sayings* (Yu Hsuan Yu Lu).

PART III. *The Diamond Cutter of Doubts*, a Commentary on the Diamond Sūtra, by Ch'an Master Han Shan.

PART IV. *A Straight Talk on the Heart Sūtra*, by Ch'an Master Han Shan.

Master Hsu Yun's Prerequisites of the Ch'an training, Ch'an Training and Daily Lectures at two Ch'an weeks are very useful guides, not only for Western practisers of Ch'an but also for adherents of the sect in the East. In these chapters, all useful informations are given, and difficult terms and profound meanings are fully explained in abundant footnotes so that even a beginner can practise the Mind Dharma without a teacher.

The stories of ancient masters and their sayings quoted by Master Hsu Yun are found in the following Ch'an collections:

The Transmission of the Lamp (Ching Te Ch'uan Teng Lu),
Five Lamps Meeting at the Source (Wu Teng Hui Yuan),
Finger Pointing at the Moon (Shui Yueh Chai Chih Yueh Lu),
Imperial Selection of Ch'an Sayings (Yu Hsuan Yu Lu),
The Sayings of Ancient Masters (Ku Tsun Su Yu Lu),
Stories of Eminent Monks (Kao Seng Ch'uan), and
Stories of Eminent Upāsakas (Ch'u Shih Ch'uan).

The master quoted also some very interesting passages from the Śūraṅgama Sūtra (Leng Yen Ching) for meditators undergoing Ch'an training.

In order to acquaint readers with the Ch'an terminology and language of the uncreate, as Upāsaka P'ang Yun called it, 'The Master's Arrival at

Ts'ao Ch'i' is added after the first three chapters. In this fourth chapter, readers will find themselves in exactly the same Ch'an atmosphere as in the monasteries in China where the language of the absolute is spoken to reveal that which is inconceivable and inexpressible.

This chapter will take readers right into the heart of Ts'ao Ch'i, a district through which the Ts'ao stream still winds its course and where in A.D. 502 an Indian master erected Pao Lin (Precious Wood) monastery, predicting that some 170 years later a flesh-and-blood Bodhisattva would come there to turn the Wheel of the Supreme Vehicle. This Precious Wood was the source of the five Ch'an sects of China. Readers will follow master Hsu Yun who will lead them to the Ts'ao Ch'i Gate, the Monastery Gate, the Maitreya Hall, the Wei To Hall, the Han Shan Hall, the Buddha Hall, the Abbot's room and, finally, the Dharma Hall where Hui Neng sat on the Altar seat to expound the unsurpassed Dharma and liberated an unlimited number of living beings.

Master Hsu Yun was Abbot of Ku Shan monastery in Fu Chien (Fukien) Province. In 1934, one evening he beheld in his meditation the Sixth Patriarch, who said to him: 'This is the time for you to go back.' The next morning, the master said to his senior disciple Kuan Pen: 'My causal life is coming to an end. Yesterday I saw the Sixth Patriarch who called me back.' In the fourth moon of the same year, one night in a dream, he saw the Patriarch who thrice urged him to 'go back'. Some time later, he received from the provincial governor telegrams inviting him to come to Ts'ao Ch'i to take charge of the monastery of the Sixth Patriarch which was in the same deplorable condition as found by Han Shan over three hundred years before.

The Dharma words in this chapter have only one aim: the direct pointing at the mind for the realization of self-nature and attainment of Buddhahood according to the Transmission handed down by past Patriarchs.

My master, the Venerable Hsu Yun, was the son of Officer Hsiao Yu T'ang of Chuan Chou Prefecture, Fukièn Province. He was born at the hour Yin of the last day of the seventh month of the year K'eng Tsu in the twentieth year of Tao Kuang reign (26 August 1840 between 3 and 5 a.m.). His mother died immediately after his birth. At the age of 11 two little girls were selected for his wives but were later converted to Buddhism by their 'nominal' husband; after his father's death, the two young ladies, with his stepmother, entered a nunnery and became later two enlightened nuns. At 13, he already thought of 'leaving home', but was prevented by his father. At 19, together with a cousin, he ran away from his house and entered Ku Shan monastery where his head was shaved and he was given the name 'Ku Yen' with aliases Yen Ch'e and Te Ch'ing. At 28, he went to stay in a grotto for three years. At 30, he left the grotto and wandered from place to place seeking instruction. A master taught him to practise the hua t'ou: 'Who is dragging a corpse here?' At 43, he went to P'u T'o, thence to the Five Peaked Mountain. During his journey on foot, he was caught in a heavy snowfall, became gravely ill, and was twice saved by a beggar named Wen Chi, who gave him food. During his conversation with the beggar, the latter asked him some strange questions somewhat similar to those put to master Wu Chu (*see* story of Wu Chu, on page 139). The master was still unenlightened and did not realize that *Wen* Chi was but *Wen* Shu, the Chinese name of Mañjuśrī, who came to his rescue. After his journey to the Five Peaked Mountain, he went West and reached Lhasa, thence he continued his travels to Bhutan, India, Ceylon and Burma before returning to China, where he rebuilt many monasteries, including those of the founders of Ch'an sects. He also travelled extensively in Malaya and Thailand where his followers are numerous.

Master Hsu Yun was the Dharma successor to all the five Ch'an sects of China and is considered the right Dharma eye of the present generation. The number of his followers is very great and cannot be counted. His disciples are everywhere and include an abbot, monks and nuns in Hawaii.

PART II of the book contains the stories of six eminent Ch'an masters with their sayings, and describes the circumstances leading to their enlightenment. Readers will understand the meaning of the term 'kung an' after reading these stories. This Part II serves as prelude to longer stories which will be presented in our Series Two of Ch'an and Zen Teaching, in which all techniques and devices used by the ancients will be discussed in detail.

PARTS III and IV present respectively the Diamond Sūtra and Heart Sūtra with comprehensive commentaries by Ch'an master Han Shan, who wrote them after his own enlightenment in the sixteenth century. These two wisdom sūtras are indispensable to Ch'an practisers wishing to disentangle themselves from illusions so that the potentialities inherent in them can be activated to the full and they become ready for instantaneous awakening. It is impossible for us to have a chance to meet enlightened masters in this period of decline of the Dharma and these two sūtras will fill the gap.

It is true that some ancient masters urged their disciples not to read sūtras during their training, but as soon as the latter had been awakened they immediately began to read the whole Tripitaka which they could then understand from end to end. There were recalcitrant disciples who clung to the names and terms found in the sūtras and quoted them when arguing among themselves or with their teachers. Moreover, when a sūtra is not well explained and thoroughly understood, the excellent teaching is wrongly interpreted and can easily be more harmful than the demon's words. But nothing is more fallacious than the contention that sūtras can be dispensed with, especially in this period of decline of the Doctrine when enlightened masters are almost undiscoverable. Also misleading is the presumption that the rules of morality and discipline can be disregarded, for without morality and discipline the deluded man can indulge in discriminations and discernings and will thus be bound to return to the six worlds of existence.

PARTS II, III and IV are also preceded each by a Foreword giving useful explanations. All brackets are mine.

UPĀSAKA LU K'UAN YÜ.

Hongkong, 22 May 1959.

PART I

MASTER HSU YUN'S DISCOURSES AND DHARMA WORDS

I

Prerequisites of the Ch'an Training

(From the Hsu Yun Ho Shang Fa Hui)

THE object of Ch'an training is to realize the mind for the perception of (self-) nature, that is to wipe out the impurities which soil the mind so that the fundamental face of self-nature can really be perceived. Impurities are our false thinking and clinging (to things as real). Self-nature is the meritorious characteristic of the Tathāgata wisdom which is the same in both Buddhas and living beings. If one's false thinking and grasping are cast aside, one will bear witness to the meritorious characteristic of one's Tathāgata wisdom and will become a Buddha, otherwise one will remain a living being. For since countless aeons, our own delusion has immersed us in the (sea of) birth and death. Since our defilement has (already) lasted so long, we are unable instantly to free ourselves from false thinking in order to perceive our self-nature. This is why we must undergo Ch'an training. The prerequisite of this training is the eradication of false thinking. As to how to wipe it out, we have already many sayings of Śākyamuni Buddha and nothing is simpler than the word 'Halt' in His saying: 'If it halts, it is Enlightenment (Bodhi).[1]

The Ch'an sect from its introduction by Bodhidharma after his arrival in the East until after the passing of the Sixth Patriarch, spread widely all over the country and enjoyed great prosperity, unknown before and after that period. However, the most important thing taught by Bodhidharma and the Sixth Patriarch was only this: 'Expel all concurrent causes; do not give rise to a single thought.' To expel all concurrent causes is to lay them down.[2] Therefore, these two sentences: 'Expel all concurrent causes. Do not give rise to a single thought', are the prerequisites of Ch'an training. If these two sentences are not put into actual practice, not only will the training be ineffective, but also it will be

[1] The full sentence is: The mad mind does not halt; if it halts, it is Bodhi, i.e. enlightenment.
[2] In Ch'an terminology, 'to lay down causes or thoughts' is to lay down the heavy load of causes or thoughts to free the mind from defilement.

impossible to start it, for in the midst of causes which rise and fall, thought after thought, how can you talk about Ch'an training?

Now we know that (the sentences): 'Expel all concurrent causes. Do not give rise to a single thought' are the prerequisites of Ch'an training; how can we fulfil these prerequisites? Those of high spirituality are able to halt for ever the arising of a single thought until they reach (the state of) birthlessness and will thereby instantaneously realize enlightenment (bodhi) without any more ado. Those of lower spirituality will deduce the underlying principle[1] from facts[2] and will thoroughly understand that the self-nature is fundamentally pure and clean and that distress (kleśa)[3] and enlightenment as well as birth, death and Nirvāṇa are all empty names having no connexion whatever with self-nature; that phenomena are like a dream, an illusion, a bubble and a shadow; and that the four basic elements constituting the physical body, as well as mountains, rivers and the great earth which are within self-nature, are just like bubbles in the sea. These phenomena rise and fall following one another in succession without interfering with the essence (of self-nature). Therefore, one should not follow illusion in its creation, stay, change and annihilation and give rise to feelings of joy, sadness, attachment and rejection. One should lay down everything with which one's body is burdened, thus becoming exactly like a dead man. The outcome will be that sense-organs, sense-data and consciousness will vanish and that concupiscence, anger, stupidity and love will be eliminated. When all our feelings of joy and sadness, of the cold of hunger and the warmth of one's fill, of honour and dishonour, of birth and death, of happiness and misery, of blessing and calamity, of praise and censure, of gain and loss, of safety and danger, and of handicap and help, are all cast aside, this is the true laying down (of everything). To lay down a thing is to lay down everything for ever, and this is called the laying down of all concurrent causes. When all concurrent causes have been laid down, false thinking will vanish with the non-arising of differentiation and the elimination of all attachments. When one reaches this state of the non-arising of a single thought, the brightness of self-nature will appear in full.[4] Then only can the prerequisites of Ch'an training be entirely fulfilled. Further efforts in the true training and real instrospection will be required if one wishes to be qualified for realizing the mind for the perception of self-nature.

Recently, Ch'an Buddhists often came to inquire (about all this). As

[1] Underlying principle: theory, noumenon.
[2] Facts: activity, practice, phenomenon.
[3] Kleśa: distress, worry, trouble and whatever causes them.
[4] This is the state described in Han Shan's 'Song of the Board-bearer'.

to the Dharma, fundamentally there is no such thing, because as soon as it is expressed in words, the meaning will not be true. Just see clearly that mind is Buddha and there will be no more ado. This is self-evident and all talks of practice and realization are the demon's words. Bodhidharma, who came to the East to 'directly point at man's mind for the perception of self-nature leading to the attainment of Buddhahood', clearly indicated that all living beings on earth were Buddhas. The outright cognizance of this pure and clean self-nature together with complete harmony with it, without contamination from attachment (to anything)[1] and without the least mental differentiation, while walking, standing, sitting and lying by day or night[2] is nothing but the self-evident Buddha(hood). It does not require any application of mind or use of effort. Moreover, there is no place for either action or deed, and no use for words, speech and thought. For this reason, it is said that the attainment of Buddhahood is the most free and easy thing which relies only on oneself and does not depend on others. If all living beings on this earth are not willing to pass long aeons through the successive four kinds of birth[3] in the six realms of existence[4] to stay permanently immersed in the sea of suffering, and if they wish to attain Buddhahood with the accompanying enjoyment of true eternity, true bliss, true personality and true purity,[5] they should sincerely believe the true words of the Buddha and Patriarchs, and lay down all (attachments) without thinking of either good or evil; all of them will certainly be able to become Buddhas on the spot. All Buddhas. Bodhisattvas and Patriarchs of past generations did not take the vow of liberating all living beings without warrant for so doing; they did not take vain vows and did not tell a deliberate lie.

The (qualification) above referred to, is in the state provided by nature.[6] Moreover, the Buddha and Patriarchs had expounded it again and again, and their injunction in this respect had also been repeated; theirs were true words, words corresponding to reality, which did not contain an atom of falsehood and deception. However, all living beings on this earth have been, for countless aeons, deluded and sunk in the bitter ocean of birth and death, rising and falling in their endless transmigrations. Being deluded, confused and upset, they turn their back on enlightenment and unite with impurities. They are just like real gold thrown into a manure

[1] Even attachment to the self-nature is also an impurity which should be cast aside.

[2] Literally 'during the two six-hour periods of the day'. Each day is divided into two six-hour periods, one for day-time and one for night-time.

[3] Birth from eggs, wombs and humidity, and by transformation.

[4] Worlds of gods (devas), men, spirits (asuras), animals, hungry ghosts and hells.

[5] The four transcendental realities in Nirvāṇa expounded in the Mahāparinirvāṇa Sūtra.

[6] i.e. 'self-so', so of itself, natural, of course, self-existing, the self-existent.

pit where it not only falls into disuse but is also deplorably soiled. Because of His great mercy, the Buddha was compelled to set up 84,000[1] Dharma doors (to enlightenment) so that living beings of different natural capacities could use them to cure the 84,000 ailments caused by their habitual concupiscence, anger, stupidity and love. In the same way you are taught to use a shovel, brush, water and cloth to wash, brush, polish and scrub the dirty piece of gold. Therefore, the Dharma doors expounded by the Buddha are all excellent Dharmas which enable one to see through birth and death and to attain Buddhahood, the only question being the adaptability or otherwise of individual potentialities. These Dharma doors should not be divided arbitrarily into superior or inferior ones. Those introduced into China are: the Ch'an Sect (Tsung), the Discipline School (Lu Tsung), the Teaching School (Chiao Tsung), the Pure Land School (Chin Tsung), and the Yoga School (Mi Tsung). Of these five Dharma doors, it is up to each man to choose the one which is suitable to his natural character and inclination, and he will surely reach his goal if he only sticks to it long enough without change of mind and deeply penetrates it.

Our sect advocates the Ch'an training. This training centres on 'realization of mind (and) perception of self-nature', that is an exhaustive investigation into one's fundamental face. The Dharma door which consists in the 'clear awakening to the self-mind and through perception of the fundamental nature' has been handed down ever since the Buddha held up a flower until after Bodhidharma's coming to the East, with frequent changes in the method of practice. Up to the T'ang (935) and Sung (1278) dynasties, most adherents of the Ch'an sect became enlightened after hearing a word or sentence. The transmission from master to disciple did not exceed the sealing of mind by mind, and there was no fixed Dharma (taught). In their questions and answers (the role played by a master) was only to untie the bonds (fettering his disciple)[2] according to available circumstances, just like the giving of an appropriate medicine for each particular ailment. In and after the Sung dynasty, human potentialities became duller, and the instructions given by the masters were not carried out by their disciples. For instance, when they were taught to 'lay down everything' and 'not to think of either good or evil', practisers could not lay down anything and could not stop thinking of either good

[1] The digits *8* and *4* symbolize respectively the eighth Vijñāna or Consciousness and the *four* basic elements of the physical body, and mean the deluded self-nature (8) held in bondage in the illusory body (4), i.e. Space. The three following zeros symbolize Time, and so long as one remains under delusion, it will be immaterial to add 10, 100, or 1,000 zeros at the end of the number. However, when one attains enlightenment in one finger-snap, the digits 8 and 4 or Space will disappear and the line of zeros, or Time, will have no meaning.

[2] i.e. freeing his disciples from restraint caused by delusion.

or evil. Under these circumstances, the ancestors and masters were compelled to devise a 'poison-against-poison' method by teaching their followers to inquire into a kung an[1] or look into a hua t'ou.[2] Their disciples were even taught to hold a meaningless hua t'ou as firmly as possible (in their minds), without loosening their grip even for the shortest possible moment, in the same way as a rat will (stubbornly) bite the board of a coffin at a fixed spot until it has made a hole. The aim of this method was to use a single thought to oppose and arrest myriad thoughts because the masters had no alternative. It was like an operation which became imperative when poison had been introduced into the body. There were many kung ans (devised by the ancients but) later only hua t'ous were taught such as: 'Who is dragging this corpse here?'[3] and 'What was my fundamental face before I was born?' In the present day, the masters use the hua t'ou: 'Who is the repeater of Buddha's name?'

All these hua t'ous have only one meaning which is very ordinary and has nothing peculiar about it. If you look into him 'Who is reciting a sūtra?', 'Who is holding a mantra?', 'Who is worshipping Buddha?', 'Who is taking a meal?', 'Who is wearing a robe?', 'Who is walking on the road?', or 'Who is sleeping?', the reply to 'Who?' will invariably be the same: 'It is Mind.' Word arises from Mind and Mind is head of (i.e. ante-) Word. Thought arises from Mind and Mind is head of Thought. Myriad things come from Mind and Mind is head of myriad things. In reality, a hua t'ou is the head of a thought (i.e. ante-thought). The head of thought is nothing but Mind. To make it plain, before a thought arises, it is a hua t'ou. From the above, we know that to look into a hua t'ou is to look into the Mind. The fundamental face before one's birth is Mind. To look into one's fundamental face before one's birth is to look into one's mind. Self-nature is Mind (and) to 'turn inwards the hearing to hear the self-nature' is to 'turn inward one's contemplation to contemplate the self-mind'.

The sentence: 'The perfect shining on the pure Awareness' means this: 'the pure awareness' is mind and 'to shine on' is to look into. Mind is Buddha and to repeat the Buddha's-(name) is to contemplate the

[1] Kung an, or kōan in Japanese = A dossier, or case-record; a cause, public laws, regulations; case-law. Problems set by Ch'an masters upon which thought is concentrated as a means to attain inner unity and illumination. The meaning of a kung an is irrevocable and kung an is as valid as the law.

[2] Hua t'ou = ante-word, or ante-thought, i.e. the mind before it is stirred by a thought. It is the mind in its undisturbed condition. The holding of a hua t'ou in the mind is the looking into the self-mind until its realization. It is also the turning inward of the faculty of hearing to hear the self-nature, for the disentanglement of mind (subject) from external objects.

[3] i.e. who is dragging here this physical body of yours?

Buddha. To contemplate Buddha is to contemplate mind. Therefore, to 'look into a hua t'ou' or 'to look into him who repeats the Buddha's name' is to contemplate the mind or to contemplate the pure essence of awareness of the self-mind, or to contemplate the self-natured Buddha. Mind is self-nature, is awareness and is Buddha, having neither form nor location, and being undiscoverable. It is clean and pure by nature, penetrates everywhere in the Dharmadhātu, does not enter or leave, neither comes nor goes, and is fundamentally the self-evident pure Dharmakāya Buddha.

A practiser should keep under control all his six sense-organs and take good care of this hua t'ou by looking into where a thought usually arises, until he perceives his pure self-nature, free from all thoughts. This continuous, close, quiet and indifferent investigation will lead to a still and shining[1] contemplation (the outcome of which will be) the outright non-existence of the five constituent elements of being (skandhas)[2] and the wiping out of both body and mind, without the least thing being left behind. Thereafter, this absolute immutability (should be maintained) in every state, while walking, standing, sitting and lying by day or night. As time goes on, this achievement will be brought to perfection, resulting in the perception of self-nature and the attainment of Buddhahood, with the elimination of all distress and suffering.

Ancestor Kao Feng said:[3] 'When a student looks into a hua t'ou with the same steadiness with which a broken tile when thrown into a deep pond plunges straight down 10,000 changs to the bottom,[4] if he fails to become awakened in seven days, anyone can chop off my head and take it away.' Dear friends, these are the words of an experienced master: they are true and correspond to reality, they are not deceitful words to cheat people.

Then why in the present generation are there not even a few men who attain enlightenment in spite of the great number who hold a hua t'ou (in their minds)? This is because their potentialities are not so sharp as those of the ancients. It is also because students are confused about the correct method of training and of holding a hua t'ou. They go to various places in the four quarters, seeking instruction, and the result is that when they get old, they are still not clear about the meaning of a hua t'ou and

[1] The essence of the mind is still and its function is shining.

[2] The 5 skandhas: form, feeling, ideation, reaction and consciousness.

[3] Kao Feng was the teacher of Chung Feng whose 'Sayings of Chung Feng' (Chung Feng Kuang Lu) were read by Han Shan before the latter began his Ch'an training. (See Han Shan's Autobiography.)

[4] Chang: a measure of ten Chinese feet.

how to look into it. They pass their whole lives clinging to words and names, and applying their minds to the tail of the hua t'ou.[1] They inquire into (the sentences): 'Look into him who repeats the Buddha's name' and 'Take care of the hua t'ou', and the more they look and inquire into these sentences, the more they get away from what these sentences stand for.[2] Thus how can they be awakened to the self-evident Wu Wei (Transcendental) Supreme Reality, and how can they ascend the undisturbable Royal Throne? When gold powder is thrown into their eyes, they are blinded: how then can they send out the great illuminating ray? What a pity! What a pity! They are all good sons and good daughters who leave their homes in quest of the truth, and their determination is above the average. What a pity if they labour to no purpose! (For this reason) an ancient master said: 'It is better to remain unenlightened for a thousand years than to tread the wrong path for a day.'

Self-cultivation for awakening to the truth is easy and is (also) difficult. For example, when we turn on the electric light, if we know how, in a finger-snap there will be light and the darkness which has lasted for a myriad years will disappear. If one does not know how to turn on the light, the electric wires will be interfered with and the lamp will be damaged, resulting in an increase of passions and ignorance. There are also some people who, while undergoing Ch'an training and looking into the hua t'ou, get entangled with demons and become insane, while others vomit blood and fall sick.[3] Are the fire of ignorance bursting into flame and the deep-rooted view of self and other[4] not the obvious causes of all this? Therefore, practisers should harmonize body with mind and become calm, free from all impediments and from (the view of) self and other so as to bring about a perfect unison with their latent potentialities. Fundamentally, this method used in Ch'an training is invariably the same, but the training is both difficult and easy to beginners as well as to old hands.

Where does its difficulty lie for a beginner? Although his body and

[1] When the sentence 'who repeats the Buddha's name?' is merely repeated by a practiser who only grasps its meaning, he thinks of the 'tail' of the hua t'ou, instead of its head or ante-word, that is the mind. Thus he wrongly applies his mind to 'tail' instead of 'head'.

[2] The master means that these people fail because they set their discriminating minds on grasping the meaning of these sentences, whereas in the training, their minds should first be disentangled from all discriminations.

[3] If an evil thought is allowed to slip into the concentration of mind while holding a hua t'ou, this thought will replace the hua t'ou and may grow out of proportion and become difficult to subdue. If it be a strong desire which cannot be satisfied, the resultant frustration may cause insanity. One's breath should never be interfered with, and concentration of mind should never be on the chest as it may affect the lungs and cause the vomiting of blood.

[4] View of dualism which should be wiped out.

mind are mature for it, he is still confused about the method of undergoing it, and since his practice is ineffective, he will either become impatient or spend his time in dozing with this result: 'A beginner's training in the first year, an old hand's training in the second, and no training in the third year.'

Where does its easiness lie for a beginner? It only requires a believing, a long enduring and a mindless mind. A believing mind is, firstly, belief that this mind of ours is fundamentally Buddha, not differing from all Buddhas and all living beings of the three times in the ten directions of space, and secondly, belief that all Dharmas expounded by Śākyamuni Buddha can enable us to put an end to birth and death and to attain Buddhahood. A long enduring mind consists in the choice of a method to be put into continuous practice in the present lifetime, in the next life, and in the life after next. The Ch'an training should be continued in this manner; the repetition of the Buddha's name should be continued in this manner; the holding of a mantra (mystic incantation) should be continued in this manner and the study of sūtras, which consists in putting into practice the teaching heard (i.e. learned from the Scriptures), should be continued in this manner. The practice of any Dharma door (to enlightenment) must be based on Śīla[1] and if the training is undergone in this manner, there is no reason why it will not be successful. The old master Kuei Shan[2] said: 'Anybody practising this Dharma without backsliding in three successive lives can surely expect to attain the Buddha-stage.' The old master Yung Chia said: 'If I utter deceitful words to cheat living beings, I shall be prepared to fall into the tongue-snatching hell for aeons as numberless as atoms.'

By mindlessness is meant the laying down of everything[3] so that the practiser will become like a dead man who, while following others in their normal activities, does not give rise to the least differentiation and attachment, and lives as a mindless religious man.

After a beginner has acquired these three kinds of mind, if he undergoes the Ch'an training and looks into, for instance, the hua t'ou: 'Who is the repeater of Buddha's name?'. he should silently repeat a few times: 'Amitābha Buddha' and then look into him who thinks of the Buddha and where this thought arises. He should know that this thought does not arise either from his mouth or body. If it arises from either his mouth or body, why when he dies, cannot his body and mouth, which still exist,

[1] Śīla = precept, command, prohibition, discipline, rule, morality.

[2] Master *Kuei* Shan and his disciple *Yang* Shan were founders of the Kuei Yang Sect (Ikyō in Japanese), one of the five Ch'an Sects in China.

[3] i.e. free from all attachments, which are likened to a burden which one should lay down.

give rise to this thought? Therefore, he knows that this thought arises from his mind. Now he should watch (and locate) where his mind gives rise to this thought and keep on looking into it, like a cat ready to pounce on a mouse, with his exclusive attention concentrated upon it, free from a second thought. However, its sharpness and dullness should be in equal proportions. It should never be too sharp for that sharpness may cause illness. If the training is undergone in this manner, in every state, while walking, standing, sitting and lying, it will be effective as time goes on, and when cause comes to fruition, like a ripe melon which automatically falls, anything it may happen to touch or come into contact with, will suddenly cause his supreme awakening. This is the moment when the practiser will be like one who drinks water and who alone knows whether it is cold or warm, until he becomes free from all doubts about himself and experiences a great happiness similar to that when meeting one's own father at the cross-roads.

Where do both easiness and difficulty lie for an old hand? By old hand is meant one who has called on learned masters for instruction and has undergone the training for many years during which his body and mind were mature for it and he was clear about the method which he could practise comfortably without experiencing any handicap. The difficulty met by a monk who is an old hand lies in this feeling of comfort and clearness in which he stops and stays. Thus, because of his stay in this illusion-city, he does not reach the place of precious things (i.e. the perfect Nirvāṇa). He is fit only for stillness but is unfit for disturbance and his training is, therefore, not completely effective for really full use. In the worst case, the practiser will, when coming into contact with his surroundings, give rise to feelings of like and dislike and of acceptance and rejection, with the result that his false thinking, both coarse and fine, will remain as firm as before. His training will be likened to the soaking of a stone in water and will become ineffective. As time goes on, weariness and laziness will slip into his training which will become fruitless in the end. When such a monk is aware of this, he should immediately give rise to the hua t'ou again and rouse his spirits to take a step forward from the top of a hundred-foot pole (he has reached)[1] until he reaches the top of the highest peak on which he will firmly stand or the bottom of the deepest ocean where he will walk (in every direction). He will cast away (his last link with the unreal) and will walk freely everywhere, meeting

[1] This state of stillness is fully described in Han Shan's 'Song of the Board-bearer' (see Han Shan's Autobiography) and in Avalokiteśvara Bodhisattva's 'Complete Enlightenment' when he said: 'Both the hearing and its object came to an end but I did not stay where they ended.' (See Master Hsu Yun's 'Daily Lectures', pages 89 and 92).

face to face (lit. substance to substance, or essence to essence) with Buddhas and Patriarchs. Where is the difficulty? Is this not easy?

Hua t'ou is One-Mind. This One-Mind of yours and mine is neither within nor without nor between the two. It is also within, without and between the two and is like Space which is immutable and is all-embracing. Therefore, the hua t'ou should not be pulled up or pushed down. If it is pulled up, it will cause disturbance, and if it is pushed down, it will cause dullness, and so will be in contradiction with the mind-nature[1] and not in line with the 'mean'.[2] Everybody is afraid of false thinking which he finds difficult to control, but I tell you, dear friends, do not be afraid of false thinking and do not make any effort to control it. You have only to be aware of it but should not cling to it, follow it or push it away. It will suffice to discontinue your thinking and it will leave you alone. Hence, the saying: 'The rise of falsehood should be immediately cognized, and once cognized, it will quit.'

However, in his training, if the practiser can turn this false thinking to his own advantage, he will look into where it arises and will notice that it has no independent nature of its own. At once, he will realize the non-existence of this very thinking and will recover his fundamental mindless nature, followed immediately by the manifestation of his pure self-natured Dharmakāya Buddha which will appear on the spot.

In reality, the real and the false are the same (in nature); the living and the Buddhas are not a dualism; and birth-death and Nirvāṇa as well as enlightenment (bodhi) and distress (kleśa) all belong to our self-mind and self-nature and should not be differentiated, should not be either liked or disliked and should not be either grasped or rejected. This mind is pure and clean and fundamentally is Buddha. Not a single Dharma is required (in the quest of enlightenment). Why so much complication? Ts'an![3]

[1] Mind-nature: immutable mind-body, the existing fundamental pure mind, the all, the Tathāgata-garba.

[2] Mean: between the two extremes.

[3] Ts'an: to inquire, investigate, look into. Usually at the end of a meeting, a master utters this word to urge his disciples to inquire into or ponder over the real meaning.

2

The Ch'an Training

(From the Hsu Yun Ho Shang Fa Hui)

MASTER HSU YUN'S DISCOURSE IN THE CH'AN HALL

(DEAR friends,) you have been coming frequently to ask for my instruction and I really feel ashamed (of my incompetence). (Every day) from morning to evening, you have been all hard at work splitting firewood, tilling the fields, moving earth and carrying bricks. In spite of this, you still remember your religious duties; this earnestness of yours does indeed warm the heart of other people. I, Hsu Yun, feel really ashamed of my incompetence in religion and lack of virtue. I am not qualified to give instruction and can only pick up a few sentences left behind by the ancients in reply to your questions.

PRELIMINARIES TO THE METHOD OF TRAINING

There are many kinds of method but I will deal briefly with them.

PREREQUISITES OF THE PERFORMANCE OF RELIGIOUS DUTY

(1) *Firm belief in the (law of) causality*

Whoever one may be, especially if striving to perform one's religious duty, one should believe firmly in the law of causality. If one lacks this belief and does whatever one likes, not only will one fail in the performance of religious duty, but also there will be no escape from this law (of causality) even in the three unhappy ways.[1] An ancient master said: 'If one wishes to know the causes formed in a previous life, one can find them in how one fares in the present life; if one wishes to know the effects in the next life, one can find them in one's deeds in the present life.' He

[1] By going to (*a*) the hell of fire, (*b*) the hell of blood, where the inhabitants devour each other like animals and (*c*) the Asipattra hell of swords, where the leaves and grass are sharp-edged swords.

also said: 'The karma of our deeds will never be wiped out even after hundreds and thousands of aeons (but) as soon as conditions become ripe, we will have to bear the effects ourselves.' The Śūraṅgama Sūtra says: 'If the causal ground is not a true one, the ripening (fruit) will be distorted.' Therefore, when one sows a good cause, one will reap a good fruit (and) when one sows an evil cause, one will reap an evil fruit; when one sows melon (seeds) one will gather melons (and) when one sows beans, one will gather beans. This is the plain truth. As I am talking about the law of causality, I will tell you two stories to illustrate it.

The first story is about the massacre of the Śākya clansmen by the Crystal King (Virūdhaka).[1] Before the advent of Śākyamuni Buddha, there was near Kapila town a village inhabited by fishermen, and in it was a big pond. It happened that because of a great drought, the pond ran dry and all the fish were caught and eaten by the villagers. The last fish taken was a big one and before it was killed, a boy who never ate fish, played with it and thrice knocked its head. Later, after Śākyamuni Buddha's appearance in this world, King Prasenajit[2] who believed in the Buddha-dharma, married a Śākya girl who then gave birth to a prince called Crystal. When he was young, Crystal had his schooling in Kapila which was then inhabited by the Śākya clansmen. One day, while playing, the boy ascended to the Buddha's seat and was reprimanded by others who dragged him down. The boy cherished a grudge against the men and when he became king, he led his soldiers to attack Kapila, killing all its inhabitants. At the same time, the Buddha suffered from a headache which lasted three days. When His disciples asked Him to rescue the poor inhabitants, the Buddha replied that a fixed Karma could not be changed. By means of his miraculous powers, Maudgalyāyana[3] rescued five hundred Śākya clansmen and thought he could give them refuge in his own bowl which was raised up in the air. When the bowl was brought down, all the men had been turned into blood. When asked by His chief disciples, the Buddha related the story (kung an) of the villagers who in days gone by had killed all the fish (in their pond); King Crystal had been the big fish and his soldiers the other fish in the

[1] This story was related by the Buddha himself.

[2] King of Śrāvastī and a contemporary of the Buddha. He was killed by his son, Virūḍhaka, known as the Crystal King and the Evil Born King, who supplanted him.

[3] Mahā-Maudgalyāyana, or Maudgalaputra, was one of the ten chief disciples of the Buddha, and was specially noted for his miraculous powers; formerly an ascetic, he agreed with Śāriputra that whichever first found the truth would reveal it to the other. Śāriputra found the Buddha and brought Maudgalyāyana to Him; the former is placed on His right, the latter on His left.

pond; the inhabitants of Kapila who were now killed had been those who ate the fish; and the Buddha Himself had been the boy who thrice knocked the head of the big fish. (Karma was) now causing Him to suffer from a headache for three days in retribution for His previous act. Since there could be no escape from the effects of a fixed Karma, the five hundred Śākya clansmen, although rescued by Maudgalyāyana, shared the same fate. Later, King Crystal was reborn in a hell. (As cause produces effect which in turn becomes a new cause) the retribution (theory) is inexhaustible. The law of causality is really very dreadful.

The second story is that of (Ch'an master) Pai Chang who liberated a wild fox.[1] One day, after a Ch'an meeting, although all his disciples had retired, the old master Pai Chang noticed an elderly man who remained behind. Pai Chang asked the man what he was doing and he replied: 'I am not a human being but the spirit of a wild fox. In my previous life, I was the head-monk of this place. One day, a monk asked me, "Does a man practising self-cultivation, still become involved in the (theory of) retribution?" I replied, "No, he is free from the (theory of) retribution." For this (reply) alone, I got involved in retribution and have now been the spirit of a wild fox for five hundred years, and am still unable to get away from it. Will the master be compassionate enough to enlighten me on all this.' Pai Chang said to the old man: 'Ask me the same question (and I will explain it to you).' The man then said to the master: 'I wish to ask the master this: Does one who practises self-cultivation still get involved in the (theory of) retribution?' Pai Chang replied: 'He is not blind to cause and effect.' Thereupon, the old man was greatly awakened; he prostrated himself before the master to thank him and said: 'I am indebted to you for your (appropriate) reply to the question and am now liberated from the fox's body.[2] I live in a (small) grotto on the mountain behind and hope you will grant me the usual rites for a dead monk.' The following day, Pai Chang went to a mountain

[1] This story is recorded in 'The Transmission of the Lamp' (Ching Te Ch'uan Teng Lu) and other Ch'an collections.

[2] In his previous life, the old monk had already succeeded in disentangling his mind from its attachment to the phenomenal. However, he could not get away from Saṁsāra because of the karma of misguiding his former disciple about retribution. In his present transmigration, he had realized a singleness of mind about leaving the world of animals and had thereby acquired the occult power of transforming his fox's body into that of an old man. However, he still clung to the dual view of the existence of ego (subject) and fox (object) and could not free himself from this last bondage. Pai Chang's words had a tremendous effect on the old man, releasing his mind from his doubt about his self-nature which fundamentally was pure and contained neither cause nor effect. Being free from this last bond, his self-nature now returned to normal and could function without further handicap; it could hear the master's voice by means of its function. When function operated normally, its essence manifested itself; hence enlightenment.

behind (his monastery), where in a (small) grotto he probed the ground with his staff and discovered a dead fox for whom the usual funeral rites for a dead monk were held.

(Dear) friends, after listening to these two stories, you will realize that the law of causality is indeed a dreadful (thing). Even after His attainment of Buddhahood, the Buddha still suffered a headache in retribution (for His former act). Retribution is infallible and fixed karma is inescapable. So we should always be heedful of all this and should be very careful about creating (new) causes.

(2) *Strict observance of the rules of discipline (commandments)*

In striving to perform one's religious duty, the first thing is to observe the rules of discipline. For discipline is the fundamental of the Supreme Bodhi; discipline begets immutability and immutability begets wisdom. There is no such thing as self-cultivation without observance of the rules of discipline. The Śūraṅgama Sūtra which lists four kinds of purity, clearly teaches us that cultivation of Samādhi (-mind) without observance of the rules of discipline, will not wipe out the dust (impurities). Even if there be manifestation of much knowledge with dhyāna, this also will cause a fall into (the realm of) māras (evil demons) and heretics. Therefore, we know that observance of the rules of discipline is very important. A man observing them is supported and protected by dragon-kings and devas, and respected and feared by māras and heretics. A man breaking the rules of discipline is called a big robber by the ghosts who make a clean sweep of even his footprints. Formerly, in Kubhāna state (Kashmir), there was nearby a monastery a poisonous dragon which frequently played havoc in the region. (In the monastery) five hundred arhats gathered together but failed to drive away the dragon with their collective power of Dhyāna-samādhi. Later, a monk came (to the monastery) where he did not enter into Dhyāna-samādhi; he merely said to the poisonous dragon: 'Will the wise and virtuous one leave this place and go to some distant one.' Thereupon, the poisonous dragon fled to a distant place. When asked by the arhats what miraculous power he had used to drive away the dragon, the monk replied: 'I did not use the power of Dhyāna-samādhi; I am only very careful about keeping the rules of discipline and I observe a minor one with the same care as a major one.' So, we can see that the collective power of five hundred arhats' Dhyāna-samādhi cannot compare with a monk's strict observance of the rules of discipline.

If you (retort and) ask me (why) the Sixth Patriarch said:

'Why should discipline be observed if the mind is (already) impartial?
Why should straightforward men practise Ch'an?'[1]

I will ask you back this question: 'Is your mind already impartial and straightforward; if the (lady) Ch'ang O came down from the moon[2] with her naked body and embraced you in her arms, would your heart remain undisturbed; and if someone without any reason insults and beats you, will you not give rise to feelings of anger and resentment? Can you refrain from differentiating between enmity and affection, between hate and love, between self and other, and between right and wrong? If you can do all this, then you can open your mouth widely to talk, otherwise it is useless to tell a deliberate lie.'

(3) *A firm faith*

A firm believing mind is the fundamental of one's training for performing one's religious duty, because faith is the mother (or begetter) of the beginning (or source) of right doctrine, and because without faith, no good will derive therefrom. If we want to be liberated from (the round of) births and deaths, we must first have a firm believing mind. The Buddha said that all living beings on earth had (inherent in them) the meritorious Tathāgata wisdom which they could not realize solely because of their false thinking and grasping. He also expounded all kinds of Dharma doors (to enlightenment) to cure (all kinds of) ailments from which living beings suffered. We should, therefore, believe that his words are not false and that all living beings can attain Buddhahood. But why have we failed to attain Buddhahood? It is because we have not gone into training according to the (correct) method. For example, we believe and know that bean curd can be made with soybean but if we do not start making it, soybean cannot turn into bean curd (for us). Now assuming that soybean is used for making bean curd, we shall still fail to make it if we do not know how to mix it with gypsum. If we know the method, we will grind the soybean (put the powder in water), boil it, take out the bean grounds and add a suitable quantity of gypsum powder; thus we will certainly get bean curd. Likewise, in the performance of our religious duty, Buddhahood will be unattainable not only because of lack of training, but also because of training not in conformity with the (correct) method. If our self-cultivation is practised according to the (correct) method, without either backsliding or regret, we are bound to attain Buddhahood.

[1] See 'The Altar Sūtra of the Sixth Patriarch,' Chapter III.
[2] The name of a very beautiful lady who, according to a popular tale, stole the elixir of life and fled with it to the moon where she was changed into a frog.

Therefore, we should firmly believe that fundamentally we are Buddhas; we should also firmly believe that self-cultivation performed according to the (correct) method is bound to result in the attainment of Buddhahood. Master Yung Chia said (in his Song of Enlightenment):

> 'When the real is attained, neither ego nor dharma exist,
> And in a moment the avici karma[1] is eradicated.
> If knowingly I lie to deceive living beings, my tongue
> Will be pulled out for aeons uncountable as dust and sand.'[2]

The old master was very compassionate and took this boundless vow to urge those coming after him to develop a firm believing mind.

(4) *Adoption of the method of training*

After one has developed a firm faith, one should choose a Dharma door (to enlightenment) for one's training. One should never change it, and when one's choice has been made, either for repetition of the Buddha's name, or for holding a mantra, or for Ch'an training, one should stick to it for ever without backsliding and regret. If today the method does not prove successful, tomorrow it shall be continued; if this year it does not prove successful, next year it shall be continued; and if in the present lifetime it does not prove successful, it shall be continued in the next life. The old master Kuei Shan said: 'If one practises it in each succeeding reincarnation, the Buddha-stage can be expected.' There are some people who are irresolute in their decisions; today after hearing a learned man praise the repetition of Buddha's name, they decide to repeat it for a couple of days and tomorrow, after hearing another learned man praise Ch'an training, they will try it for another two days. If they like to play in this manner, they will go on doing so until their death without succeeding in getting any result. Is it not a pity?

METHOD OF CH'AN TRAINING

Although there are many Dharma doors (to enlightenment), the Buddha, Patriarchs and Ancestors[3] were agreed that the Ch'an training was the unsurpassed wonderful door. In the Śūraṅgama assembly, the Buddha ordered Mañjuśrī to choose between the (various modes of)

[1] Avīci is the last and deepest of the eight hells, where the culprits suffer, die, and are instantly reborn to suffering without interruption.
[2] As punishment for verbal sins.
[3] The Patriarchs are the six Patriarchs of China. The Ancestors are the great Ch'an Masters who came after the Patriarchs. Hsu Yun is now called an Ancestor.

complete enlightenment, and (he chose) Avalokiteśvara Bodhisattva's (method) of using the faculty of hearing, as the best. When we turn back the hearing to hear our self-nature, this is (one of the methods of) Ch'an training. This place is a Ch'an hall in which we should discuss this Ch'an training.

ESSENTIALS OF CH'AN TRAINING

Our daily activities are performed within the truth itself. Is there a place that is not a Bodhimaṇḍala?[1] Fundamentally a Ch'an hall is out of place; moreover Ch'an does not mean sitting (in meditation). The so-called Ch'an hall and the so-called Ch'an sitting are only provided for people (who encounter) insurmountable obstructions (of their own) and who are of shallow wisdom in this period of decadence (of the Dharma).

When one sits in this training, one's body and mind should be well controlled. If they are not well controlled a small harm will be illness and a great harm will be entanglement with the demon, which is most regrettable. In the Ch'an hall, when incense sticks are burned for your walking or sitting, the aim is to ensure the control of body and mind. Besides this, there are many ways to control body and mind, but I will deal briefly with the essential ones.

When sitting in Ch'an meditation, the correct position is the natural one. The waist should not be pushed forward, for to do so is to pull upward the inner heat with the result that after the sitting, there will be tears, bad breath, uneasy respiration, loss of appetite and even vomiting of blood. Neither should the waist be drawn backward with dropped head, for this can easily cause dullness. As soon as dullness is felt, the meditator should open his eyes wide, pull up his waist and gently shake his buttocks, and dullness will disappear automatically.

If the training is undergone in hot haste, one will feel a certain annoying dryness in the chest. In this case, it will be advisable to stop the training for the time a half-inch of the incense stick takes to burn, and resume when one feels at ease again. If one does not proceed in this manner, one will, as time goes on, develop a hot and excitable character, and in the worst case, one may thereby become insane or get entangled with demons.

When the Ch'an sitting (in meditation) becomes effective, there will be (mental) states which are too many to enumerate, but if you do not cling to them, they will not hinder you. This is just what the proverb

[1] Bodhimaṇḍala: truth-plot, holy site, place of enlightenment.

says: 'Don't wonder at the wonderful and the wonderful will be in full retreat.' Even if you see evil spirits of all kinds coming to disturb you, you should take no notice of them and you should not be afraid of them. Even if Śākyamuni Buddha comes to lay His hand on your head[1] and prophesies (your future Buddhahood) you should not take any notice of all this and should not be delighted by it. The Śūraṅgama Sutra says: 'A perfect state is that in which the mind is undisturbed by the saintly; an interpretation of the saintly is entanglement with all demons.'

HOW TO BEGIN THE TRAINING: DISTINCTION BETWEEN HOST AND GUEST

How should one start the (Ch'an) training? In the Śūraṅgama assembly, Ārya Ājñātakauṇḍinya talked about the two words 'Foreign Dust'[2] and this is just where we should begin our training. He said: 'For instance, a traveller stops at an inn where he passes the night or takes his meal, and as soon as he has done so, he packs and continues his journey, because he has no time to stay longer. As for the host (of the inn), he has nowhere to go. My deduction is that the one who does not stay is the guest and the one who does stay is the host. Therefore, a thing is foreign when it does not stay. Again in a clear sky, when the sun rises and sunlight enters (the house) through an opening, the dust is seen moving in the ray of light whereas the empty space is unmoving. Therefore, that which is still is voidness and that which moves is dust.'

Foreign dust illustrates false thinking and voidness illustrates self-nature, that is the permanent host who does not follow the guest in the latter's coming and going. This serves to illustrate the eternal (unmoving) self-nature which does not follow false thinking in its sudden rise and fall. Therefore, it is said: 'If one is unmindful of all things, one will meet with no inconvenience when surrounded by all things.' By dust which moves of itself and does not inconvenience voidness which is clearly still, one means that false thinking rises and falls by itself and does not hinder the self-nature which is immutable in its Bhūtatathatā (suchness, thatness) condition. This is the meaning of the saying: 'If the mind does not arise, all things are blameless.'

[1] A custom of Buddha in teaching His disciples, from which the burning of spots on the head of a monk is said to have originated. The eventual vision of the Buddha is merely an impure creation of the deluded mind and does not really represent Him in His Dharmakāya which is inconceivable. Many meditators mistake such visions for the real and become involved with demons. (See Śūraṅgama Sūtra.)

[2] See Master Hsu Yun's 'Daily Discourses', page 94.

(The meaning of) the above word 'foreign' is coarse and (that of) 'dust' is fine. Beginners should clearly understand (the difference between) 'host' and 'guest' and will thus not be 'drifted about' by false thinking. By advancing further, they will be clear about 'voidness' and 'dust' and thus will experience no inconvenience from false thinking. It is said: 'When (false thinking) is known, there will be no harm.' If you inquire carefully into and understand all this, over half of what the training means will become quite clear to you.

HUA T'OU AND DOUBT

In ancient times, the Patriarchs and Ancestors directly pointed at the mind for realization of self-nature and attainment of Buddhahood. Like Bodhidharma who 'quietened the mind' and the Sixth Patriarch who only talked about 'perception of self-nature', all of them just advocated the outright cognizance (of it) without any more ado. They did not advocate looking into a hua t'ou, but later they discovered that men were becoming unreliable, were not of dogged determination, indulged in playing tricks and boasted of their possession of precious gems which really belonged to others. For this reason, these ancestors were compelled to set up their own sects, each with its own devices; hence, the hua t'ou technique.

There are many hua t'ous, such as: 'All things are returnable to One, to what is (that) One returnable?'[1] 'Before you were born, what was your real face?'[2] but the hua t'ou: 'Who is repeating Buddha's name?' is widely in use (today).

What is hua t'ou? (lit. word-head). Word is the spoken word and head is that which precedes word. For instance, when one says 'Amitābha-Buddha', this is a word. Before it is said it is a hua t'ou (or ante-word). That which is called a hua t'ou is the moment before a thought arises. As soon as a thought arises, it becomes a hua wei (lit. word-tail). The moment before a thought arises is called 'the un-born'. That void which is neither disturbed nor dull, and neither still nor (one-sided) is called 'the unending'. The unremitting turning of the light inwards on oneself, instant after instant, and exclusive of all other things, is called 'looking into the hua t'ou' or 'taking care of the hua t'ou'.

[1] All things are returnable to One-mind, to what is One-mind returnable?

[2] This hua t'ou is sometimes wrongly translated in the West as: Before your parents *were born*, what was your *original* face? There are two errors here. The first is probably due to the wrong interpretation of the Chinese character 'sheng', which means 'born' or 'to give birth'. Then 'original' is wrong because it suggests creation or a beginning. The self-nature has no beginning, being outside time. The correct rendering is: Before your parents gave birth to you, what was your fundamental face?'

When one looks into a hua t'ou, the most important thing is to give rise to a doubt. Doubt is the crutch of hua t'ou.[1] For instance, when one is asked: 'Who is repeating Buddha's name?' everybody knows that he himself repeats it, but is it repeated by the mouth or by the mind? If the mouth repeats it, why does not it do so when one sleeps? If the mind repeats it, what does the mind look like? As mind is intangible, one is not clear about it. Consequently some slight feeling of doubt arises about 'WHO'. This doubt should not be coarse; the finer it is, the better. At all times and in all places, this doubt alone should be looked into unremittingly, like an ever-flowing stream, without giving rise to a second thought. If this doubt persists, do not try to shake it; if it ceases to exist, one should gently give rise to it again. Beginners will find the hua t'ou more effective in some still place than amidst disturbance. However, one should not give rise to a discriminating mind; one should remain indifferent to either the effectiveness or ineffectiveness (of the hua t'ou) and one should take no notice of either stillness or disturbance. Thus, one should work at the training with singleness of mind.

(In the hua t'ou): 'Who is repeating the Buddha's name?' emphasis should be laid upon the word 'Who', the other words serving only to give a general idea of the whole sentence. For instance (in the questions): 'Who is wearing this robe and eating rice?', 'Who is going to stool and is urinating?', 'Who is putting an end to ignorance?', and 'Who is able to know and feel?', as soon as one lays emphasis upon (the word) 'Who', while one is walking or standing, sitting or reclining, one will be able to give rise to a doubt without difficulty and without having to use one's faculty of thought to think and discriminate. Consequently the word 'Who' of the hua t'ou is a wonderful technique in Ch'an training. However, one should not repeat the word 'Who' or the sentence 'Who is repeating the Buddha's name?' like (adherents of the Pure Land School) who repeat the Buddha's name. Neither should one set one's thinking and discriminating mind on searching for him who repeats the Buddha's name. There are some people who unremittingly repeat the sentence: 'Who is repeating the Buddha's name?'; it would be far better merely to repeat Amitābha Buddha's name (as do followers of the Pure Land School) for this will give greater merits. There are others who indulge in thinking of a lot of things and seek after everything here and there, and call this the rising of a doubt; they do not know that the more they think, the more their false thinking will increase, just like someone who wants to ascend but is really descending. You should know all this.

[1] Doubt is as indispensable to hua t'ou as crutches are to the cripples.

Usually beginners give rise to a doubt which is very coarse; it is apt to stop abruptly and to continue again, and seems suddenly familiar and suddenly unfamiliar. This is (certainly) not doubt and can only be their thinking (process). When the mad (wandering) mind has gradually been brought under control, one will be able to apply the brake on the thinking process, and only then can this be called 'looking into' (a hua t'ou). Furthermore, little by little, one will gain experience in the training and then, there will be no need to give rise to the doubt which will rise of itself automatically. In reality, at the beginning, there is no effective training at all as there is only (an effort) to put an end to false thinking. When real doubt rises of itself, this can be called true training. This is the moment when one reaches a 'strategic gateway' where it is easy to go out of one's way (as follows).

Firstly, there is the moment when one will experience utter purity and boundless ease[1] and if one fails to be aware of and look into the same, one will slip into a state of dullness. If a learned teacher is present, he will immediately see clearly that the student is in such a state and will strike the meditator with the (usual) flat stick, thus clearing away the confusing dullness; a great many are thereby awakened to the truth.[2]

Secondly, when the state of purity and emptiness appears, if the doubt ceases to exist, this is the unrecordable state[3] in which the meditator is likened to one sitting on a withered tree in a grotto, or to soaking stones with water.[4] When one reaches this state, one should arouse (the doubt) to be immediately followed by one's awareness and contemplation (of this state). Awareness (of this state) is freedom from illusion; this is wisdom. Contemplation (of this state) wipes out confusion; this is imperturbability. This singleness of mind will be thoroughly still and

[1] Lit. utter purity and extreme lightness. When the meditator succeeds in putting an end to all his thoughts, he will step into 'the stream' or correct concentration in which his body and its weight seem to disappear completely and to give way to a bright purity which is as light as air; he will feel as if he is about to be levitated.

[2] Lit. thus clearing away the fog that darkens the sky. As soon as the confusing dullness is cleared away, the self-nature, now free from hindrance, is able to function normally and will actually receive the beating, hence enlightenment.

[3] Avyākṛta or Avyākhyāta, in Sanskrit; unrecordable, either as good or bad; neutral, neither good nor bad, things that are innocent and cannot be classified under moral categories.

[4] When the mind is disentangled from the sense-organs, sense-data and consciousness, one reaches a state described as: 'holding fast to the top of a pole', or 'silent immersion in stagnant water' or 'sitting on the clean white ground'. (See Han Shan's 'Song of the Board-bearer'.) One should take a step forward in order to get out of this state called 'a life', the fourth of the four lakṣaṇas (of an ego, a personality, a being and a life) mentioned in the Diamond Sūtra, otherwise the result one will achieve is no better than 'soaking stones with water' which never penetrates stones. If from the top of a hundred-foot pole one takes a step forward, one will reach the top of a high peak from which one will release one's last hold and leap over the phenomenal.

shining, in its imperturbable absoluteness, spiritual clearness and thorough understanding, like the continuous smoke of a solitary fire. When one reaches this stage, one should be provided with a diamond eye[1] and should refrain from giving rise to anything else, as if one does, one will (simply) add another head upon one's head.[2]

Formerly, when a monk asked (Master) Chao Chou: 'What should one do when there is not a thing to bring with self?' Chao Chou replied: 'Lay it down.' The monk said: 'What shall I lay down when I do not bring a thing with me?' Chao Chou replied: 'If you cannot lay it down, carry it away.'[3] This is exactly the stage (above mentioned) which is like that of a drinker of water who alone knows whether it is cold or warm. This cannot be expressed in words and speeches, and one who reaches this stage will clearly know it. As to one who has not reached it, it will be useless to tell him about it. This is what the (following) lines mean:

> 'When you meet a fencing master, show to him your sword.
> Do not give your poem to a man who's not a poet.'[4]

TAKING CARE OF A HUA T'OU AND TURNING INWARD THE HEARING TO HEAR THE SELF-NATURE

Someone may ask: 'How can Avalokiteśvara Bodhisattva's "method of turning inward the hearing to hear the self-nature" be regarded as

[1] Diamond eye: indestructible eye of Wisdom.

[2] A superfluous and unnecessary thing that will obstruct the training.

[3] The monk became thoroughly awakened after hearing Chao Chou's reply. His first question means: 'What should one do when one becomes disentangled from sense-organs, sense-data and consciousnesses?' He did not know that he was still entangled with this awareness of ego and preservation of ego. (See Han Shan's commentary on The Diamond Cutter of Doubts). Chao Chou's reply 'Lay it down' means: 'Lay down even the thought you are still burdened with, for this very thought of not carrying a thing with you holds you in bondage.' The monk argued: 'As I do not carry a single thing with me, what shall I lay down?' Chao Chou replied: 'If you really have got rid of all your false thinking, there will only remain your self-nature which is pure and clean and which you should carry away with you, because you cannot get rid of it.' The monk, now released from his awareness of ego or last bondage, realized that only his self-nature remained which was free from all impediments and which he could not get rid of, for Chao Chou told him to carry it away. It was this very self-nature of his, now pure and clean, which actually heard the master's voice, hence his enlightenment.

[4] These two lines come from Lin Chi (Rinzai in Japanese) whose idea was that one could talk about enlightenment with an enlightened person and that it was useless to do so when meeting a deluded man, for the truth was inexpressible and could only be realized after rigorous training. The first line 'When you meet a fencing master, show to him your sword' was illustrated when Han Shan met Ta Kuan and sat cross-legged face to face with him for forty days and nights without sleeping. (See Han Shan's Autobiography). The second line 'Do not give your poem to a man who's not a poet' was proved by the Sixth Patriarch, who urged his disciples not to discuss the Supreme Vehicle with those who were not of the same sect, but to bring their palms together to salute them and make them happy. (See *The Altar Sūtra of the Sixth Patriarch.*)

Ch'an training?' I have just talked about looking into the hua t'ou; it means that you should unremittingly and one-pointedly turn the light inwards on 'that which is not born and does not die' which is the hua t'ou. To turn inwards one's hearing to hear the self-nature means also that you should unremittingly and one-pointedly turn inwards your (faculty of) hearing to hear the self-nature. 'To turn inwards' is 'to turn back'. 'That which is not born and does not die' is nothing but the self-nature. When hearing and looking follow sound and form in the worldly stream, hearing does not go beyond sound and looking does not go beyond form (appearance), with the obvious differentiation. However, when going against the mundane stream, the meditation is turned inwards to contemplate the self-nature. When 'hearing' and 'looking' are no longer in pursuit of sound and appearance, they become fundamentally pure and enlightening and do not differ from each other. We should know that what we call 'looking into the hua t'ou' and 'turning inwards the hearing to hear the self-nature' cannot be effected by means of the eye to look or the ear to hear. If eye and ear are so used, there will be pursuit after sound and form with the result that one will be turned by things (i.e. externals); this is called 'surrender to the (mundane) stream'.[1] If there is singleness of thought abiding in that 'which is not born and does not die', without pursuing sound and form, this is 'going against the stream'; this is called 'looking into the hua t'ou' or 'turning inwards the hearing to hear the self-nature'.

EARNESTNESS ABOUT LEAVING SAṂSĀRA[2] AND DEVELOPING A LONG ENDURING MIND

In the Ch'an training, one should be in earnest in one's desire to leave the realm of birth and death, and develop a long enduring mind (in one's striving). If the mind is not earnest it will be impossible to give rise to the doubt, and the striving will be ineffective. Lack of a long enduring mind will result in laziness and the training will not be continuous. Just develop a long enduring mind and the doubt will rise of itself. When doubt rises trouble (kleśa) will come to an end of itself. As the ripe moment comes (it will be like) running water which will form a channel.[3]

I will now tell you a story I personally witnessed. In the year K'eng

[1] i.e. to accord with the world, its ways and customs; to die.
[2] Realm of birth and death.
[3] i.e. success is bound to follow.

Tsu (1900), when eight world powers sent their expeditionary forces to Peking (after the Boxer rebellion), I followed Emperor Kuang Hsu and Empress-Dowager Tz'u Hsi when they fled from the capital. We had to hurry towards Shen Hsi (Shensi) province; each day we walked several tens of miles, and for several days we had no rice to eat. On the road, a peasant offered some creepers of sweet potato[1] to the (hungry) emperor, who found them savoury and asked the man what they were. You can imagine that when the emperor who used to put on airs and had an awe-inspiring reputation, had to run some distance he became very hungry. When he ate creepers of sweet potato, he gave up all his airs and awe-inspiring attitude. Why did he walk on foot, become hungry and lay down everything? Because the allied forces wanted his life and he had only one thought, that of running for his life. Later, when peace had been concluded, he returned to the capital, putting on once more his airs with his awe-inspiring reputation. Again he would no longer walk in the street and did not feel hungry. If he did not find some food savoury, once more he could not swallow it. Why was he (again) unable to lay down everything now? Because the allied forces no longer wanted his life and because his mind was not set on escaping. If he now applied the same mind (previously) set on running for his life to perform his religious duty, was there anything he could not do? This was due to the fact that he did not have a long enduring mind, and as soon as favourable conditions prevailed, his former habits appeared again.

Dear friends, the murderous demon of impermanence is constantly looking for our lives and will never agree to conclude peace with us! Let us hastily develop a long enduring mind to get out of birth and death. Master Yuan Miao of Kao Feng said: 'If one sets a time limit for success in the Ch'an training, one should act like a man who has fallen to the bottom of a pit one thousand chang deep.[2] His thousand and ten-thousand thoughts are reduced to a single idea on how to escape from the pit. He keeps it up from morning to evening and from evening (to the following) morning, and has no other thought. If he trains in this way and does not realize the truth in three, five or seven days, I shall be guilty of a verbal sin for which I shall fall into the hell where tongues are pulled out.' The old master was earnest in his great mercy and being apprehensive that we would not develop a long enduring mind, he took this great vow to guarantee (our successes).

[1] In China, only starving people eat creepers of sweet potato which is used as food for pigs.

[2] Chang: a measure of ten Chinese feet.

DIFFICULTY AND EASINESS IN CH'AN TRAINING

There is difficulty and easiness in the Ch'an training, both for beginners and for old practisers.

DIFFICULTY FOR BEGINNERS: THE REMISS MIND

The most common defects of a beginner lie in his inability to lay down his habits of false thinking; of (self-indulgence in) ignorance caused by pride and jealousy; of (self-inflicted) obstructions caused by concupiscence, anger, stupidity and love; of laziness and gluttony; and of (attachment to) right and wrong, to selfness and otherness. With a belly (breast) filled with all the above (defects), how can he be responsive to the truth? Others are young gentlemen[1] who are unable to get rid of their habits and are incapable of the least condescension and of enduring the smallest trouble; how can they undergo the training in performance of their religious duties? They never think of our original teacher, Sakyaṃuni Buddha, and of His standing when He left home. Some people who know a little literature, use their knowledge of it to interpret the ancients' sayings, boast of their unequalled abilities and regard themselves as superiors.[2] When seriously ill, they cannot bear their sufferings with patience. When they are about to die, they lose their heads and realize that their usual knowledge is useless. Thus their repentance will be tardy.

Some are serious in their religious duties but do not know where to begin their training. Others are afraid of false thinking and are unable to put an end to it. So they worry about it all day long and blame their karmic obstructions for it, thus falling away in their religious enthusiasm. Some want to resist false thinking to the death by angrily clenching their fists to keep up their spirits and by thrusting out their chests and widely opening their eyes as if there is really something very important to do. They want to fight to a finish against their false thinking; not only will they fail to drive it away but they will thereby vomit blood or become insane. There are people who are afraid of falling into voidness but they do not know they are thus giving rise to the 'demon'. Consequently, they can neither wipe out voidness nor attain awakening. There are those who set their minds on the quest of awakening and who do not know that to seek awakening and to desire Buddhahood are nothing but a great falsehood; they do not know that gravel cannot be turned into

[1] Literally 'sons of officials'; equivalent of the French term 'fils à papa'.
[2] One of the ten wrong views.

rice and they will thus wait until the year of the donkey for their awakening.[1]

There are (also) those who can manage to sit (in meditation) during the time one or two incense sticks take to burn and thereby experience some joy, but this is only likened to the blind black tortoise which stretched its head through the hole of a floating log.[2] It is just a rare chance and not (the result of) true training. Moreover, the demon of joy has already slipped into their minds. There are cases of the enjoyable state of purity and cleanness realizable in stillness but not realizable in disturbance and for this reason meditators avoid disturbing conditions and look for quiet places. They do not realize that they have already agreed to become servants of the demon of both stillness and disturbance.[3]

There are many cases like the above. It is really difficult for beginners to know the correct method of training; awareness without contemplation will lead to confusion and instability, and contemplation without awareness will result in immersion in stagnant water.

EASINESS FOR BEGINNERS: LAYING DOWN OF (THE BURDEN OF) THINKING AND GIVING RISE TO A SINGLE THOUGHT

Although the training seems difficult, it becomes very easy once its method is known. Where does easiness lie for beginners? There is nothing ingenious in it because it lies in 'laying down'. Laying down what? (The burden of) distress (kleśa) caused by ignorance. How does one lay it down? You have all been at the bedside of a dead man. If you try to scold him a few times, he will not be excited. If you give him a few strokes of the staff he will not strike back. Formerly he indulged in ignorance but now he cannot do so any more. Formerly he longed for reputation and wealth but now he no longer wants it. Formerly he was contaminated by habits but now he is free from them. Now he does not make distinctions and lays down everything. Dear friends, please look at

[1] Animals and birds were chosen by the ancients as symbols for lunar years, such as a rat, buffalo, tiger, rabbit, dragon, snake, horse, sheep, monkey, chicken, dog and pig. As a donkey was not one of them, the year of the donkey can never come round, i.e. these people can never attain enlightenment.

[2] The Saṁyuktāgama Sūtra says: 'There was a blind tortoise countless aeons old which stretched out its head once every century. There was a log with a hole through it, floating in the sea and tossed about by high waves raised by winds of gale force. The tortoise stretched its head through the hole. . . .' This shows the rareness of the chance as compared with the difficulty of the blind black tortoise succeeding in putting its head through the hole in the floating log.

[3] i.e. differentiation between stillness and disturbance.

all this. When we have breathed our last, this physical body of ours will become a corpse. Because we cherish this body, we are unable to lay down everything, with the resultant creation of self and other, right and wrong, like and dislike, and acceptance and rejection. If we only regard this body as a corpse, we will not cherish it and will certainly not consider it as ours. (If so) is there anything we cannot lay down?

We only have to lay down everything, day and night, no matter whether we walk, stand, sit or recline, in the midst of either stillness or disturbance, and whether busy or not; throughout our bodies, within and without, there should be only a doubt, a uniform, harmonizing and continuous doubt, unmixed with any other thought, in other words, a hua t'ou which is likened to a long sword leaning against the sky, which we will use to cut down a demon or Buddha should either appear. Thus we will not fear false thinking; who then will disturb us; who will distinguish between disturbance and stillness and who will cling to existence and non-existence? If there be fear of false thinking, this fear will increase false thinking. If there be awareness of purity, this purity will immediately be impure. If there be fear of falling into non-existence, there will immediately be a fall into existence. If there be desire to attain Buddhahood, there will immediately be a fall into the way of demons. (For this reason) it is said: 'The carrying of water and fetching of firewood are nothing but the wonderful Truth. The hoeing of fields and the cultivation of soil are entirely Ch'an potentialities.' This does not mean that only the crossing of legs for sitting in meditation can be regarded as Ch'an training in the performance of one's religious duty.

DIFFICULTY FOR OLD PRACTISERS: INABILITY TO TAKE A STEP FORWARD AFTER REACHING THE TOP OF A HUNDRED-FOOT POLE

Where does difficulty lie for an old practiser? In his training, when his doubt has become genuinely real, his awareness and contemplation are still linked with the (realm) of birth and death, and lack of awareness and contemplation is (the cause of) his fall into (the realm of) non-existence. It is already difficult to reach these stages, but there are many who are unable to get beyond them, and are content to stand on the top of a hundred-foot pole without knowing how to take a step forward. Others who, after reaching these stages, are able to achieve in the stillness some wisdom which enables them to understand a few kung ans left behind by the ancients; they also lay down the doubt, thinking they have attained a thorough awakening, and compose poems and gāthās, twinkle their eyes and raise their eyebrows, calling themselves enlightened; they do not know that they are servants of the demon.[1]

There are also those who misunderstand the meaning of Bodhidharma's (words:)

> 'Put an end to the formation of all causes without, and have no panting heart within; then with a mind like a wall,[2] you will be able to enter the Truth.'

and the Sixth Patriarch's (words:)

> 'Do not think of either good or evil; at this very instant, what is the Venerable Hui Ming's real face?'[3]

They think that sitting with crossed legs like withered logs in a grotto is the best pattern. These people mistake an illusion-city for a place of precious things,[4] and take a foreign land for their native village. The story of the old lady burning the hut serves to scold these (logs of) dead wood.[5]

EASINESS FOR OLD PRACTISERS: CONTINUATION OF CLOSE AND UNINTERRUPTED CH'AN TRAINING

Where does easiness lie for old practisers? It lies only in the absence of self-satisfaction and the continuation of the close and uninterrupted (Ch'an) training; the closeness should be much closer, the continuance much more continuous and the subtleness much more subtle. When the ripe moment comes, the bottom of the barrel will drop off of itself;[6] otherwise one will have to call on enlightened masters who will help one to pull out (the remaining) nail or stake (of obstruction).

[1] Ancient masters used to twinkle their eyes and raise their eyebrows to reveal the self-mind to their disciples. In the above text, those who have only made some progress but are still unenlightened, ape the ancients to prove their attainment of the truth.

[2] When the mind is like a wall, it will remain indifferent to all externals.

[3] See *The Altar Sūtra of the Sixth Patriarch*.

[4] Quotation from the Lotus Sūtra in which the Buddha urged His disciples not to stay in the illusion-city or incomplete Nirvāṇa but to strive to reach the Perfect Nirvāṇa.

[5] An old lady supported a Ch'an monk for twenty years and used to send every day a sixteen-year-old girl to bring him food and offerings. One day, the old lady ordered the girl to ask him this question: 'How is "it" at this very moment?' The monk replied:

'A withered log in a cold cave
After three winters has no warmth'.

The girl gave the monk's reply to the old lady who said: 'I have been making offerings to one who can prove only that he is a worldly fellow.' Thereupon, she sent him away and set fire to the hut. (See *The Imperial Selection of Ch'an Sayings*). The monk reached only the top of a hundred-foot pole but refused to take a step forward. As he was only dead wood, the old lady was angry, sent him away and destroyed the hut.

[6] i.e. the bottom of the barrel full of black lacquer, or ignorance; when it drops off, the barrel will be emptied of lacquer and enlightenment will be attained.

Master Han Shan's Song is:[1]

High on a mountain peak[2]
Only boundless space is seen.[3]
How to sit in meditation, no one knows.[4]
The solitary moon shines o'er the icy pool,[5]
But in the pool there is no moon;[6]
The moon is in the night-blue sky.[7]
This song is chanted now,
(But) there's no Ch'an in the song.[8]

The first two lines show that that which is truly eternal is solitary and does not belong to anything else, and that it shines brightly over the world without encountering any obstruction. The following (third) line shows the wonderful body of Bhūtatathatā[9] which worldly men do not know and which cannot be located[10] (even) by all Buddhas of the three times; hence the three words: 'no one knows'. The next three (fourth, fifth and sixth) lines show the old master's expedient expounding of this state. The last two lines (seventh and eighth) give a special warning to all of us, lest we mistake the finger for the moon,[11] that is none of these words are Ch'an.[12]

[1] Han Shan (Cold Mountain) should not be confounded with Han Shan (Silly Mountain) whose autobiography has been translated by me into English.

[2] The high purpose of one desirous of escaping from mortality.

[3] The magnitude of his high aim.

[4] Worldly men turn their backs on the transcendental which they do not know.

[5] The solitary moon symbolizes enlightenment which is independent of the phenomenal and is the absolute which does not brook interference from any quarter. The pool is a symbol of the self-nature which avoids all worldly things and is disentangled from them. The line means the attainment of enlightenment by self-nature.

[6] The self-nature is fundamentally pure and clean and does not gain anything, even the moon, symbol of enlightenment, when it is awakened, or lose anything, when it is under delusion. If there be a moon, or enlightenment in it, it will not be absolute and will not be pure and clean.

[7] The enlightened self-nature neither comes nor goes for it is immutable and pervades everywhere in the Dharmadhātu, symbolized by the blue sky which is pure and clean.

[8] The song is chanted in praise of that which is pure and clean and does not contain an atom of Ch'an, because Ch'an is only an empty name with no real nature.

[9] Bhūtatathatā: the real, thus always, or eternally so; i.e. reality as contrasted with unreality, or appearance, and the unchanging or immutable as contrasted with form and phenomena. Bhūta is substance, that which exists; tathatā is suchness, thusness, i.e. such is its nature.

[10] If it can be located anywhere, it will not be the absolute and will not be all-embracing.

[11] When a finger points towards the moon, wise men look at the moon whereas the ignorant look at the finger and do not see the moon, or the truth. This parable was used by the Buddha when teaching His disciples.

[12] Readers will notice that footnotes (2) to (8) on this page seem somewhat different from Master Hsu Yun's commentary on the song, and will realize that Han Shan's poem was excellent in that it can be interpretated either 'perpendicularly' or 'horizontally' as the learned ancients put it, provided there be no deviation from its main purport. My footnotes describe a student striving to achieve enlightenment whereas my master Hsu Yun describes the state of an enlightened master. Gāthās and poems chanted by the ancients are like a prism or spectrum of multi-levelled meanings, as Mr. I. Groupp, an American Buddhist of New York, ably puts it.

CONCLUSION

My talk is like a heap of things and is also (like what we call) the drag of creepers[1] and an interfering interruption (because) wherever there are words and speeches, there is no real meaning.[2] When the ancient masters received their students, either they used their staffs (to beat them) or they shouted (to wake them up)[3] and there were not so many complications. However, the present cannot be compared with the past, and it is, therefore, imperative to point a finger at the moon.[4] Dear friends, please look into all this; after all, who is pointing his finger and who is looking at the moon?[5]

[1] Creepers: unnecessary things which do not concern the real.

[2] Words and speeches cannot express the inexpressible. Real meaning is the reality which cannot be described and expressed.

[3] Beating and shouting are to reveal the master's self-nature which beats and shouts and the student's self-nature which is beaten and hears the shout. Thus beating and shouting are in accord with Bodhidharma's direct pointing at the self-mind for realization of the self-nature for attainment of Buddhahood.

[4] The finger is an expediency used to reveal the moon, or enlightened self-nature, but one should not cling to the finger and overlook the moon which is pointed at.

[5] One who points at the moon and one who looks at the moon are the self-mind of the master and the self-mind of the student respectively, again a direct pointing at the self-mind for realization of self-nature and attainment of Buddhahood, as taught by Bodhidharma.

3

Daily Lectures at Two Ch'an Weeks

given at the Jade Buddha Monastery, Shanghai, in 1953

(from the Hsu Yun Ho Shang Nien P'u)

THE FIRST WEEK

The First Day

THE Venerable Wei Fang, abbot (of this monastery), is very compassionate indeed, and the chief monks are also earnest in their efforts to spread the Dharma. In addition, all the laymen (upāsakas) here are keen in their studies of the truth and have come to sit in meditation during this Ch'an week. All have asked me to preside over the meeting and this is really an unsurpassable (co-operating) cause. However, for the last few years, I have been ill and am, therefore, unable to give long lectures.

The World Honoured One spent over forty years in expounding the Dharma, exoterically and esoterically, and his teaching is found in the twelve divisions[1] of the Mahāyāna canon in the Tripiṭaka. If I am asked to give lectures, the most I can do is to pick up words already spoken by the Buddha and Masters.

As to the Dharma of our sect, when the Buddha ascended to his seat for the last time, he held up and showed to the assembly a golden flower of sandalwood, offered to him by the king of the eighteen Brahmalokas (Mahābrahmā Devarāja). All men and gods (devas) who were present, did not understand the Buddha's (meaning). Only Mahākāśyapa (acknowledged it with a) broad smile. Thereupon the World Honoured One declared to him: 'I have the treasure of the correct Dharma eye, Nirvāṇa's wonderful mind and the formless Reality which I now transmit to you.'

[1] The 12 divisions of the Mahāyāna canon are: (1) sūtra, the Buddha's sermons; (2) geya, metrical pieces; (3) gāthā, poems or chants; (4) nidāna, sūtras written by request or in answer to a query, because certain percepts were violated and because of certain events; (5) itivṛttaka, narratives; (6) jātaka, stories of former lives of Buddha; (7) adbhuta-dharma, miracles; (8) avadāna, parables, metaphors, stories, illustrations; (9) upadeśa, discourses and discussions by question and answer; (10) udāna, impromptu, or unsolicited addresses; (11) vaipulya, expanded sūtras; (12) vyākaraṇa, prophecies.

This was the transmission outside of teaching, which did not make use of scriptures and was the unsurpassed Dharma door of direct realization.

Those who came afterwards, got confused about it and (wrongly) called it Ch'an (Dhyāna in Sanskrit and Zen in Japanese). We should know that over twenty kinds of Ch'an are enumerated in the Mahāprajñā-pāramitā Sūtra, but none of them is the final one.

The Ch'an of our sect does not set up (progressive) stages and is, therefore, the unsurpassed one. (Its aim) is the direct realization leading to the perception of the (self-) nature and attainment of Buddhahood. Therefore, it has nothing to do with the sitting or not sitting in meditation during a Ch'an week. However, on account of living beings' dull roots and due to their numerous false thoughts, ancient masters devised expediencies to guide them. Since the time of Mahākāśyapa up to now, there have been sixty to seventy generations. In the Tang and Sung dynasties (619–1278), the Ch'an sect spread to every part of the country and how it prospered at the time! At present, it has reached the bottom of its decadence (and) only those monasteries like Chin Shan, Kao Min and Pao Kuan, can still manage to present some appearance. This is why men of outstanding ability are now so rarely found and even the holding of Ch'an weeks has only a name but lacks its spirit.

When the Seventh Ancestor[1] Hsing Szu of Ch'ing Yuan Mountain asked the Sixth Patriarch: 'What should one do in order not to fall into the progressive stages?'[2] the Patriarch asked: 'What did you practise of late?' Hsing Szu replied: 'I did not even practise the Noble Truths.'[3] The Patriarch asked: 'Then falling into what progressive stages?' Hsing Szu replied: 'Even the Noble Truths are not practised, where are the progressive stages?' The Sixth Patriarch had a high opinion of Hsing Szu.

Because of our inferior roots, the great masters were obliged to use expediencies and to instruct their followers to hold (and examine into) a sentence called hua t'ou. As Buddhists (of the Pure Land School) who used to repeat the Buddha's name (in their practice) were numerous, the great masters instructed them to hold (and examine into the hua t'ou): 'Who is the repeater of the Buddha's name?' Nowadays, this expedient is adopted in Ch'an training all over the country. However, many are

[1] Hsing Szu inherited the Dharma from the Sixth Patriarch and was called the Seventh Ancestor because his two Dharma-descendants Tung Shan and Ts'ao Shan founded the Ts'ao Tung sect, which was one of the five Ch'an sects in China.

[2] Of the method of gradual enlightenment which took many aeons to enable an adherent to attain the Buddha-stage.

[3] The four Noble Truths are: Misery; the accumulation of misery, caused by passions; the extinction of passions, being possible; and the doctrine of the Path leading to extinction of passions.

not clear about it and merely repeat without interruption the sentence: 'Who is the repeater of the Buddha's name?' Thus they are repeaters of the hua t'ou, and are not investigators of the hua t'ou ('s meaning). To investigate is to inquire into. For this reason, the four Chinese characters 'chao ku hua t'ou' are prominently exhibited in all Ch'an halls. 'Chao' is to turn inward the light, and 'ku' is to care for. These (two characters together) mean 'to turn inward the light on the self-nature'. This is to turn inward our minds which are prone to wander outside, and this is called investigation of the hua t'ou. 'Who is the repeater of the Buddha's name?' is a sentence. Before this sentence is uttered, it is called a hua t'ou (lit. sentence's head). As soon as it is uttered, it becomes the sentence's tail (hua wei). In our inquiry into the hua t'ou, this (word) 'Who' should be examined: What is it before it arises? For instance, I am repeating the Buddha's name in this hall. Suddenly someone asks me: 'Who is repeating the Buddha's name?' I reply: 'It is I.' The questioner asks again: 'If you are the repeater of the Buddha's name, do you repeat it with your mouth or with your mind? If you repeat it with your mouth, why don't you repeat it when you sleep? If you repeat it with your mind, why don't you repeat it after your death?' This question will cause a doubt to arise (in our minds) and it is here that we should inquire into this doubt. We should endeavour to know where this 'Who' comes from and what it looks like. Our minute examination should be turned inward and this is also called 'the turning inward of the hearing to hear the self-nature'.

When offering incense and circumambulating in the hall, one's neck should touch the (back of the wide) collar of the robe, one's feet should follow closely the preceding walker, one's mind should be set at rest and one should not look to the right or to the left. With a single mind, the hua t'ou should be well cared for.

When sitting in meditation, the chest should not be pushed forward. The prāṇa (vital energy) should neither be brought upward nor pressed down, and should be left in its natural condition. However, the six sense organs should be brought under control, and all thoughts should be brought to an end. Only the hua t'ou should be gripped and the grip should never loosen. The hua t'ou should not be coarse for it will float up and cannot be brought down. Neither should it be fine, for it will become blurred with the resultant fall into the void. In both cases, no result can be achieved.

If the hua t'ou is properly looked after, the training will become easier and all former habits will be brought automatically to an end. A beginner will not find it easy to hold the hua t'ou well (in his mind), but he should not worry about it. He should neither hope for awakening nor seek wisdom, for the purpose of this sitting in meditation in the Ch'an week is already the attainment of awakening and wisdom. If he develops a mind in pursuit of these ends, he puts another head upon his own head.[1]

Now we know that we should give rise only to a sentence called hua t'ou which we should care for. If thoughts arise, let them rise and if we disregard them, they will vanish. This is why it is said: 'One should not be afraid of rising thoughts but only of the delay in being aware of them.' If thoughts arise, let our awareness of them nail the hua t'ou to them. If the hua t'ou escapes from our grip, we should immediately bring it back again.

The first sitting in meditation can be likened to a battle against rising thoughts. Gradually the hua t'ou will be well gripped and it will be easy to hold it uninterruptedly during the whole time an incense stick takes to burn.[2] We can expect good results when it does not escape from our grip any more.

The foregoing are only empty words; now let us exert our efforts in the training.

The Second Day

To sit in meditation during a Ch'an week is the best method which sets a time limit for realizing the truth by personal experience. This method was not used in ancient times for the ancients had sharp roots (and did not require it). It has gradually been put into use since the Sung dynasty (fell in 1278). In the Ch'ing dynasty (1662–1910), it was brought into vogue and the Emperor Yung Cheng used to hold frequent Ch'an weeks in the imperial palace. He entertained the highest regard for the Sect and his own attainment of Ch'an samādhi was excellent. Over ten persons realized the truth under the imperial auspices and Master T'ien Hui Ch'e of the Kao Min monastery at Yang Chou attained enlightenment during these meetings (in the palace). The emperor also revised and improved for observance the rules and regulations of the Sect, which flourished and produced so many men of ability. The (strict observance of) rules and regulations is, therefore, of paramount importance.

[1] A Ch'an term which means an unwanted thing which hinders self-realization.
[2] Usually one hour. The longer sticks take an hour and a half to burn.

This method of setting a time limit for personal experience of the truth is likened to a scholars' examination. The candidates sit for it and write their compositions according to the subjects, for each of which a time limit is set. The subject of our Ch'an week is Ch'an meditation. For this reason, this hall is called the Ch'an hall. Ch'an is dhyāna in Sanscrit and means 'unperturbed abstraction'. There are various kinds of Ch'an, such as the Mahāyāna and Hīnayāna Ch'ans, the material and immaterial Ch'ans, the Śrāvakas' and the Heretics' Ch'an. Ours is the unsurpassed Ch'an. If one succeeds in seeing through the doubt (mentioned yesterday) and in sitting on and cracking the life-root,[1] one will be similar to the Tathāgata.

For this reason, a Ch'an hall is also called a Buddha's selecting place. It is called a Prajñā hall. The Dharma taught in this hall is the Wu Wei Dharma.[2] Wu Wei means 'not doing'. In other words, not a (single) thing can be gained and not a (single) thing can be done. If there be doing (saṁskṛta),[3] it will produce birth and death. If there is gain, there will be loss. For this reason, the sūtra says: 'There are only words and expressions which have no real meaning.' The recitation of sūtras and the holding of confessional services pertain to doing (saṁskṛta) and are only expediencies used in the teaching school.

As to our Sect, its teaching consists in the direct (self-) cognizance for which words and expressions have no room. Formerly, a student called on the old master Nan Chuan and asked him: 'What is Tao?' Nan Chuan replied: 'The ordinary mind[4] is the truth.' Every day, we wear robes and eat rice; we go out to work and return to rest; all our actions are performed according to the truth.[5] It is because we bind ourselves in every situation that we fail to realize that the self-mind is Buddha.

When Ch'an Master Fa Ch'ang of Ta Mei Mountain called for the first time on Ma Tsu, he asked the latter: 'What is Buddha?' Ma Tsu replied: 'Mind is Buddha.' Thereupon, Ta Mei[6] was completely

[1] Life-root. A root, or basis for life, or reincarnation, the nexus of Hīnayāna between two life-periods, accepted by Mahāyāna as nominal but not real. The Chinese idiom 'to sit on and to crack' is equivalent to the Western term 'to break up'.

[2] Wu Wei. Asaṁskṛta in Sanscrit, anything not subject to cause, condition or dependence; out of time, eternal, inactive, supramundane.

[3] Saṁskṛta. Yu Wei in Chinese, active, creative, productive, functioning, causative, phenomenal, the process resulting from the laws of karma.

[4] Ordinary mind = undiscriminating mind.

[5] Without discrimination, the acts of wearing clothes and eating and all our activities are nothing but the functions of the self-nature; and One reality is all reality. On the other hand if the mind discriminates when one wears one's robe or takes one's meal, everything around one will be the phenomenal.

[6] Ta Mei. In deference to him, the master was called after the name of the mountain where he stayed.

enlightened. He left Ma Tsu and proceeded to the Szu Ming district where he lived in a hermitage formerly belonging to Mei Tsu Chen.

In the Chen Yuan reign (A.D. 785–804) of the T'ang dynasty, a monk who was a disciple of Yen Kuan and went to the mountain to collect branches of trees for making staffs, lost his way and arrived at the hut. He asked Ta Mei: 'How long have you stayed here?' Ta Mei replied: 'I see only four mountains which are blue and yellow.'[1] The monk said: 'Please show me the mountain track so that I can get out of here.' Ta Mei replied: 'Follow the stream.'[2]

Upon his return the monk reported what he saw in the mountain to Yen Kuan who said: 'I once saw a monk in Chiang Hsi (province) but I have had no news of him since. Is it not that monk?'

Then Yen Kuan sent the monk (to the mountain) to invite Ta Mei to come (to his place). In reply, Ta Mei sent the following poem:

A withered log in the cold forest
Does not change heart for several springs,
The woodcutter will not look at it.
How can a stranger hunt it?
A lotus pond yields boundless store of clothing:
More fir cones drop from pines than you can eat.
When worldly men discover where you live
You move your thatched hut far into the hills.[3]

Ma Tsu heard of Ta Mei's stay on the mountain and sent a monk to ask him this question: 'What did you obtain when you called on the great master Ma Tsu and what prompted you to stay here?' Ta Mei replied: 'The great master told me that mind was Buddha and that is why I came to stay here.' The monk said: 'The great master's Buddha Dharma is different now.' Ta Mei asked: 'What is it now?' The monk replied: 'He says it is neither mind nor Buddha.'[4] Ta Mei said: 'That old man is causing confusion in the minds of others and all this will have no end. Let him say that it is neither mind nor Buddha. As far as I am concerned, Mind is Buddha.'

[1] The mountains are immutable and symbolize the unchanging self-nature, whereas their colours (blue and yellow) change and symbolize appearance, i.e. the phenomenal. Ta Mei's reply meant that his self-nature was the same and beyond time.

[2] If your mind wanders outside, it will follow the stream of birth and death.

[3] When the mind is free from passions, it is like a withered log which is indifferent to its surroundings and does not 'grow' any more in spite of the spring, the season of the year in which trees begin to grow after lying dormant all winter. A mind free from delusion remains unchanged and indifferent to all changes in its surrounding and to those who hunt after it.

[4] Because his disciples clung to his saying: 'Mind is Buddha,' Ma Tsu said to them: 'It is neither mind nor Buddha' so that they ceased to cling, which was the cause of their delusion.

When the monk returned and reported the above dialogue to Ma Tsu, the latter said: 'The plum is now ripe.'[1]

This shows how the ancients were competent and concise. Because of our inferior roots and perverted thinking, the masters taught us to hold a hua t'ou (in our minds) and they were obliged to use this expedient. Master Yung Chia said: 'After the elimination of the ego and dharma, the attainment of reality will destroy the Avīci hell in a moment (kṣaṇa). If I tell a lie to deceive living beings, I will consent to fall into the hell where the tongue is pulled out (as punishment for my verbal sin).'[2] Master Yuan Miao of Kao Feng said: 'Ch'an training is like throwing into a deep pond a tile which sinks to the bottom.' When we hold a hua t'ou, we must look into it until we reach its 'bottom' and 'crack' it. Master Yuan Miao also swore: 'If someone holding a hua t'ou without giving rise to a second thought, fails to realize the truth, I will be (ready) to fall into the hell where the tongue is pulled out.' The sole reason why (we do not succeed in our practice) is because our faith (in the hua t'ou) is not deep enough and because we do not put an end to our (wrong) thinking. If we are firmly determined to escape from the round of births and deaths, a sentence of the hua t'ou will never escape from our grip. Master Kuei Shan said: 'If in every reincarnation we (can hold it firmly) without backsliding, the Buddha stage can be expected.'

All beginners are inclined to give rise to all kinds of (false) thoughts; they have a pain in the legs and do not know how to undergo the training. The truth is that they should be firm in their determination to escape from the round of births and deaths. They should stick to the hua t'ou and no matter whether they walk, stand, sit or lie, they should grasp it. From morning to evening, they should look into this (word) 'Who' until it becomes as clear as 'the autumn moon reflected in a limpid pool'. It should be clearly (and closely) inquired into and should be neither blurred nor unsteady. (If this can be achieved) why worry about the Buddha stage which seems unattainable?

If the hua t'ou becomes blurred, you can open your eyes wide and raise your chest gently; this will raise your spirits. At the same time, it should not be held too loosely, nor should it be too fine, because if it is too fine, it will cause a fall into emptiness and dullness. If you fall into emptiness, you will perceive only stillness and will experience liveliness.

[1] Ta Mei means 'Big Plum'. Ma Tsu confirmed that master Ta Mei was ripe, i.e enlightened.

[2] Quotation from Yung Chia's 'Song of Enlightenment'. Avīci is the last and deepest of the eight hot hells, where sinners suffer, die, and are instantly reborn to suffering, without interruption. Kṣaṇa is the shortest measure of time, as kalpa is the longest.

At this moment, the hua t'ou should not be allowed to escape from your grip so that you can take a step forward after you have reached 'the top of the pole'.[1] Otherwise, you will fall into dull emptiness and will never attain the ultimate.

If it is loosely gripped, you will be easily assailed by false thoughts. If false thoughts arise, they will be difficult to suppress.

Therefore, coarseness should be tempered with fineness and fineness with coarseness to succeed in the training and to realize the sameness of the mutable and immutable.

Formerly I was at Chin Shan and other monasteries and when the Karmadāna[2] received the incense sticks which he had ordered (previously), his two feet ran[3] with great speed as if he flew (in the air) and the monks who followed him were also good runners. As soon as the signal was given, all of them looked like automata. (Thus) how could wrong thoughts arise (in their minds)? At present (although) we also walk (after sitting in meditation), what a great difference there is between then and now!

When you sit in meditation, you should not push up the hua t'ou for this will cause its dimness. You should not hold it in your chest for it causes pain in the chest. Neither should you press it down, for it will expand the belly and will cause your fall into the realm of the five aggregates (skandhas)[4] resulting in all kinds of defect. With serenity and self-possession, only the word 'Who' should be looked into with the same care with which a hen sits on her egg and a cat pounces on a mouse. When the hua-t'ou is efficiently held, the life-root will automatically be cut off.

This method is obviously not an easy one for beginners, but you must exert yourselves unceasingly. Now I give you an example. Self-cultivation is likened to making fire with a piece of flint. We must know the method of producing a fire and if we do not know it, we will never light a fire

[1] The instant one perceives only stillness and experiences liveliness; it is called in Ch'an parlance 'reaching the top of a hundred-foot pole'. All masters advised their disciples not to abide in this state which was not real. Master Han Shan composed 'The Song of the Board-bearer' to warn his followers against 'silent immersion in stagnant water'. This state is called 'life' and is the fourth of the four signs (lakṣaṇa) mentioned in the Diamond Sūtra. (See Part 3.)

[2] Karmadāna: the duty-distributor, second in command of a monastery.

[3] After a meditation, the monks used to march quickly in single file to relax their legs, preceded by the Karmadāna and followed by the abbot.

[4] Realm of the five skandhas: the present world as the state of the five aggregates. The best place in which to hold the hua t'ou is between the pit of the stomach and the navel. A meditator may have all kinds of visions before his attainment of enlightenment, and these visions belong to the realm of the five skandhas, i.e. are creations of his mind. His master would instruct him to remain indifferent, to neither 'accept' nor 'reject' these visions which will disappear before the meditator makes further progress in the right direction.

even if we break the flint in pieces. The method consists in using a bit of tinder and a steel. The tinder is held under the flint and the steel strikes the upper part of the flint so as to direct the spark to the tinder which will catch it. This is the only method of starting a fire (with a flint).

Although we know quite well that Mind is Buddha, we are still unable to accept this as a fact. For this reason, a sentence of the hua t'ou has been used as the fire-starting-steel. It was just the same when formerly the World Honoured One became thoroughly enlightened after gazing at the stars at night. We are not clear about the self-nature because we do not know how to start a fire. Our fundamental self-nature and the Buddha do not differ from each other. It is only because of our perverted thinking that we are (still) not liberated. So the Buddha is still Buddha and we are still ourselves. Now as we know the method, if we could inquire into it, it would indeed be an unsurpassing co-operating cause! I hope that everyone here will, by exerting himself, take a step forward from the top of a hundred-foot pole and will be elected (Buddha) in this hall so that he can pay the debt of gratitude he owes to the Buddha high above and deliver living beings here below. If the Buddha Dharma does not produce men of ability, it is because no one is willing to exert himself. Our heart is full of sadness when we talk about this (situation). If we really have deep faith in the words uttered under oath by Masters Yung Chia and Yuan Miao, we are sure we will also realize the truth. Now is the time to exert yourselves!

The Third Day

Time passes quickly (indeed); we have only just opened this Ch'an week and it is already the third day. Those who have efficiently held the hua t'ou (in their minds) have (been able to) clear up their passions and wrong thoughts; they can now go straight home.[1] For this reason, an ancient (master) said:

> Self-cultivation has no other method;
> It requires but knowledge of the way.
> If the way only can be known,
> Birth and death at once will end.

[1] To go straight home. A Ch'an idiom meaning the return to the self-nature, i.e. realization of the real. 'Home' is our self-natured Buddha.

Our way consists in laying down our baggage[1] and our home is very near. The Sixth Patriarch said: 'If the preceding thought does not arise, it is mind. If the following thought does not end, it is Buddha.'[2]

Fundamentally, our four elements are void and the five aggregates (skandhas) are non-existent. It is only because of (our) wrong thoughts which grasp (everything) that we like the illusion of the (impermanent) world and are thereby held in bondage. Consequently, we are unable to (perceive) the voidness of the four elements and (to realize) the non-existence of birth and death. However, if in a single thought, we can have an experience of that which is not born, there will be no need for those Dharma doors expounded by Śākyamuni Buddha. (If so) can it still be said that birth and death cannot be brought to an end? On that account, the brightness of our Sect's Dharma really illumines the boundless space in the ten directions.

Master Teh Shan was a native of Chien Chou town in Szu Ch'uan. His lay surname was Chou. He left home at the age of twenty. After being fully ordained, he studied the Vinaya-piṭaka[3] which he mastered. He was well-versed in the teaching of the noumenal and phenomenal as expounded in the sūtras. He used to teach the Diamond Prajñā and was called 'Diamond Chou'.

Said he to his schoolmates:

> When a hair swallows the ocean[4]
> The nature-ocean[5] loses naught.
> To hit a needle's point with mustard seed
> Shakes not the needle's point.[6]
> (Of) śaikṣa and aśaikṣa[7]
> I know and I alone.

When he heard that the Ch'an Sect was flourishing in the South, he could not keep his temper and said: 'All who leave home take a

[1] Baggage: our body, mind and all the seeming which we hold dear.

[2] That which has no birth and death, i.e. the eternal self-nature.

[3] Vinaya-piṭaka. One of the three divisions of the canon or Tripiṭaka. It emphasizes the discipline. The other two divisions are: sūtras (sermons) and śāstras (treatises).

[4] The two forms of Karma resulting from one's past are: (1) the resultant person, symbolized by a *hair*, and (2) the dependent condition or environment, e.g. country, family, possessions, etc., symbolized by the *ocean*. These two forms being illusory only, they penetrate each other without changing the self-nature, or the nature-ocean (see footnote 5) which is beyond time and space.

[5] Nature-ocean. The ocean of the Bhūtatathatā, the all-containing, immaterial nature of the Dharmakāya.

[6] The appearance of a Buddha is as rare as the hitting of a needle's point with a fine mustard-seed thrown from a devaloka. Even an accurate hit does not move the immutable needle's point.

[7] Śaikṣa, need of study; aśaikṣa, no longer learning, beyond study, the state of arhatship, the fourth of the śrāvaka stages; the preceding three stages requiring study. When the arhat is free from all illusion, he has nothing more to study.

thousand aeons to learn the Buddha's respect-inspiring deportment[1] and ten thousand aeons to study the Buddha's fine deeds; (in spite of this) they are still unable to attain Buddhahood. How can those demons in the south dare to say that the direct indication of the mind leads to the perception of the (self-) nature and attainment of Buddhahood? I must (go to the south,) sweep away their den and destroy their race to repay the debt of gratitude I owe the Buddha.'

He left Szu Ch'uan province with Ch'ing Lung's Commentary[2] on his shoulders. When he reached Li Yang, he saw an old woman selling tien hsin (lit. mind-refreshment)[3] on the roadside. He halted, laid down his load and intended to buy some pastries to refresh his mind. The old woman pointed at the load and asked him: 'What is this literature?' Teh Shan replied: 'Ch'ing Lung's Commentary.' The old woman asked: 'Commentary on what sūtra?' Teh Shan replied: 'On the Diamond Sūtra.' The old woman said: 'I have a question to ask you; if you can answer it, I will offer you mind-refreshment. If you cannot reply, (please) go away. The Diamond Sūtra says: "The past, present and future mind cannot be found." What do you want to refresh?'

Teh Shan remained speechless. He (left the place and) went to the Dragon Pond (Lung T'an) monastery. He entered the Dharma hall and said: 'I have long desired to see the Dragon Pond, but as I arrive here, neither is the pond seen nor does the dragon appear.' Hearing this, (Master) Lung T'an came out and said: 'You have really arrived at the Dragon Pond.'[4] Teh Shan remained speechless; he then (made up his mind to) stay at the monastery.

One night, while he was standing (as an attendant) by Lung T'an, the latter said to him: 'It is late now, why don't you go back to your quarters?' After wishing his master good night, he withdrew but returned and said: 'It is very dark outside.' Lung T'an lit a paper-torch and handed it to him. When Teh Shan was about to take the torch, Lung T'an blew out the light.[5]

[1] Dignity in walking, standing, sitting and lying.

[2] A Commentary on the Diamond Sūtra by Tao Yin of the Ch'ing Lung monastery.

[3] Tien hsin, pastry, snack, refreshment to keep up one's spirits.

[4] Lung T'an was an enlightened master. The sentence: 'You have really arrived at the Dragon Pond' means: 'You have really attained the state of Lung T'an or enlightenment for the real is invisible and does not appear before the eyes of the unenlightened'. Teh Shan did not understand its meaning and remained speechless. This was the second time he remained speechless, the first being when the old woman asked him about the past, present and future mind. He was still unenlightened but became later an eminent Ch'an master after his awakening.

[5] Lung T'an was an eminent master and knew the moment was ripe to enlighten Teh Shan. The latter perceived the master's self-nature through its function which blew out the torch. At the same time, Teh Shan perceived also that which 'saw' the torch blown out, i.e. his own nature.

Thereupon Teh Shan was completely enlightened and made his obeisance to the master (to thank him). Lung T'an asked him: 'What have you seen?' Teh Shan replied: 'In future, I will entertain no more doubt about the tips of the tongues of the old monks all over the country.'[1]

The following day, Lung T'an ascended to his seat and said to the assembly: 'There is a fellow whose teeth are like sword-leaf trees and whose mouth is like a blood bath.[2] He receives a stroke of the staff but does not turn his head.[3] Later, he will set up my doctrine on the top of a solitary peak.'[4]

In front of the Dharma hall, Teh Shan laid on the ground all the sheets of the Ch'ing Lung Commentary in a heap and raising a torch said: 'An exhaustive discussion of the abstruse is like a hair placed in the great void (and) the exertion to the full of all human capabilities is like a drop of water poured into the great ocean.' Then he burned the manuscript. He bade farewell to his master and left the monastery.

He went straight to Kuei Shan (monastery) and carrying his baggage under his arm, he entered the Dharma hall which he crossed from its east to its west side and then from its west to its east side. He looked at the abbot (Master Kuei Shan) and said: 'Anything? Anything?' Kuei Shan was sitting in the hall but paid no attention to the visitor. Teh Shan said: 'Nothing, nothing,' and left the hall.[5]

When he reached the front door of the monastery, he said to himself: 'Be that as it may, I should not be so careless.' Then, he turned back and again entered the hall in full ceremony. As he crossed its threshold, he took out and raised his cloth rug (niṣīdana),[6] calling: 'Venerable

[1] Old monks all over the country: a Chinese idiom referring to eminent Ch'an masters who were intransigent and exacting when teaching and guiding their disciples. Readers may learn about these masters by studying their sayings which seem ambiguous but are full of deep meaning.

[2] A fellow who was awe-inspiring like the two hells where there are hills of swords or sword-leaf trees and blood baths as punishments for sinners. Lung T'an foretold the severity with which Teh Shan would receive, teach and train his disciples. Those wishing to familiarize themselves with these awe-inspiring things should read Dr. W. Y. Evans-Wentz's *The Tibetan Book of the Dead* (Oxford University Press).

[3] Ch'an masters frequently used their staffs to strike their disciples to provoke their awakening. The stroke of the staff here referred to Teh Shan's enlightenment after 'seeing' the torch blown out by his master. Teh Shan did not turn his head, because he was really enlightened and did not have any more doubt about his self-nature.

[4] Will be an outstanding Ch'an master.

[5] This walk from east to west and then from west to east meant the 'coming' and 'going' which were non-existent in the Dharmadhātu wherein the Dharmakāya remained immutable and unchanging. Teh Shan's question: 'Anything? Anything?' and the reply: 'Nothing, Nothing,' served to emphasize the nothingness in space.

[6] Niṣīdana, a cloth for sitting on.

Upādhyāya!'[1] As Kuei Shan was about to pick up a dust-whisk,[2] Teh Shan shouted[3] and left the hall.

That evening, Kuei Shan asked the leader of the assembly: 'Is the newcomer still here?' The leader replied: 'When he left the hall, he turned his back to it, put on his straw sandals and went away.'[4] Kuei Shan said: 'That man will later go to some lonely peak where he will erect a thatched hut; he will scold Buddhas and curse Patriarchs.'[5]

Teh Shan stayed thirty years at Li Yang. During the persecution of Buddhists by the Emperor Wu Tsung (A.D. 841–846) of the T'ang dynasty, the master took refuge in a stone hut on the Tu Fou mountain (in A.D. 847). At the beginning of Ta Chung's reign, prefect Hsieh T'ing Wang of Wu Ling restored the veneration of Teh Shan monastery and named it Ko Teh Hall. He was looking for a man of outstanding ability to take charge of the monastery when he heard of the master's reputation. In spite of several invitations, Teh Shan refused to descend the (Tu Fou) mountain. Finally, the prefect devised a stratagem and sent his men falsely to accuse him of smuggling tea and salt in defiance of the law. When the master was brought to the prefecture, the prefect paid obeisance to him and insistently invited him to take charge of the Ch'an hall where Teh Shan spread widely the Sect's teaching.

Later, people talked about Teh Shan's shouting and Lin Chi's[6] caning. If we can discipline ourselves like these two masters, why should we be unable to put an end to birth and death? After Teh Shan, came Yen T'ou and Hsueh Feng. After Hsueh Feng, came Yun Men and Fa Yen,[7] and also state master Teh Shao and ancestor Yen Shou of

[1] Upādhyāya, a general term for a monk.

[2] The duster used by the ancients consisted of long horse hairs attached to the end of its handle. It was used to reveal the function of the self-nature.

[3] The shout was to reveal that which uttered it, i.e. the self-nature.

[4] Teh Shan took out and raised his niṣīdana, calling: 'Venerable Upādhyāya' to show the function of that which took out and raised the niṣīdana and called Kuei Shan. When the latter was about to take the duster to test the visitor's enlightenment, Teh Shan shouted just to indicate the presence of the substance of that which called on the host. Teh Shan left the hall and went away to show the return of function to the substance. Thus Teh Shan's enlightenment was complete, because both function and substance, or Prajñā and Samādhi were on a level. Therefore, he did not require any further instruction and any test of his attainment would be superfluous. For this reason, Kuei Shan praised the visitor, saying: 'That man will later go to some solitary peak . . . will scold Buddhas and Patriarchs.'

[5] Teh Shan would 'scold' unreal Buddhas and 'curse' unreal Patriarchs who existed only in the impure minds of deluded disciples, for the latter's conditioned and discriminating minds could create only impure Buddhas and impure Patriarchs. Teh Shan's teaching was based only on the absolute Prajñā which had no room for worldly feelings and discernings, the causes of birth and death.

[6] Lin Chi was the founder of the Lin Chi Sect, one of the five Ch'an Sects of China.

[7] Yun Men and Fa Yen were respective founders of the Yun Men and Fa Yen Sects, two of the five Ch'an Sects in China.

the Yung Ming (monastery). They were all 'produced' by (Teh Shan's) staff.

During the past successive dynasties, the Sect was kept going by great ancestors and masters. You are here to hold a Ch'an week and you understand very well this unsurpassed doctrine which will enable (us) without difficulty to attain direct (self-) cognizance and liberation from birth and death. However, if you trifle with it and do not train seriously, or if from morning to evening, you like to behold the 'demon in the bright shadow' or to make your plans inside 'the den of words and expressions', you will never escape from birth and death.[1] Now, all of you, please exert yourselves diligently.

The Fourth Day

This is the fourth day of our Ch'an week. You have exerted yourselves in your training; some of you have composed poems and gāthās and have presented them to me for verification. This is not an easy thing but those of you who have made efforts in this manner, must have forgotten my two previous lectures. Yesterday evening, I said:

> Self-cultivation has no other method;
> It requires but knowledge of the way.

We are here to inquire into the hua t'ou which is the way we should follow. Our purpose is to be clear about birth and death and to attain Buddhahood. In order to be clear about birth and death, we must have recourse to this hua t'ou which should be used as the Vajra King's[2] precious sword to cut down demons if demons come and Buddhas if Buddhas come[3] so that no feelings will remain and not a single thing (dharma) can be set up. In such a manner, where could there have been wrong thinking about writing poems and gāthās and seeing such states as voidness and brightness?[4] If you made your efforts (so wrongly), I really do not know where

[1] If while sitting in meditation one only takes delight in false visions or in the wrong interpretation of sūtras and sayings, one will never attain the real.

[2] The strongest or sharpest precious sword.

[3] i.e. false visions of demons and Buddhas in one's meditation.

[4] Beginners usually see the voidness and brightness as soon as all thoughts are discarded. Although these visions indicate some progress in the training, they should not be taken as achievements. The meditator should remain indifferent to them as they are only the creation of the deluded mind and should hold firm the hua t'ou.

your hua t'ou went. Experienced Ch'an monks do not require further talks about this, but beginners should be very careful.

As I was apprehensive that you might not know how to undergo your training, I talked during the last two days about the purpose of sitting in meditation in a Ch'an week, the worthiness of this method devised by our Sect and the way of making efforts. Our method consists in concentrating pointedly on a hua t'ou which should not be interrupted by day or night in the same way as running water. It should be spirited and clear and should never be blurred. It should be clearly and constantly cognizable. All worldly feelings and holy interpretations should be cut down (by it). An ancient (master) said:

> Study the truth as you would defend a citadel
> Which, when besieged, (at all costs) must be held.
> If intense cold strikes not to the bone,
> How can plum blossom fragrant be?

These four lines came from (Master) Huang Po and have two meanings. The first two illustrate those who undergo the (Ch'an) training and who should hold firm the hua t'ou in the same manner as the defence of a citadel which no foe must be allowed to enter. This is the unyielding defence (of the citadel). Each of us has a mind which is the eighth consciousness (vijñāna), as well as the seventh, sixth and the first five consciousnesses. The first five are the five thieves of the eye, ear, nose, tongue and body. The sixth consciousness is the thief of mind (manas). The seventh is the deceptive consciousness (kliṣṭa-mano-vijñāna) which from morning to evening grasps the eighth consciousness' 'subject' and mistakes it for an 'ego'. It incites the sixth to lead the first five consciousnesses to seek external objects (such as) form, sound, smell, taste and touch. Being constantly deceived and tied the eighth consciousness-mind is held in bondage without being able to free itself. For this reason we are obliged to have recourse to this hua t'ou and use its 'Vajra King's Precious Sword' to kill all these thieves so that the eighth consciousness can be transmuted into the Great Mirror Wisdom, the seventh into the Wisdom of Equality, the sixth into the Profound Observing Wisdom and the first five consciousnesses into the Perfecting Wisdom.[1] It is of paramount importance first to transmute the sixth and seventh consciousnesses, for they play the leading role and because of their power in discriminating and discerning. While you were seeing the voidness and the brightness and composing poems and gāthās, these two consciousnesses performed their (evil)

[1] Cf. Sūtra of the Sixth Patriarch.

functions. Today, we should use this hua t'ou to transmute the discriminating consciousness into the Profound Observing Wisdom and the mind which differentiates between ego and personality into the Wisdom of Equality. This is called the transmutation of consciousness into wisdom and the transformation of the worldly into the saintly. It is important not to allow these thieves who are fond of form, sound, smell, taste, touch and dharma, to attack us. Therefore, this is likened to the defence of a citadel.

The last two lines:

> If intense cold strikes not to the bone
> How can plum blossom fragrant be?

illustrate living beings in the three worlds of existence[1] who are engulfed in the ocean of birth and death, tied to the five desires,[2] deceived by their passions, and unable to obtain liberation. Hence the plum blossom is used as an illustration, for these plum trees spring into blossom in snowy weather. In general, insects and plants are born in the spring, grow in summer, remain stationary in autumn and lie dormant in winter. In winter, insects and plants either die or lie dormant. The snow also lays the dust which is cold and cannot rise in the air. These insects, plants and dust are likened to our mind's wrong thinking, discerning, ignorance, envy and jealousy resulting from contamination with the three poisons.[3] If we rid ourselves of these (impurities), our minds will be naturally comfortable and plum blossoms will be fragrant in the snow. But you should know that these plum trees blossom in the bitter cold and not in the lovely bright spring or in the mild breeze of charming weather. If we want our mind-flowers to bloom, we cannot expect this flowering in the midst of pleasure, anger, sorrow and joy or (when we hold the conception of) ego, personality, right and wrong. If we are confused about these eight kinds of mind, the result will be unrecordable.[4] If evil actions are committed, the result will be evil. If good actions are performed, the result will be good.

There are two kinds of unrecordable nature; that of dreams and of dead emptiness. The unrecordable nature of dreams is that of illusory things appearing in a dream and unconnected with usually well-known

[1] World of desire, world of form and formless world.

[2] The five desires arising from the objects of the five senses, things seen, heard, smelt, tasted and touched.

[3] The three poisons are: concupiscence or wrong desire, hate or resentment, and stupidity.

[4] i.e. neutral, neither good nor bad, things that are innocent or cannot be classified under moral categories.

daily activities. This is the state of an independent mind-consciousness (mano-vijñāna).[1] This is also called an independent unrecordable state.

What is the unrecordable dead emptiness? In our meditation, if we lose sight of the hua t'ou while dwelling in stillness, there results an indistinctive voidness wherein there is nothing. The clinging to this state of stillness is a Ch'an illness which we should never contract while undergoing our training. This is the unrecordable dead emptiness.

What we have to do is throughout the day to hold without loosening our grip the hua t'ou which should be lively, bright, undimmed and clearly and constantly cognizable. Such a condition should obtain no matter whether we walk or sit. For this reason, an ancient master said:

'When walking, naught but Ch'an; when sitting, naught but Ch'an. Then body is at peace whether or no one talks or moves.'

Ancestor Han Shan said:

High on a mountain peak
Only boundless space is seen.
How to sit in meditation, no one knows.
The solitary moon shines o'er the icy pool,
But in the pool there is no moon;
The moon is in the night-blue sky.
This song is chanted now,
(But) there's no Ch'an in the song.[2]

You and I must have a co-operating cause, which is why I have this opportunity of addressing you on the (Ch'an) training. I hope you will exert yourselves and make steady progress, and will not wrongly apply your minds.

I will tell you another story, a kung an (or kōan in Japanese). After the founder of the Hsi T'an (Siddham in Sanskrit) monastery on the Cock's Foot (Chi Tsu) mountain had left home, he called on enlightened masters (for instruction) and made very good progress in his training. One day, he stopped at an inn, and heard a girl in a bean-curd shop singing this song:

Bean-curd Chang and Bean-curd Li![3]
While your heads rest on the pillow,
You think a thousand thoughts,
Yet tomorrow you will sell bean-curd again.

[1] i.e. when the sixth consciousness is independent of the first five.
[2] See page 47 for comment.
[3] Chang and Li are the Chinese equivalents of Smith and Brown.

The master was sitting in meditation and upon hearing this song, he was instantaneously awakened.[1] This shows that when the ancients underwent the training, there was no necessity of doing it in a Ch'an hall for experiencing the truth. The (self-) cultivation and training lie in the One-Mind. So, all of you, please don't allow your minds to be disturbed in order not to waste your time. Otherwise, you will be selling bean-curd again tomorrow morning.[2]

The Fifth Day

About this method of (self-) cultivation, it can be said that it is both easy and difficult. It is easy because it is really easy and it is difficult because it is really difficult.

It is easy because you are only required to lay down (every thought), to have a firm faith in it (the method) and to develop a lasting mind. All this will ensure your success.

It is difficult because you are afraid of enduring hardships and because of your desire to be at ease. You should know all worldly occupations also require study and training before success can be achieved. How much more so when we want to learn (wisdom) from the sages in order to become Buddhas and Patriarchs. Can we reach our goal if we (act) carelessly?

Therefore, the first thing is to have a firm mind in our self-cultivation and performance of the truth. In this, we cannot avoid being obstructed by demons. These demoniacal obstructions are the (external) karmic surroundings caused by our passions for all form, sound, smell, taste, touch and dharma as enumerated in my talk yesterday. This karmic environment is our foe through life and death. For this reason, there are many sūtra expounding Dharma masters who cannot stand firm on their own feet while in the midst of these surroundings because of their wavering religious mind.[3]

The next important thing is to develop an enduring mind. Since our

[1] In his meditation, the master had already discarded all thoughts and upon hearing the song, he instantly perceived that which heard the song, i.e. the self-nature. This is called Avalokiteśvara's complete enlightenment by means of hearing, or the successful turning inward of the faculty of hearing to hear the self-nature.—Cf. Śūraṇgama Sūtra.

[2] Bean-curd is made of soy-bean and is very cheap, so that only poor people make it for sale. For this reason, they are never satisfied with their lot and always want to do something more profitable.

[3] The mind which is bent on the right way, which seeks enlightenment.

birth in this world, we have created boundless karmas and if we now wish to cultivate ourselves for the purpose of escaping from birth and death, can we wipe out our former habits all at once? In olden times, ancestors such as Ch'an master Ch'ang Ch'ing, who sat in meditation until he had worn out seven mats, and (Ch'an master) Chao Chou who wandered from place to place (soliciting instruction) at the age of eighty after having spent forty years in meditating on the word 'Wu' (*lit.* No) without giving rise to a thought in his mind. They finally obtained complete enlightenment, and the princes of the Yen and Chao states revered them and made offerings to them. In the Ch'ing dynasty, Emperor Yung Cheng (1723–35) who had read their sayings and had found these excellent, bestowed upon them the posthumous title of 'Ancient Buddha'. This is the resultant attainment after a whole life of austerity. If we can now wipe out all our former habits to purify our One-thought, we will be on an equality with Buddhas and Patriarchs. The Śūraṅgama Sūtra says:

> 'It is like the purification of muddy water stored in a clean container; left unshaken in complete calmness, the sand and mud will sink to the bottom. When the clear water appears, this is called the first suppression of the intruding evil element of passion.[1] When the mud has been removed leaving behind only the clear water, this is called the permanent cutting off of basic ignorance.'[2]

Our habitual passions are likened to mud and sediment, which is why we must make use of the hua t'ou. The hua t'ou is likened to alum used to clarify muddy water in the same manner as passions are brought under control. If in his training, a man succeeds in achieving the sameness of body and mind with the resultant appearance of the condition of stillness, he should be careful and should never abide in it. He should know that it is (only) an initial step but that ignorance caused by passions is still not wiped out. This is (only) the deluded mind reaching the state of purity, just like muddy water which, although purified, still contains mud and sediment at the bottom. You must make additional efforts to advance further. An ancient master said:

> Sitting on a pole top one hundred feet in heighth[3]
> One will still perceive (that) which is not real.
> If from the pole top one then takes a step
> One's body will appear throughout the Universe.

[1] Āgantu-kleśa in Sanskrit, the foreign atom, or intruding element, which enters the mind and causes distress and delusion. The mind will be pure only after the evil element has been removed.

[2] Water is the symbol of self-nature and mud of ignorance caused by passions.

[3] A state of empty stillness in which all thoughts have ceased to arise and Prajñā is not yet attained.

If you do not take a step forward, you will take the illusion-city for your home and your passions will be able to rise (again). If so, it will be difficult for you to become even a self-enlightened person.[1] For this reason, the mud must be removed in order to retain the (clear) water. This is the permanent wiping out of the basic ignorance and only then can Buddhahood be attained. When ignorance has been permanently wiped out, you will be able to appear in bodily form in the ten directions of the Universe to expound the Dharma, in the same manner as Avalokiteśvara Bodhisattva who can appear in thirty-two forms and who, in manifesting to teach the Dharma, can choose the most appropriate form to liberate a responsive living being. You will be free from restraint and will enjoy independence and comfort (everywhere) even in a house of prostitution, a public bar, the womb of a cow, a mare or a mule, in paradise or hell.

On the other hand, a discriminating thought will send you down to the turning wheel of births and deaths. Formerly, Ch'in Kuai[2] who had (in a former life) made offerings of incense and candles to Kṣitigarbha Bodhisattva but did not develop an enduring mind (in his training) because of his failure to wipe out his ignorance caused by passions, was the victim of his hatred-mind (in his following reincarnation). This is just an example.

If your believing-mind is strong and your enduring-mind does not retrograde, you will, in your present bodily form, be able to attain Buddhahood, even if you are only an ordinary man.

Formerly there was a poor and miserable man who joined the order (saṅgha) at a monastery. Although he was keen to practise (self-) cultivation, he did not know the method. As he did not know whom to ask about it, he decided to toil and moil every day. One day, a wandering monk came to the monastery and saw the man toiling. The monk asked him about his practice and the man replied: 'Every day, I do this kind of hard work. Please show me the method of (self-) cultivation.' The monk replied: 'You should inquire into (the sentence:) "Who is the repeater of Buddha's name?" ' As instructed by the visiting monk, the man managed to bear the word 'Who' in mind while he did his daily work. Later, he went to stay in a grotto on an islet to continue his training, using leaves for clothing and plants for food. His mother and sister who were still living, heard of his retreat in a grotto on an islet where he endured hardships in his self-cultivation. His mother sent his sister to take him a roll

[1] In contrast with a Bodhisattva who seeks self-enlightenment to enlighten the multitude.
[2] A statesman of the Sung dynasty, through whom Yueh Fei, a good commander, was executed; he is universally execrated for this and his name is now synonymous with traitor.

of cloth and some provisions. When she arrived, she saw him seated (in meditation). She called him but he did not reply, and she shook him but he did not move. Seeing that her brother neither looked at nor greeted her but continued his meditation in the grotto, she was enraged, left the roll of cloth and provisions there and returned home. Thirteen years later, his sister went again to visit him and saw the same roll of cloth still lying in the same place.

Later a hungry refugee came to the grotto wherein he saw a monk in ragged garments; he entered and begged for food. The monk (got up and) went to the side of the grotto to pick some pebbles which he placed in a pot. After cooking them for a while, he took them out and invited the visitor to eat them with him. The pebbles looked like potatoes and when the visitor had satisfied his hunger, the monk said to him: 'Please do not mention our meal to outsiders.'

Some time later, the monk thought to himself: 'I have stayed here so many years for my (self-) cultivation and should now form (propitious) causes (for the welfare of others).' Thereupon, he proceeded to Hsia Men[1] where on the side of a road, he built a thatched hut offering free tea (to travellers). This took place in Wan Li's reign (1573–1619) about the time the empress mother passed away. The emperor wanted to invite eminent monks to perform (Buddhist) ceremonies for the welfare of his deceased mother. He first intended to invite monks in the capital but at the time, there were no eminent monks there. (One night) the emperor saw in a dream his mother who said that there was one in the Chang Chou prefecture of Fu Chien province. The emperor sent officials there to invite local monks to come to the capital for the ceremonies. When these monks with their bundles set out on their journey to the capital, they passed by the hut of the poor monk who asked them: 'Venerable masters, what makes you so happy and where are you going?' They replied: 'We have received the emperor's order to proceed to the capital to perform ceremonies for the spirit of the empress mother.' The poor monk said: 'May I go with you?' They replied: 'You are so miserable, how can you go with us?' He said: 'I do not know how to recite sūtras but I can carry your bundles for you. It is worth while to pay a visit to the capital.' Thereupon, he picked up the bundles and followed the other monks to the capital.

When the emperor knew that the monks were about to arrive, he ordered an official to bury a copy of the Diamond Sūtra under the doorstep of the palace. When the monks arrived, they did not know anything

[1] Hsia Men, Amoy, a town on the south coast of Fukien province.

about the sūtra, crossed the doorstep and entered the palace one after another. When the miserable monk reached the threshold, he knelt upon his knees and brought his palms together but did not enter (the palace). In spite of the door-keepers who called him and tried to drag him in, he refused to enter. When the incident was reported to the emperor who had ordered the burial of the sūtra, he realized that the holy monk had arrived and came personally to receive him. He said: 'Why don't you enter the palace?' The monk replied: 'I dare not, because a copy of the Diamond Sūtra has been buried in the ground.' The emperor said: 'Why don't you stand on your head to enter it?' Upon hearing this, the monk placed his hands upon the ground and somersaulted into the palace. The emperor had the greatest respect for him and invited him to stay in the inner palace.

When asked about the altar and the ceremony, the monk replied: 'The ceremony will be held tomorrow morning, in the fifth watch of the night. I will require only one altar with one leading[1] banner and one table with incense, candles and fruit for offerings (to Buddhas).' The emperor was not pleased with the prospect of an unimpressive ceremony and was at the same time apprehensive that the monk might not possess enough virtue to perform it. (To test his virtue), he ordered two maids of honour to bathe the monk. (During and) after the bath, his genital organ remained unmoved. The maids of honour reported this to the emperor whose respect for the monk grew the greater for he realized now that the visitor was really holy. Preparation was then made according to the monk's instruction and the following morning, the monk ascended to his seat to expound the Dharma. Then he ascended to the altar, joined his palms together (to salute) and holding the banner, went to the coffin, saying:

> In reality I do not come;
> (But) in your likes you are one-sided.
> In one thought to realize there is no birth
> Means that you will leap o'er the deva realms.

After the ceremony, the monk said to the emperor: 'I congratulate you on the liberation of her majesty the Empress Mother.' As the emperor was doubting the efficiency of a ceremony which ended in such a manner, he heard in the room the voice of the deceased saying: 'I am now liberated; you should bow your thanks to the holy master.'

The emperor was taken aback, and his face beamed with delight. He paid obeisance to the monk and thanked him. In the inner palace, a vegetarian banquet was offered to the master. Seeing that the emperor

[1] To lead the spirit of the deceased to the Pure Land.

was wearing a pair of coloured trousers, the monk fixed his eyes on them. The emperor asked him: 'Does the Virtuous One like this pair of trousers?' and taking them off he offered them to the visitor who said: 'Thank your Majesty for his grace.' Thereupon, the emperor bestowed upon the monk the title of State Master Dragon Trousers. After the banquet, the emperor led the monk to the imperial garden where there was a precious stūpa. The monk was happy at the sight of the stūpa and stopped to admire it. The emperor asked 'Does the State Master like this stūpa?' The visitor replied: 'It is wonderful!' The emperor said: 'I am willing to offer it to you with reverence.' As the host was giving orders to remove the stūpa to Chang Chou, the monk said: 'There is no need, I can take it away.' After saying this, the monk placed the stūpa in his (long) sleeve, rose in the air and left. The emperor stunned and overjoyed at the same time, praised the unprecedented occurrence.

Dear friends, it is a (wonderful) story indeed and it all came about simply because from the time he left his home, the monk never used his discriminating mind and had a lasting faith in the truth. He did not care for his sister who came to see him, paid no attention to his ragged garments, and did not touch the roll of cloth lying thirteen years in the grotto. We must now ask ourselves if we can undergo our training in such a manner. It would be superfluous to talk about our inability to follow the monk's example when our sisters come to see us. It is enough to mention the attitude we take after our meditation when, while walking, we cannot refrain from gazing at our leader when he offers incense or at our neighbour's movements. If our training is done in this manner, how can our hua t'ou be firmly held?

Dear friends, you have only to remove the mud and retain the water. When the water is clear, automatically the moon will appear.[1] Now it is time to give rise to your hua t'ou and to examine it closely.

The Sixth Day

The ancients said: 'Days and months pass quickly like a shuttle (and) time flies like an arrow.' Our Ch'an week began only the other day and will come to an end tomorrow. According to the standing rule, an examination will be held tomorrow morning, for the purpose of a Ch'an

[1] Water is the symbol of self-nature and the moon of enlightenment.

week is to set a time limit for experiencing (the truth). By experiencing, it means awakening to and realization (of the truth). That is to say, the experiencing of one's fundamental self and the realization of the Tathāgata's profound nature. This is called the experiencing and realization (of the truth).

Your examination is for the purpose of ascertaining the extent to which you have reached attainment during these seven days and you will have to disclose your achievement to the assembly. Usually this examination is called the collection of (the bill of) fare[1] from all of you. (This means that) you must all appear for this examination. In other words, all of you must be awakened (to the truth) so that you can expound the Buddha Dharma for the liberation of all the living. Today, I am not saying I expect that you must all be awakened to the truth. If even one of you is awakened, I can (still) collect this bill of fare. That is to say, one person will pay the bill for the meals served to the whole assembly. If all of us develop a skilful and progressive mind in quest of the truth, we will all be awakened to it. The ancients said:

> 'It is easy for a worldly man to win Buddhahood,
> (But) hard indeed is it to bring wrong thinking to an end.'

It is only because of our insatiable desires since the time without beginning that we now drift about in the sea of mortality, within which there are 84,000 passions and all sorts of habits which we cannot wipe out. (In consequence), we are unable to attain the truth and to be like Buddhas and Bodhisattvas who are permanently enlightened and are free from delusion. For this reason, (Master) Lien Ch'ih said:

> It is easy to be caught up in the causes of pollution,[2]
> (But) to earn truth producing karma is most hard.[3]
> If you cannot see behind what can be seen,
> Differentiated are (concurrent) causes,
> (Around you) are but objects which, like gusts of wind,
> Destroy the crop of merits (you have sown).[4]
> The passions of the mind e'er burst in flames,
> Destroying seeds of Bodhi (in the heart).
> If recollection[5] of the truth be as (intense as) passion,

[1] Lit. cost of the dumplings.
[2] Nidāna or cause of pollution, which connects illusion with the karmic miseries of reincarnation.
[3] Good karma which leads to enlightenment.
[4] Accumulation of merits leading to realization of the truth.
[5] Smṛti in Sanskrit.

Buddhahood will quickly be attained.
If you treat others as you treat the self,
All will be settled (to your satisfaction).
If self is not right and others are not wrong,
Lords and their servants will respect each other.
If the Buddha-dharma's constantly before one,
From all passions this is liberation.

How clear and how to the point are these lines! The (word) pollution means (the act of) making unclean. The realm of worldly men is tainted with desires of wealth, sensuality, fame and gain as well as anger and dispute. To them, the two words 'religion' and 'virtue' are only obstacles. Every day, they give way to pleasure, anger, sorrow and joy and long for wealth, honour, glory and prosperity. Because they cannot eliminate worldly passions, they are unable to give rise to a single thought of the truth. In consequence, the grove of merits is ruined and all seeds of Bodhi are destroyed. If they are indifferent to all worldly passions; if they give equal treatment to friends and foes; if they refrain from killing, stealing, committing adultery, lying and drinking intoxicating liquors; if they are impartial to all living beings; if they regard other people's hunger as their own; if they regard other people's drowning as if they get drowned themselves; and if they develop the Bodhi mind, they will be in agreement with the truth and will also be able to attain Buddhahood at a stroke. For this reason, it is said: 'If recollection of the truth be (as intense) as passions, Buddhahood will quickly be attained.' All Buddhas and saints appear in the world to serve the living, by rescuing them from suffering, by bestowing happiness upon them and by aiding them out of pity.

We can practise self-denial as well as compassion for others, thus foregoing all sorts of enjoyment. (If we can do so), no one will have to endure suffering and there will remain nothing that cannot be accomplished. It will follow that we will be able to obtain the full fruit of our reward, in the same manner as a boat rises automatically with the tide. When dealing with others, if you have a compassionate and respectful mind, and are without self-importance, arrogance and deception, they will certainly receive you with respect and courtesy. On the other hand, if you rely on your abilities and are unreasonable, or if you are double-faced aiming only at (your own enjoyment of) sound, form, fame and wealth, the respect with which they may receive you, will not be real. For this reason, Confucius said: 'If you respect others, they will always respect you. If you have sympathy for others, they will always have sympathy for you.'

The Sixth Patriarch said:

'Although their faults are theirs and are not ours, should we discriminate, we too are wrong.'[1]

Therefore, we should not develop a mind which discriminates between right and wrong and between self and others. If we serve other people in the same manner as Buddhas and Bodhisattvas did, we will be able to sow Bodhi seeds everywhere and will reap the most excellent fruits. Thus, passions will never be able to hold us in bondage.

The twelve divisions of the Mahāyāna's Tripiṭaka were expounded by the World Honoured One because of our three poisons, concupiscence, anger and stupidity. Therefore, the aims of the twelve divisions of this Tripiṭaka are: discipline (śīla) imperturbability (samādhi) and wisdom (prajñā). Their purpose is to enable us to wipe out our desires, to embrace (the four infinite Buddha states of mind): kindness (maitrī), pity (karuṇā), joy (muditā)[2] and indifference (upekṣā)[3] and all modes of salvation,[4] to eliminate the delusion of ignorance and the depravity of stupidity, to achieve the virtue of complete wisdom and to embellish the meritorious Dharmakāya. If we can take such a line of conduct, the Lotus treasury[5] will appear everywhere.

Today, most of you who have come for this Ch'an week, are virtuous laymen (upāsakas). You should subdue your minds in an appropriate manner and get rid of all bondages. I will now tell you another kung an so that you can follow the example (given by those mentioned in it). If I do not tell it, I am afraid you will not acquire the Gem and will go home empty-handed, and (at the same time) I will be guilty of a breach of trust. Please listen attentively:

In the T'ang dynasty, there was an upāsaka whose name was P'ang Yun, alias Tao Hsuan, and whose native town was Heng Yang in Hu Nan province. He was originally a Confucian scholar and since his youth, he realized (the futility of) passions and was determined in his search for the truth.

At the beginning of Chen Yuan's reign (A.D. 785–804), he heard of master Shih T'ou's learning and called on him (for instruction). (When

[1] Quotation from a hymn chanted by the Sixth Patriarch—(Cf. *Altar Sūtra*, Chapter II).

[2] Joy on seeing others rescued from suffering.

[3] Rising above these emotions, or giving up all things, e.g. distinctions of friend and foe, love and hate, etc.

[4] The Six Pāramitās are: dāna (charity), śīla (discipline), kṣānti (patience or endurance), vīrya (zeal and progress), dhyāna (meditation) and prajñā (wisdom).

[5] Lotus treasury: Lotus store, or Lotus world, the Pure Land of all Buddhas in their Sambhogakāya, or Reward bodies.

he saw the master), he asked him: 'Who is the man who does not take all dharmas as his companions?'[1] Shih T'ou stretched out his hand to close P'ang Yun's mouth and the visitor immediately understood the move.[2]

One day, Shih T'ou asked P'ang Yun: 'Since you have seen this old man (i.e. me), what have you been doing each day?' P'ang Yun replied: 'If you ask me what I have been doing, I do not know how to open my mouth (to talk about it).' Then he presented the following poem to Shih T'ou:

> There is nothing special about what I do each day;
> I only keep myself in harmony with it,[3]
> Everywhere I neither accept nor reject anything.
> Nowhere do I confirm or refute a thing.[4]
> Why do people say that red and purple differ?[4]
> There's not a speck of dust on the blue mountain.[5]
> Supernatural powers and wonder-making works
> Are but fetching water and the gathering of wood,[6]

Shih T'ou approved of the poem and asked P'ang Yun: 'Will you join the Saṇgha order or will you remain a layman (upāsaka)?' P'ang Yun replied: 'I will act as I please', and did not shave his head.[7]

Later, P'ang Yun called on (master) Ma Tsu and asked him: 'Who is the man who does not take all dharmas as his companions?' Ma Tsu replied: 'I will tell you this after you have swallowed all the water in the West River.'[8] Upon hearing this, P'ang Yun was instantaneously awakened

[1] In plain English the question means: Who is the man who has no more attachments to things, or the phenomenal?

[2] In Shih T'ou's move, P'ang Yun perceived that which stretched out the hand to close his mouth and became awakened to the self-nature which was invisible and manifested itself by means of its function.

[3] After enlightenment one attends to one's daily task as usual, the only difference being that the mind no longer discriminates and harmonizes with its surroundings.

[4] Mind is now free from all conceptions of duality.

[5] The blue mountain symbolizes that which is immutable and free from dust, or impurities. A misprint occurs in the printed text, so I have followed the ancient version of the story of Upāsaka P'ang Yun.

[6] Carrying water and fetching wood are the functions of that which possesses supernatural powers and accomplishes wonderful works; in other words, the self-nature which is immaterial and invisible, can be perceived only by means of its functions which are no longer discriminative.

[7] He did not join the Saṇgha order.

[8] The one who has no more attachment to worldly things is the enlightened self-nature which is beyond description. Ma Tsu gave this reply, because when one attains enlightenment, his body or substance pervades everywhere and contains everything, including the West River which is likened to a speck of dust inside the immense universe; he knows everything and does not require any description of himself.—A misprint in the text has been corrected.

to the profound doctrine. He stayed two years at the monastery (of Ma Tsu).

Since his complete realization of his fundamental nature, the Upasaka gave up all worldly occupations, dumped into the Hsiang River his whole fortune amounting to 10,000 strings of gold and silver (coins) and made bamboo-ware to earn his living.

One day, while chatting with his wife on the doctrine of the unborn, the Upāsaka said: 'Difficult! Difficult! Difficult! (It is like unpacking and) distributing ten loads of sesame seeds on the top of a tree.'[1]

His wife interjected: 'Easy! Easy! Easy! A hundred blades of grass are the masters' indication.'[2]

Hearing their dialogue, their daughter Ling Chao said laughingly: 'Oh, you two old people! How can you talk like that?' The Upāsaka said to his daughter: 'What, then, would you say?' She replied: 'It is not difficult! And it is not easy! When hungry one eats and when tired one sleeps.'[3]

P'ang Yun clapped his hands, laughed and said: 'My son will not get a wife; my daughter will not have a husband. We will all remain together to speak the language of the un-born.'[4] Since then, his dialectic powers became eloquent and forcible and he was admired everywhere.

When the Upāsaka left (master) Yo Shan, the latter sent ten Ch'an monks to accompany him to the front door (of the monastery). Pointing his finger at the falling snow, the Upāsaka said to them: 'Good snow! The flakes do not fall elsewhere.' A Ch'an monk named Ch'uan asked him: 'Where do they fall?' The Upāsaka slapped the monk in the face, and Ch'uan said: 'You can't act so carelessly.' The Upāsaka replied: 'What a Ch'an monk you are! The god of the dead will not let you pass.' Ch'uan asked: 'Then what does the (Venerable) Upāsaka mean?' The Upāsaka

[1] The Patriarchs' doctrine was very profound and was as difficult to teach as the unpacking and distributing of sesame seeds on the top of a tree, an impossible thing for an unenlightened man.

[2] In order to wipe out the conception of difficulty, the wife said the doctrine was easy to expound for even the dewdrops on blades of grass were used by eminent masters to give the direct indication of *that which* saw these dewdrops. This was only easy for enlightened people.

[3] If it is said that the doctrine is difficult to understand, no one will try to learn it. If it is said that it is easy to understand, people will take it as easy and never attain the truth. So the daughter took the middle way by saying that it was neither difficult nor easy. Her idea was that one who is free from discrimination and who eats when hungry and sleeps when tired, is precisely the one meant by eminent masters. Therefore, the doctrine is not difficult for an enlightened man and not easy for an unenlightened man, thus wiping out the two extremes which have no room in the absolute.

[4] This sentence is omitted in the Chinese text and is added here to be in accord with Master Hsu Yun's lecture.

slapped him again and said: 'You see like the blind and you talk like the dumb.'[1]

The Upāsaka used to frequent places where sūtras were explained and commented on. One day, he listened to the expounding of the Diamond Sūtra, and when the commentator came to the sentence on the non-existence of ego and personality, he asked: '(Venerable) Sir, since there is neither self nor other, who is now expounding and who is listening?' As the commentator could not reply, the Upāsaka said: 'Although I am a layman, I comprehend something.' The commentator asked him: 'What is the (Venerable) Upāsaka's interpretation?' The Upāsaka replied with the following poem:

> There is neither ego nor personality,
> Who is distant then and who is intimate?
> Take my advice and quit your task of comment
> Since that cannot compare with the direct quest of the truth.
> The nature of the Diamond Wisdom
> Contains no foreign dust.[2]
> The words 'I hear', 'I believe' and 'I receive'
> Are meaningless and used expediently.

After hearing the poem, the commentator was delighted (with the correct interpretation) and praised (the Upāsaka).

One day, the Upāsaka asked Ling Chao: 'How do you understand the ancients' saying: "Clearly there are a hundred blades of grass; clearly these are the Patriarchs' indication?"' Ling Chao replied: 'Oh you old man, how can you talk like that?' The Upāsaka asked her: 'How would you say it?' Ling Chao replied: 'Clearly there are a hundred blades of grass; clearly these are the Patriarchs' indication.'[3] The Upāsaka laughed (approvingly).

[1] All Ch'an masters had compassion for unenlightened people and never missed a chance to enlighten them. Yo Shan sent ten Ch'an monks to accompany the eminent visitor to the front of the monastery so that they could learn something from him. Out of pity, the Upāsaka said: 'Good snow! The flakes do not fall elsewhere!', to probe the ability of the monks and to press them hard so that they could realize their self-minds for the attainment of Buddhahood. However, the monks seemed ignorant and did not realize that since the mind created the snow, the snow could not fall outside the mind. If they could only perceive *that which* slapped the unenlightened monk in the face, they would realize their self-nature. A serious monk would, under the circumstances, devote all his attention to inquiring into the unreasonable conduct of the visitor and would at least make some progress in his training.

[2] i.e. free from external impurities.

[3] The daughter seemed at first to criticize her father and then repeated the same sentence to confirm what he had said. Similar questions and answers are found frequently in Ch'an texts where Ch'an masters wanted to probe their disciples' abilities by first criticizing what they said. Any hesitation on the part of the disciples would disclose that they only repeated others' sayings without comprehending them. This was like a trap set to catch unenlightened disciples who claimed that they had realized the truth. When a disciple was really enlightened, he would remain undisturbed and would ask back the question. When the master was satisfied that the disciple's understanding was genuine, he would simply repeat the same sentence to give more emphasis to what the disciple had said.

(When he knew that) he was about to die, he said to Ling Chao: '(Go out and) see if it is early or late; if it is noon, let me know.' Ling Chao went out and returned, saying: 'The sun is in mid-heaven, but unfortunately is being swallowed by the heaven-dog[1]. (Father) why don't you go out to have a look?' Thinking that her story was true, he left his seat and went outside. Thereupon, Ling Chao (taking advantage of her father's absence) ascended to his seat, sat with crossed legs and with her two palms brought together, and passed away.

When the Upāsaka returned, he saw that Ling Chao had died and said, with a sigh: 'My daughter was sharp-witted and left before me.' So he postponed his death for a week, (in order to bury his daughter).

When magistrate Yu Ti came to inquire after his health, the Upāsaka said to him:

> Vow only to wipe out all that is;
> Beware of making real what is not.[1]
> Life in this (mortal) world
> A shadow is, an echo.

After saying this, he rested his head on the magistrate's knees and passed away. As willed by him, his body was cremated and the ashes were thrown into the lake.

His wife heard of his death and went to inform her son of it. Upon hearing the news, the son (stopped his work in the field), rested his chin on the handle of his hoe and passed away in a standing position. After witnessing these three successive events, the mother retired (to an unknown place) to live in seclusion.

As you see, the whole family of four had supernatural powers and could do works of wonder and these laymen who were also upāsakas like you, were of superior attainments. At present, it is impossible to find men of such outstanding ability not only among you upāsakas (and upāsikās) but also among monks and nuns who are no better than myself, Hsu Yun. What a disgrace!

Now let us exert outselves again in our training!

[1] i.e. eclipse of the sun.

[2] Existence and non-existence are two extremes which should be wiped out before one can attain the absolute reality.

The Seventh Day

Dear friends, allow me to congratulate you for the merits you have accumulated in the Ch'an week which comes to an end today. According to the standing rule, those of you who have experienced and realized (the truth) should come forward in this hall as did candidates who sat for a scholar's examination held previously in the imperial palace. Today, being the day of posting the list of successful graduates, should be one for congratulations. However, (the venerable) abbot has been most compassionate and (has decided to) continue this Ch'an meeting for another week so that we can all make additional efforts for further progress (in self-cultivation).

All the masters who are present here and are old hands in this training, know that it is a wonderful opportunity for co-operation and will not throw away their precious time. But those who are beginners, should know that it is difficult to acquire a human body[1] and that the question of birth and death is important. As we have human bodies, we should know that it is difficult to get the chance to hear the Buddha Dharma and meet learned teachers. Today you have come to the 'precious mountain'[2] and should take advantage of this excellent opportunity to make every possible effort (in your self-cultivation) in order not to return home empty-handed.

As I have said, our Sect's Dharma which was transmitted by the World Honoured One when he held up a flower to show it to the assembly, has been handed down from one generation to another. Although Ānanda was a cousin of the Buddha and left home to follow him as an attendant, he did not succeed in attaining the truth in the presence of the World Honoured One. After the Buddha had entered nirvāṇa, his great disciples assembled in a cave (to compile sūtras) but Ānanda was not permitted by them to attend the meeting. Mahākāśyapa said to him: 'You have not acquired the World Honoured One's Mind Seal, so please pull down the banner-pole in front of the door.' Thereupon, Ānanda was thoroughly enlightened. Then Mahākāśyapa transmitted to

[1] i.e. to be reborn in the human world. The realm of human beings is difficult of attainment; it is one of suffering and is the most suitable for self-cultivation, for human beings have more chance to study the Dharma in order to get rid of their miseries. The other five worlds of existence either enjoy too much happiness (devas and asuras) or endure too much suffering (animals, hungry ghosts and hells), thus having no chance to learn the Dharma.

[2] The Sūtra of Contemplation of Mind says: 'Like a handless man who cannot acquire anything in spite of his arrival at the precious mountain, one who is deprived of the "hand" of Faith, will not acquire anything even if he finds the Triple Gem.'

him the Tathāgata's Mind Seal, making him the second Indian Patriarch. The transmission was handed down to following generations, and after the Patriarchs Aśvaghoṣa and Nāgārjuna, Ch'an master Hui Wen of T'ien T'ai mountain in the Pei Ch'i dynasty (A.D. 550–78) after reading (Nāgārjuna's) Mādhyamika Śāstra, succeeded in realizing his own mind and founded the T'ien T'ai School.[1] At the time, our Ch'an Sect was very flourishing. Later, when the T'ien T'ai School fell into decadence, State master Teh Shao (a Ch'an master) journeyed to Korea (where the only copy of Chih I's works existed), copied it and returned to revive the Sect.

Bodhidharma who was the twenty-eighth Indian Patriarch, came to the East where he became the first (Chinese) Patriarch. From his transmission (of the Dharma) until the (time of the) Fifth Patriarch, the Mind-lamp shone brilliantly. The Sixth Patriarch had forty-three successors among whom were (the eminent) Ch'an masters Hsing Szu and Huai Jang. Then came (Ch'an master) Ma Tsu who had eighty-three successors. At the time, the Right Dharma reached its zenith and was held in reverence by emperors and high officials. Although the Tathāgata expounded many Dharmas, the Sect's was the unsurpassed one.

As to the Dharma which consists in repeating only the name of Amitābha (Buddha), it was extolled by (Ch'an Patriarchs) Aśvaghoṣa and Nāgārjuna,[2] and after master Hui Yuan,[3] Ch'an master Yen Shou of the Yung Ming monastery became the Sixth Patriarch of the Pure Land Sect (Chin T'u Tsung), which was subsequently spread by many other Ch'an masters.

After being propagated by Ch'an master I Hsing, the Esoteric Sect[4] spread to Japan but disappeared in China where there was no one to succeed to the master.

[1] The nine Patriarchs of the T'ien T'ai sect are: (1) Nāgārjuna, (2) Hui Wen of the Pei Ch'i dynasty, (3) Hui Ssu of Nan Yo, (4) Chih Che, or Chih I, (5) Kuan Ting of Chang An, (6) Fa Hua, (7) T'ien Kung, (8) Tso Ch'i and (9) Chan Jan of Ching Ch'i. The 10th, Tao Sui was considered a patriarch in Japan, because he was the teacher of (the Japanese) Dengyo Daishi who brought the Tendai system to that country in the ninth century. The T'ien T'ai (or Tendai in Japanese) Sect bases its tenets on the Lotus, Mahāparinirvāṇa and Mahāprajñāpāramitā Sūtras. It maintains the identity of the Absolute and the world of phenomena, and attempts to unlock the secrets of all phenomena by means of meditation.

[2] The 12th and 14th Patriarchs of the Ch'an sect respectively. Readers will notice that these two Patriarchs and many other Ch'an masters were not sectarian and extolled also the Pure Land School which was also a Dharma door expounded by the Buddha.

[3] Hui Yuan was an eminent master of the Pure Land Sect.

[4] Chen Yen Tsung, also called 'True Word' Sect, or Shingon in Japanese. The founding of this Sect is attributed to Vairocana, through Bodhisattva Vajrasattva, then through Nāgārjuna to Vajramati and to Amoghavajra.

The Dharmalakṣaṇa Sect[1] was introduced by Dharma master Hsuan Tsang but did not last very long.

Only our (Ch'an) Sect (is like a stream) which is still flowing from its remote source bringing devas into its fold and subduing dragons and tigers[2].

Lu Tung Pin, alias Shun Yang, a native of Ching Ch'uan, was one of the (famous) group of eight immortals.[3] Towards the end of the T'ang dynasty, he stood thrice for the scholar's examination but failed each time. Being disheartened, he did not return home, and one day, he met by chance in a wine-shop at Ch'ang An, an immortal named Chung Li Ch'uan who taught him the method of lengthening his span of life infinitely. Lu Tung Pin practised the method with great success and could even become invisible and fly in the air at will all over the country. One day, he paid a flying visit to the Hai Hui monastery on Lu Shan mountain; in its bell tower, he wrote on the wall:

> (After) a day of leisure when the body is at ease,
> The six organs[4] (now) in harmony, announce that all is well.
> With a gem in the pubic region[5] there's no need to search for truth,
> When mindless of surroundings, there's no need for Ch'an.

Some time later, as he was crossing the Huang Lung mountain, he beheld (in the sky) purple clouds shaped like an umbrella. Guessing that there must be some extraordinary person (in the monastery there), he entered it. It happened at the same time that in the monastery, after beating the drum, (Ch'an master) Huang Lung was ascending to his seat (to expound the Dharma). Lu Tung Pin followed the monks and entered the hall to listen to the teaching.

[1] The Dharmalakṣaṇa Sect is called Fa Hsiang in Chinese and Hossō in Japanese. This school was established in China on the return of Hsuan Tsang, consequent on his translation of the Yogācārya works. Its aim is to understand the principle underlying the nature and characteristics of all things.

[2] Maleficent beings.

[3] The immortals practise Taoism and sit in meditation with crossed legs. Their aim is to achieve immortality by putting an end to all passions, but they still cling to the view of the reality of ego and things. They live in caves or on the tops of mountains and possess the art of becoming invisible. A Chinese bhikṣu who is a friend of mine, went to North China when he was still young. Hearing of an immortal there, he tried to locate him. After several unsuccessful attempts, he succeeded finally in meeting him. Kneeling upon his knees, my friend implored the immortal to give him instruction. The latter, however, refused saying that the visitor was not of his line, i.e. Taoism. When the young man got up and raised his head, the immortal had disappeared and only a small sheet of paper was seen on the table with the word 'Good-bye' on it.

[4] According to the ancients, the six viscera are: heart, lungs, liver, kidney, stomach and gall-bladder.

[5] Pubic region, two and a half inches below the navel, on which concentration is fixed in Taoist meditation.

Huang Lung said to the assembly: 'Today there is here a plagiarist of my Dharma; the old monk (i.e. I) will not expound it.' Thereupon, Lu Tung Pin came forward and paid obeisance to the master, saying: 'I wish to ask the Venerable Master the meaning of these lines:

> A grain of corn contains the Universe:
> The hills and rivers (fill) a small cooking-pot.'

Huang Lung scolded him and said: 'What a corpse-guarding devil (you are).' Lu Tung Pin retorted: 'But my gourd holds the immortality-giving medicine.' Huang Lung said: 'Even if you succeed in living 80,000 aeons[1], you will not escape from falling into the dead void.' Forgetting all about the (fortitude advocated in his own line:)

> 'When mindless of surroundings there's no need for Ch'an.'

Lu Tung Pin burned with anger and threw his sword at Huang Lung. Huang Lung pointed his finger at the sword which fell to the ground and which the thrower could not get back. With deep remorse, Lu Tung Pin knelt upon his knees and inquired about the Buddha Dharma. Huang Lung asked: 'Let aside (the line:) "The hills, and rivers (fill) a small cooking-pot" about which I do not ask you anything. (Now) what is the meaning of: "A grain of corn contains the Universe"?'[2] Upon hearing this (question), Lu Tung Pin instantaneously realized the profound (Ch'an) meaning. Then, he chanted the following repentance-poem:

> I throw away my gourd and smash my lute.
> In future I'll not cherish gold in mercury.
> Now that I have met (the master) Huang Lung,
> I have realized my wrong use of the mind.[3]

This is the story of an immortal's return to and reliance on the Triple Gem and his entry into the monastery (Saṅghārāma) as a guardian of the

[1] The digit 8 in 80,000 symbolizes the 8th Consciousness (Vijñāna) which is an aspect of the self-nature under delusion. The sentence means that Lu Tung Pin was still unenlightened in spite of his long life.

[2] The grain of corn is created by the mind and reveals the mind which is immense and contains the whole Universe, also a creation of the mind. Being hard pressed, Lu Tung Pin instantly realized his self-mind and was awakened to the real.

[3] In ancient times, Taoists in China claimed to be able to 'extract quicksilver by smelting cinnabar', i.e. they knew the method which enabled them to become immortals, or Ṛṣis, in Sanskrit, whose existence was mentioned by the Buddha in the Śūraṇgama Sūtra. Their meditation aimed at the production of a hot current pervading all parts of the body and successful meditators could send out their spirits to distant places. They differed from Buddhists in that they held the conception of the reality of ego and of dharmas, and could not attain complete enlightenment. They used to wander in remote places, equipped with a gourd, a guitar and a 'divine' sword to protect themselves against demons. Today, adherents of the Taoist Sect are still found in great number in the Far East.

Dharma. Lu Tung Pin was also responsible for reviving the Taoist Sect at the time and was its Fifth (Tao) Patriarch in the North. The Taoist Tzu Yang also realized the mind after reading the (Buddhist) collection 'Tsu Ying Chi' and became the Fifth (Tao) Patriarch in the South.[1] Thus the Tao faith was revived thanks to the Ch'an Sect.

Confucius' teaching was handed down until Mencius after whom it came to an end. In the Sung dynasty Confucian scholars (also) studied the Buddha Dharma, and among them, (we can cite) Chou Lien Ch'i who practised the Ch'an training and succeeded in realizing his mind, and others such as Ch'eng Tzu, Chang Tzu and Chu Tzu (all famous Confucians). Therefore, the Ch'an Sect contributed (in no small measure) to the revival of Confucianism.

Nowadays, there are many people who despise the Ch'an Dharma and who even make slanderous remarks about it, thus deserving hell.[2] Today, we have this excellent opportunity of being favoured with a co-operating cause (which gathers us here). We should feel joy and should take the great vow to become objects of reverence for dragons and devas and to perpetuate the Right Dharma for ever. This is no child's play; so please make strenuous efforts to obtain more progress in your self-cultivation.

[1] Tzu Yang was an eminent Taoist who was well-versed in the Ch'an Dharma and his works attested his realization of the mind. Emperor Yung Cheng considered him a real Ch'an Buddhist and published his works in 'The Imperial Selection of Ch'an Sayings'.

[2] An evil karma which causes the sinner to be reborn in the Avīci hell. Lit: committing the Avīci-karma.

The First Day

My coming here has already caused much inconvenience to the monastery and I do not deserve the generous hospitality extended to me by the (Venerable) Abbot and group leaders. Today, I am again asked to preside over this (second Ch'an) week. I must say I am not qualified to do so. It is quite logical that the (venerable) old Dharma master Ying Tz'u who is advanced in age and Dharma years[1] should preside over this meeting. There are also in this monastery many learned and virtuous Dharma masters. I am only 'duckweed' floating on water[2] and am, therefore, a completely useless man. It would be wrong to say that I am accorded priority and courtesy because of my age.[3] Even, in the world-dharma,[4] no consideration is given to the question of age. Formerly, when the scholar's examination was held in the imperial palace, no matter whether a candidate was young or old, he called the examiner 'my old teacher' for the latter was respected (because of his rank and) not because of his age. In the Buddha Dharma also, no consideration is given to age. (I cite) Mañjuśrī Bodhisattva who very long ago attained Buddhahood and was the teacher of sixteen princes, one of whom was Amitābha Buddha. Śākyamuni Buddha was also his disciple, but when Śākyamuni Buddha attained Buddhahood, Mañjuśrī came to assist him (in teaching his disciples). Thus we know there is only One equality which is neither high nor low. Therefore, please make no mistake about all this.

As we are learning (the Dharma), we should respect (and observe) the rules and regulations (set up for the purpose). The (Venerable) Abbot has in mind the enlightenment of others, the expounding of sūtras, the holding of Ch'an meetings and the spreading of the Buddha Dharma. This is indeed a very rare opportunity.

All of you have been braving the cares and confusion of travel and

[1]The Dharma age of a monk is the number of summer or discipline years since his ordination.

[2] i.e. a man of no fixed abode. Master Hsu Yun had come from the Yun Men monastery in South China and did not yet know where he was going to settle. The Yun Men monastery was that of Ch'an master Yun Men, founder of the Yun Men Sect, one of the five Ch'an Sects in China. The monastery was rebuilt by master Hsu Yun.

[3] Master Hsu Yun was then 114 years old.

[4] World-dharma or worldly affairs.

giving yourselves a great deal of trouble to come of your own accord to attend this retreat. This shows that you have in mind the rejection of passions and desire of quiet.

In reality, you and I have only one mind but because of the difference between delusion and enlightenment, there are living beings who are busy from morning till evening without a day of rest. If we give some thought to this (state of things), we will see that no advantage can come from it. In spite of this, there are people who are busy all day long foolishly thinking of an abundance of food and clothing for themselves and anxious to find pleasure in singing and dancing. They want their children and grandchildren to have wealth and fame and their descendants to enjoy glory and prosperity. Even when they are about to breathe their last to become ghosts, they still think of protection and prosperity for their children. These people are really foolish and stupid.

There are also people who know something about good and evil and about cause and effect. They do meritorious acts which consist only in holding Buddhist ceremonies, in giving offerings to monks, in commissioning statues of Buddhas and in repairing temples and monastic buildings. Their acts contribute to the worldly[1] cause, and they hope to be rewarded with happiness in the next rebirth. Because they do not know anything about the passionless merits which are unsurpassed, they do not perform them. The Lotus Sūtra says: 'Sitting in meditation (even) for a short while is better than erecting as many seven treasure stūpas as the sandgrains in the Ganges.' For this method of sitting in meditation will enable us to wipe out our passions and to have peace of mind and body, resulting in the complete realization of the self-nature with liberation from birth and death. By 'a short while', it means a moment as short as an instant (kṣaṇa).[2] If one cleanses and purifies his mind and turns the light inwards on himself, his sitting in meditation even for an instant will (at least) enable him to sow the direct[3] cause of attainment of Buddhahood, if it does not ensure the (immediate) realization of the truth. His ultimate achievement can be expected (sooner or later). If his training is effective, Buddhahood can be attained in an instant. For this reason, Ānanda said in the Śūraṇgama Sūtra: 'The Dharmakāya can be realized without having to pass through countless aeons (kalpas).'[4]

[1] Worldly cause, or āsrava in Sanskrit, meaning 'leaking' cause; inside the passion-stream as contrasted with anāsrava, outside the passion-stream; no drip or leak.

[2] Kṣaṇa = the shortest measure of time, as kalpa or aeon, is the longest. 60 kṣaṇas equal a finger-snap, 90 a thought and 4,500 a minute.

[3] Direct cause, a true, as compared with a contributory, cause.

[4] Asaṅkhya in Sanskrit, or innumerable aeons.

However, you and I, and all other people in general, live in the midst of passions, of joy and anger, of gain and loss, of the five desires[1] and pursuits of pleasure and enjoyment. All these things are no more seen and heard as soon as we step into this Ch'an hall where our six senses are exactly like the black tortoise's six (vulnerable) parts which shrink into its shell and where nothing can disturb your minds. This is the practice of the passionless Dharma and (is also) the passionless Dharma (itself). Therefore, the merits derived from the erection of as many seven treasure stūpas as the sandgrains in the Ganges cannot be compared with those resulting from a moment spent sitting in meditation. The simile of the black tortoise comes from the (story of) the fish-eating seal which swam to catch the tortoise on the seashore. Seeing that it was attacked, the tortoise withdrew its head, tail and legs into its shell, so evading the seal's efforts to bite it.[2]

In this world, when we have no money, we are worried about our food and clothing, and when we have money, we cannot free ourselves from passions. We are thus caught and eaten by the seal. If we know of the danger to which we are exposed, we should bring our six senses under control and turn the light inwards on ourselves so that we can be liberated from mortality. Two days ago, I talked on our Sect's Dharma, dealing with the Right Dharma Eye, the Tathāgata's Mind-dharma and the basis of liberation from birth and death. Other Dharma doors[3] including the expounding of sūtras, in spite of their aims which are the arousing of faith and understanding, are only accessories[4] and do not advance the perfect (experiential) understanding. If the sūtra expounding Dharma is used to ensure liberation from birth and death, there must still be (two complementary phases) to pass through: practice and witnessing which are very difficult to achieve. For this reason, very few cases have been recorded of those who listened to the expounding of sūtras or followed other Dharma doors and who thereby attained instantaneously complete enlightenment and acquired transcendental powers. These cases were few as compared with those in the Ch'an Sect. According to our Sect, not only Ch'an monks and laymen (upāsakas) possessed

[1] The five desires arising from the objects of the five senses, things seen, heard, smelt, tasted and touched.

[2] This parable is frequently used in Buddhist Scriptures to advise us to shut the six gates of our senses so as to be detached from external surroundings.

[3] Dharma doors to enlightenment or methods of realizing the self-nature.

[4] Lit. leaves and branches in literary forms, i.e. accessories not fundamental in the experiential realization of the real. On the other hand, the Ch'an Sect aims at the direct pointing at the Buddha nature which every living being possesses and the instantaneous realization of the mind leading to the attainment of Buddhahood.

the inconceivable device, but Ch'an nuns were also of outstanding abilities.

Ch'an master Kuan Ch'i was a disciple of Lin Chi[1] but did not realize the truth in spite of having stayed several years at his master's monastery. One day, he (left his master) to call at other places (for instruction). When he arrived at a nunnery on Mo Shan mountain, a little nun reported his arrival to (Ch'an Bhikṣuṇī) Mo Shan who sent her attendant to ask him this question; 'Venerable Master, do you come here for sightseeing or for learning the Buddha Dharma?' Kuan Ch'i replied that he came for learning the Buddha Dharma. Mo Shan said: 'If you come for the Buddha Dharma, there are here also rules about beating the drum and ascending to the seat.' Thereupon, she ascended to her seat, but Kuan Ch'i bowed only and did not kneel down. Mo Shan asked him: 'What place did the Venerable Bhikṣu leave today?' He replied: 'I left the entrance to the road.' She asked him: 'Why didn't you cover it up?'[2] Kuan Ch'i could not reply and knelt down (to pay his respects), asking: 'What is Mo Shan?' She replied: 'The top of the head is not exposed.'[3] He asked: 'Who is the owner of Mo Shan (mountain)?' She replied: 'He is neither male nor female.' He shouted: 'Why does he not transform himself?' She asked back: 'He is neither a ghost nor a spirit, into what should he transform himself?'[4] He could not reply and submitted to her authority. He became a gardener at the nunnery where he stayed three years during which he was completely enlightened.

(Later) when Kuan Ch'i went to the Ch'an hall (to instruct his own disciples), he said to them: 'When I was at my father Lin Chi's place, I got a half-ladle (and) when I was at my mother Mo Shan's, I got another half-ladle, thus obtaining a full ladle which has enabled me to satisfy my hunger up to now.' Thus, although Kuan Ch'i was Lin Chi's disciple, he was also Mo Shan's Dharma successor.

[1] Founder of the Lin Chi Sect.

[2] Mo Shan's question means: If you think you are really enlightened and can dispense with kneeling, you should have realized your Dharmakāya which pervades everywhere and covers also the entrance to the road, for it is free from coming or going, and does not leave one place to come to another.

[3] The question: 'What is Mo Shan?' means: 'What is the state of the enlightened mind in the Mo Shan nunnery?' The questioner wanted a description of the Bodhi mind. The nun's reply refers to the small lump on the top of the Buddha's head which could not be seen by his disciples. Mo Shan meant that since the visitor was unenlightened, he could not perceive her Dharmakāya which was indescribable.

[4] When Kuan Ch'i asked about the owner of Mo Shan, i.e. about herself, she replied that the owner was neither male nor female for sex had nothing to do with enlightenment, and the Dharmakāya was neither male nor female. Generally, women had many more handicaps than men, and Kuan Ch'i seemed to look down upon her because of her sex and asked her why she did not change herself into a man if she was enlightened. His question showed that he was still under delusion.

We can see that among the nuns, there existed also people of real ability. There are many nuns here as well; why do not they come forward to show their abilities and reveal the Right Dharma on behalf of their predecessors? The Buddha Dharma extols equality (of sex) and we are only required to make efforts in our training without backsliding so as not to miss this (rare) opportunity.

The ancients said:

> In one hundred years or six and thirty thousand days[1],
> There is not a quiet moment to lay down mind and body.

For countless aeons, we have been floating in the sea of mortality because we have never wanted to lay down our bodies and minds in order to have quiet for our learning and self-cultivation, with the result that we have been turned round by the wheel of transmigration without a chance of liberation. For this reason, all of us should lay down both body and mind and sit in meditation for a moment with the hope that the bottom of the cask of (black) lacquer will drop off and that we will together experience the law of no-birth.[2]

The Second Day

This is the second day of the second Ch'an week. The increasing number of those who come to this meeting shows how really good-hearted are the people of Shanghai and the excellence of their blessed virtues. It also indicates every man's aversion to disturbance (caused by passions) and longing for the quiet (found in meditation), and every man's desire to escape from sorrow and to seek happiness. Generally speaking, there is more suffering than happiness in this world and, as time passes very quickly, the short space of several decades slips away in the twinkling of an eye. Even if one can live 800 years like Peng Tsu,[3] this space of time

[1] The maximum life span of each individual.

[2] In Ch'an parlance, our ignorance is symbolized by the thick black lacquer contained in a wooden cask, because nothing can be seen through it. Ch'an training will cause the bottom of the cask to drop off, thus emptying it of the black lacquer, i.e. our body and mind of delusion. This is the moment when we can perceive the real.

Law of no-birth: lit. endurance leading to the personal experiencing of the law of no-birth, or immortality, i.e. the absolute which is beyond birth and death, boundless patience or endurance being required for subduing the wandering mind.

[3] The Methuselah of China.

is (still) short in the eye of the Buddha Dharma. However, worldly men who can reach the age of seventy are rarely seen. Since you and I know that this short length of time is like an illusion and a transformation, and is really not worth our attachment (to it), we have come to this Ch'an week and this is certainly due to our having grown good roots in our former transmigrations.

This method of (self-) cultivation requires an enduring mind. Formerly, all Buddhas and Bodhisattvas reached their goal after spending many aeons in self-cultivation. The Śūraṅgama Sūtra's chapter on Avalokiteśvara's Complete Enlightenment says:

> 'I remember that long before the elapsing of as uncountable a number of aeons as there are sandgrains in the Ganges a Buddha by the name of Avalokiteśvara appeared in the world. At that time I developed the Bodhi mind and for my entry into Samādhi was instructed by Him to practise (self-) cultivation through (the faculty of) hearing.'

From the above statement, we can see that Avalokiteśvara Bodhisattva did not achieve his goal in one or two days. At the same time, he clearly told us about the method of his training. He was head (of the group of) twenty-five 'Great Ones' who attained complete enlightenment. His method consisted of (self-) cultivation of the ear which enabled him to transmute the faculty of hearing into perfection which led to (the state of) Samādhi. Samādhi means the (state of) undisturbedness. Therefore, he continued:

> (I) 'At the start, by directing the hearing (ear)
> Into the stream (of meditation), this organ became detached from its object.'

This method consists in turning the hearing inwards (on the self-nature) to hear the self-nature so that the six senses will not (wander outside to) be in touch with the six external objects. This is the collection of the six senses into the Dharma nature.[1] Therefore, he continued:

> (II) 'By wiping out (the concept of) both sound and stream-entry,
> Both disturbance and stillness
> Became clearly non-existent.'

He said again:

> (III) 'Thus advancing step by step,
> Both hearing and its object came to an end.
> But I did not stop where they ended.'

[1]Dharmata in Sanskrit, i.e. the nature underlying all things, the Bhutatathata.

He meant that we should not allow our training, by turning our hearing inwards (on the self-nature) to come to a halt; he wanted us to move forward little by little and to make additional efforts to reach (another stage about which he said as follows:)

(IV) 'When the awareness (of this state) and this state itself (were realized) as non-existent,
The awareness of voidness became all-embracing
After the elimination of both subject and object relating to voidness.
Then the disappearance of both creation and annihilation
(Resulted in) the state of Nirvāṇa becoming manifest.'

This state results from the training which consists in turning the ear inwards to hear the self-nature and after all kinds of creation and annihilation are realized as non-existent, the true mind will manifest itself. This is the (meaning of the saying:) 'When the mad mind is brought to a halt, it is Bodhi (i.e. perfect wisdom)'.

After attaining this stage, Avalokiteśvara Bodhisattva said:

'Suddenly I leaped over both the mundane and supramundane and realized an all-embracing brightness pervading the ten directions, acquiring two unsurpassed (merits). The first one was in accord with the fundamental Profound Enlightened Mind of all Buddhas high up in the ten directions, possessing the same merciful power as the Tathāgata. The second one was in sympathy with all living beings in the six realms of existence, here below in the ten directions, sharing with them the same imploration of pity.'

Today, in our study of the Buddhist doctrine for our (self-) cultivation, we should first succeed in our training by liberating all the living beings of our self-nature such as concupiscence, anger, stupidity and arrogance and by realizing the fundamentally pure and clean Profound Enlightened Real Mind.[1] Only then can we perform the Buddha work high above for the salvation of living beings here below, as did Avalokiteśvara Bodhisattva who could manifest in thirty-two different forms, each being suitable for the liberation of the corresponding individual, and only then can we possess the required (transcendental) powers. Avalokiteśvara Bodhisattva (can) appear in the world as a boy or a girl, but worldly men do not know that he has already attained Buddhahood, has no sex and

[1] The profound enlightenment of Mahāyāna, or self-enlightenment to enlighten others. The 51st and 52nd stages in the enlightenment of a Bodhisattva, or the two supreme forms of Buddha-enlightenment are respectively: (1) Samyak-saṁbodhi, or absolute universal enlightenment, omniscience, and (2) the profound enlightenment of Mahāyāna, or self-enlightenment to enlighten others. The first is the 'cause' and the second is the 'fruit', and a Bodhisattva becomes a Buddha when the 'cause is complete and the fruit is full'.

is neither an ego nor a personality, making a (particular) appearance only in response to each individual potentiality. When worldly men (in China) hear the Bodhisattva's name, thoughts of devotion and reverence for him arise. This is due to the fact that in their former lives, they had repeated his name so that the seeds previously sown in the field of their store-consciousness (ālaya-vijñāna) now develop in them. For this reason, the sūtra says:

'After entering through the hearing,
The Bodhi-seed is sown for ever.'

Today, as we come here for our self-perfuming[1] and self-cultivation, we should rely on the Dharma of the Supreme Vehicle practised and experienced by all Buddhas and Bodhisattvas. This Dharma consists in clearly recognizing the fundamental Profound Enlightened Mind; that is to say, the perception of the self-nature leading to the attainment of Buddhahood. If this mind is not recognized, Buddhahood can never be attained. In order to recognize the mind, we should begin with the performance of virtuous deeds. If every day, from morning until evening, we perform all good actions and refrain from committing evil deeds, we will accumulate merits and if in addition we hold a hua t'ou constantly (in our minds), we will be able to realize, in a moment's thought, the state of no-birth and will (thereby) attain Buddhahood instantaneously.

Dear friends, please make a profitable use of your time and do not give rise to wrong thoughts in your minds. Now is the time to give rise to a hua t'ou for your self-cultivation.

Explanatory Note:

When the Buddha expounded the Śūraṅgama Sūtra, he ordered the twenty-five 'enlightened ones' who were present, to talk about the various means by which they had attained enlightenment, so that the assembly could learn something from them. After the statements by twenty-four of the 'enlightened ones' of their realization of the real by means of the six guṇas: (1) sound, (2) sight, (3) smell, (4) taste, (5) touch and (6) idea; the five sense-organs: (7) the eye, (8) nose, (9) tongue, (10) body, and (11) mind; the six perceptions of (12) sight, (13) ear, (14) nose, (15) tongue, (16) body, and (17) faculty of mind; and the seven fundamental elements of (18) fire, (19) earth, (20) water, (21) wind, (22) space, (23) knowledge and (24) perceptibility, Avalokiteśvara Bodhisattva declared that he had attained enlightenment by means of (25) the organ of hearing. In order to teach Ānanda and the assembly, the Buddha asked Mañjuśrī for his opinion on these twenty-five

[1] i.e. to be under the beneficial influence of the fragrance of Buddha Dharma.

methods. Mañjuśrī praised the method used by Avalokiteśvara saying that he himself had also used it for his own enlightenment and that it was the most suitable one for human beings.

The following is a commentary on the verses of the Śūraṅgama Sūtra:

(I) At the start, by directing the hearing
Into the stream, this organ became detached from its object.

This was the turning of the ear inwards on the self-nature to hear it so that hearing and its object, i.e. the sound, became detached. When hearing was brought under control in this manner, the other five senses had no chance of wandering outside to get in touch with the corresponding external objects. Stream here means the inward stream of meditation, or correct concentration.

The mind was brought under control to free it from external disturbance. Could it really be controlled by using it to direct the ear inwards to hear the self-nature? The mind was already disturbed when it was directed inwards. Therefore, efforts should be made to free it from disturbance so that stillness can prevail.

(II) By wiping out (the concept of) both sound and stream-entry,
Both disturbance and stillness
Clearly became non-existent.

As the sound and stream were realized to be non-existent, both disturbance and stillness also became non-existent. The mind was thus disentangled from the guṇas, or sensation-data.

(III) Thus advancing step by step,
Both the hearing and its object came to an end;
But I did not stop where they ended.

By making additional efforts I advanced further step by step, until both hearing and sound came completely to an end. However, I did not stop there. Thus the mind was disentangled from the sense-organs. The voidness of which the meditator was aware then appeared. This incomplete or partial awareness should also be wiped out.

(IV) When the awareness (of this state) and this state itself (were realized as) non-existent,
The awareness of voidness became all-embracing,
After the elimination of subject and object relating to voidness.
Then the disappearance of creation and annihilation
(Resulted in) the state of Nirvāṇa becoming manifest.

With further progress, the meditator perceived that both the incomplete awareness (subject) of voidness and the voidness itself (object) were non-existent. After the elimination of both subject and object relating to the false conception of relative voidness, the complete awareness of the absolute voidness became all-embracing, ensuring the end of the dual conception of creation and annihilation of even subtle phenomena, perceptible only at this last stage of meditation, such as relative voidness and incomplete awareness, which were only creations of the mind. As creation existed only as a relative term and was followed by annihilation, so long as this duality existed, the mind was still held in bondage. Now as this pair of opposites was non-existent, the awareness became complete. When this last stage was reached the resultant state of Nirvāṇa became manifest. This stage ensured the instantaneous leap over both the mundane and supramundane when the meditator attained the all-embracing illumination of absolute wisdom.

Master Han Shan also followed this method and attained Samādhi during his stay on the Five Peaked Mountain. (*See* Han Shan's Autobiography.)

The holding of a hua t'ou also enables a Ch'an student to realize the disentanglement of his mind from guṇas (or external objects), sense-organs, incomplete awareness (or inner subject) and relative voidness for the same purpose of attaining the absolute voidness of complete awareness, or wisdom.

The Third Day

This is the third day of this second Ch'an week. Those who are already familiar with this training, can always control their minds no matter where they may happen to be either in the midst of disturbance or of stillness. To them, there is no difference between the first and second week or between the second and third day. But those who are beginners should endeavour to make progress in their training which they should not undergo in a careless manner, in order not to waste their (precious) time. I will now tell the beginners another story and hope they will listen to it attentively.

In every Ch'an hall, there is (a statue of) a Bodhisattva called the 'Holy Monk'. He was a cousin of the Tathāgata Śākyamuni and his name was Ārya Ājñāta-Kauṇḍinya. When the World Honoured One left home, His father sent three paternal and two maternal clansmen to go with and look after Him in the Himālayas. This cousin was one of the two maternal clansmen. After the World Honoured One had attained enlightenment, He went to the Mṛgadāva park where He expounded the Four Noble Truths and where this cousin was the first disciple awakened to the truth. This cousin was also one of His great disciples and the first to leave home. For this reason, he was called the 'Holy Monk'. He was also known as the Saṅgha Head.[1] His method of self-cultivation is clearly described in the Śūraṅgama Sūtra which says:

[1] Head of the Saṅgha order.

After I had attained enlightenment, I went to the Mṛgadāva park where I declared to Ājñāta-Kauṇḍinya and the other five bhikṣus as well as to you, the four varga,[1] that all living beings failed to realize Enlightenment (Bodhi) and attain Arhatship because they were misled by foreign dust[2] which (entering the mind) caused distress and delusion. What, at the time, caused your awakening (to the truth) for your present attainment of the holy fruit?[3]

This was the Buddha's talk about the cause of our failure to realize Bodhi and to attain Arhatship. He also asked His great disciples in the assembly about the methods they used for their awakening (to the truth). At the time, only Ājñāta-Kauṇḍinya knew this method. So he arose from his seat and replied to the World Honoured One as follows:

I am now a senior in the assembly in which I am the only one who has acquired the art of explaining because of my awakening to (the meaning of) the two words 'foreign dust' which led to my attainment of the (holy) fruit.

After saying this, he gave the following explanation (of these two words) to the World Honoured One:

World Honoured One, (foreign dust) is like a guest who stops at an inn where he passes the night or takes his meal, and as soon as he has done so, he packs and continues his journey because he has no time to stay longer. As to the host of the inn, he has nowhere to go. My deduction is that one who does not stay is a guest and one who does stay is a host. Consequently, a thing is 'foreign' when it does not stay.

Again, in a clear sky, when the sun rises and its light enters (the house) through an opening, the dust is seen moving in the ray of light whereas the empty space is unmoving. Therefore, that which is still is the void and that which moves is the dust.

How clearly he explained the two words 'host' and 'guest'! You should know that this illustration shows us how to begin our training. In other words, the real mind is the host who does not move and the moving guest is our false thinking which is likened to dust. Dust is very fine and dances in the air. It is visible only when the sunlight enters through the door or an opening. This means that false thoughts within our minds are imperceptible in the usual process of thinking. They become perceptible only when we sit in meditation during our training.

[1] The four varga, groups or orders, i.e., Bhikṣu, bhikṣuṇī, upāsaka and upāsikā; monks, nuns, male and female devotees.

[2] Foreign dust: guṅa, in Sanskrit, small particles; molecules, atoms, exhalations; element or matter, which is considered as defilement; an active conditioned principle in nature, minute, subtle and defiling to pure mind; impurities.

[3] Fruit of saintly life, i.e. Bodhi, Nirvāṇa.

In the midst of the unending rise and fall of mixed thoughts and in the tumult of false thinking, if your training is not efficient, you will not be able to act as a host; hence your failure to attain enlightenment and your drifting about in the ocean of birth and death, wherein you are a Smith in your present transmigration and will be a Jones in the next one. Thus you will be exactly like a guest who stops at an inn and will not be able to remain there for ever. However, the true mind does not act in that way; it neither comes nor goes, is not born and does not die. It does not move but remains motionless, hence the host. This host is likened to the immutable voïdness in which the dust dances. It is also like the host of an inn who always stays there for he has nowhere else to go.

Dust is like one of the passions and can be wiped out completely only when one reaches the Bodhisattva-stage. By falsehood, is meant illusion. There are eighty-eight kinds of illusory view and eighty-one of illusory thought. These (misleading) views come from the five stupid temptations,[1] and in self-cultivation, one should wipe out all of them in order to attain the first stage of the Arhat (śrota-āpanna).[2] This is the most difficult thing to do, for the cutting of illusory views is likened to the cutting (or stopping) of the flow of a forty-mile stream. Thus we can see that we should have a great measure of strength in our training. We can attain Arhatship only when we have succeeded in cutting out all misleading thoughts. This kind of self-cultivation is a gradual process.

(In our Ch'an training), we have only to make use of a hua t'ou which should be kept bright and lively and should never be allowed to become blurred and which should always be clearly cognizable. All misleading views and thoughts will thus be cut off (by the hua t'ou) at a single blow leaving behind only something like the cloudless blue sky in which the bright sun will rise. This is the brightness of the self-nature when it manifests itself.

This saint (ārya)[3] was awakened to this truth and recognized the original host. The first step in our training today is to be cognizant of the fact that the foreign dust (or guest) is moving whereas the host is motionless. If this is not clearly understood, we will not know where to begin our training, and will only waste our time as heretofore.

I hope all of you will pay great attention to the above.

[1] The five stupid temptations, or pañca-kleśa, in Sanskrit, i.e. the five dull, unintelligent, or stupid vices or agents: desire, anger or resentment, stupidity or foolishness, arrogance and doubt.

[2] One who has entered the stream of holy living or who goes against the stream of transmigration; the first stage of the Arhat.

[3] Meaning Ājñāta-Kauṇḍinya.

It is very difficult to meet with the unsurpassed Profound Dharma in a hundred, a thousand or ten thousand aeons, and the present opportunity of our gathering for a Ch'an week in this Monastery of the Jade Buddha is really afforded by an unsurpassed co-operating cause. The fact that lay men and women have come from all directions in an increasing number to attend this meeting for the sowing of the direct cause of the attainment of Buddhahood, proves that this opportunity is rarely available.

The Buddha Śākyamuni said in the Lotus Sūtra:

> If men, with minds disturbed,
> Enter a stūpa or a temple
> (And) call: Namo Buddhāya!
> Buddhahood they will attain.

In a short period of several decades, worldly men are not aware of the passing of time. Those who have money, pursue wine, sex and prosperity. Those who have no money, have to work hard for their food, clothing, shelter and travel. Thus (all of them) rarely have a moment's leisure and comfort and their sufferings are beyond description. However, if they happen to enter a Buddhist temple, they will find happiness in the majesty of its quiet. They will behold the statues of Buddhas and Bodhisattvas, and may repeat at random the Buddha's name; or they may be impressed with the sudden quiet of their (temporarily) purified minds, and praise the Tathāgata's bliss which is so rarely found (elsewhere). All this comes from their having acquired very deep good roots in their former transmigrations and provides the cause of their future attainment of Buddhahood. For, in general, what their eyes want to see is only merry-making; what their ears want to hear is only songs and music, and what their mouths want to taste is only succulent dishes and rare delicacies. All this soils their thinking and this defiled thinking produces a disturbed mind, the deluded mind of birth and death. Now, if, while in a stūpa or temple, one has a chance of calling the Buddha's name, this is the awakened mind, the pure mind and the Bodhi seed leading to attainment of Buddhahood. The Sanskrit word 'Buddha' means the Enlightened One, that is one who is (completely) enlightened and is no more deluded. When the self-nature is pure and clean, one possesses the awakened mind.

Today, we do not come here for fame and wealth and this is our awakening power which manifests itself. However, many are those who hear of the Ch'an week but do not know anything about its real meaning. They come to see this bustling meeting to satisfy their curiosity and this is (certainly) not the highest mind. Now that you have come to this place, you are like those who arrive at the mountain of precious gems and you should not return empty handed. You should develop the highest Truth-Mind, and sit in meditation during the time of the burning of an incense stick, in order to sow the direct cause of attainment of Buddhahood and to become Buddhas later on.

Formerly, Śākyamuni Buddha had a disciple whose name was Subhadra.[1] He was very poor and was all alone, without anybody to support him. His heart was full of sadness and he wanted to follow the Buddha as his disciple. One day, he went to the World Honoured One's place but it happened that He was not there.

After looking into Subhadra's former transmigrations for the purpose of finding out whether there existed some co-operating cause, the Buddha's great disciples found that in the past 80,000 aeons,[2] he had not planted any good roots. They then decided not to allow him to stay and sent him away. With a heart full of sadness, Subhadra left the place and when he reached a walled town, he thought that if his karma was so bad, it would be better for him to kill himself by knocking his head against the wall. As he was about to commit suicide, the World Honoured One happened to arrive there and asked him about his intention. Subhadra related his story to the World Honoured One who accepted him as His disciple. They returned together to His place where seven days later, Subhadra attained Arhatship. The great disciples who did not know the cause of Subhadra's attainment, asked the World Honoured One about it.

The World Honoured One said to them: 'You only know things which happened in the last 80,000 aeons, but before then Subhadra had already planted good roots. At that time, he was also very poor and gathered firewood as his means of subsistence. One day, he met a tiger on the mountains, and seeing that his escape was cut off, he hurriedly climbed a tree. The tiger saw that he was up the tree which it began to

[1] The last convert of the Buddha, 'a Brahman 120 years old'.

[2] The digit 8 in 80,000 symbolizes the eighth or store (ālaya) consciousness (vijñāna), the deluded aspect of the self-nature. So long as the self-nature is under delusion, it is controlled by the discriminating mind and will never perceive the real which is beyond all numbers. The great disciples did not perceive the unconditioned cause of the attainment of Buddhahood, and saw only worldly events occurring in the former transmigrations of Subhadra. The Buddha who possessed the Sarvajña or All-wisdom, saw clearly his new disciple's cause of Arhatship, which cause being beyond all numbers is inherent in the self-nature.

gnaw to fell it. At the critical moment, as no one came to his rescue, he had a sudden thought of the great enlightened Buddha who possessed the power of compassion and could save all sufferers. Thereupon, he called: "Namo Buddhāya! Come quickly to save me!" Upon hearing the call, the tiger went away and did not harm his life. He thus sowed the direct cause of Buddhahood which became ripe today, hence his attainment of the Arhat-stage.' After hearing the story, all the great disciples were delighted and praised the marvellous (achievement of the poor man).

Today you and I meet here under auspicious circumstances, and if we can sit in meditation during the time of the burning of a (whole) incense stick, our (resultant) good karma will exceed many times the (one narrated in the above story). We should never take this meditation as child's play. If we come here to see a bustling meeting, we will simply miss a very good opportunity.

The Fifth Day

Those of you who have a deep believing mind, are naturally making efforts in their training in this hall. The (venerable) group leaders who are experienced in this self-cultivation, are already familiar with it. However, experienced men must know the interplay of activity (phenomenon) and principle (noumenal).[1] They should probe it exhaustively and make sure that (they experience) the unhindered interdependence of the noumenal and phenomenal and of the immutable and mutable. They should not sit like dead men; they should never be immersed in the void and cling to stillness, with delight in it. If there be delight in the still surrounding and absence of (realization of) the interchange (of practice and theory), this is likened to fish in stagnant water, with no hope of jumping over the Dragon Door.[2] They are also like fish in frozen water (and) this is a fruitless type of training.

[1] i.e. practice and theory; phenomena ever change; the underlying principle, being absolute, neither changes nor acts; it is the Bhūtatathatā. When we see a flag streaming in the wind, we know that, in theory, only the mind moves and not the wind or the flag. In practice, we cannot deny that the wind blows and the flag moves. We know also that in theory mind, wind and flag are but one undivided whole. Now, how can we have an experiential realization of this sameness? If we fail to experience it, we will also fail in our self-cultivation. This is the most important phase of the meditation, which can be achieved only if we put an end to our feelings and discrimination.

[2] In ancient China, it was believed that some fish, especially carp, could jump out of the sea to become dragons. A metaphor meaning that these meditators will never obtain liberation.

In this training, beginners should be earnest (in their desire to escape) birth and death, and should develop a great mortification-mind by laying down all kinds of (productive) causes.[1] Only then, can their training be effective. If they are unable to lay down these causes, the (round of) birth and death will never come to an end. For, since we have been deluded by the seven emotions and six sexual attractions[2] from the time without beginning, we now find ourselves, from morning to evening, in the midst of sounds and forms, without knowing the permanent true-mind, hence our fall into the bitter ocean (of birth and death). As we are now awakened to the fact that there is only suffering in all worldly (situations), we can (certainly) lay down all (our thoughts of) them and (thereby) attain Buddhahood at once.[3]

The Sixth Day

In this Ch'an hall, I have noticed that many male and female participants are only beginners who do not know the (standing) rules and regulations and whose unruly behaviour interferes with the calm meditation of others. However, we are fortunate in that the Venerable Abbot is most compassionate and is doing all he can to help us achieve our religious karma.[4] (Moreover) the group leaders who have developed the unsurpassed mind bent on the right Way, are here to lead us so that we can undergo an appropriate training. This is (indeed) an opportunity rarely available in myriads of aeons.

(Therefore), we should strive resolutely to make further progress in our inner and outer training. In our inner training, we should either concentrate pointedly on the hua t'ou: 'Who is the repeater of Buddha's name?' or repeat the name of Amitābha Buddha,[5] without giving rise to

[1] i.e. all causes including feelings and passions which are productive of effects and contribute to the turning wheel of births and deaths.

[2] The seven emotions are: pleasure, anger, sorrow, joy, love, hate and desire. The six attractions arise from colour, form, carriage, voice or speech, softness or smoothness and features.

[3] Lit. on the spot.

[4] Which leads to Buddhahood.

[5] i.e. the repetition of Amitābha's name as taught by the Pure Land School; this repetition also enables the repeater to disentangle his mind from all feelings and discrimination and to attain samādhi. Cases are on record of adepts of the Pure Land School, knowing, in advance, of the time of their death. This is possible only after their attainment of samādhi which manifested itself simultaneously with prajñā, or wisdom, called the wisdom of mutual response.

desire, anger and stupidity and all kinds of thought so that the Dharma nature[1] of the Bhūtatathatā[2] can manifest itself.

In our outer training, we should not kill the living but should release all living creatures; we should transmute the ten evils[3] into the ten good virtues;[4] we should not eat meat and drink alcoholic liquors in order not to produce the sinful karma[5] of unintermittent suffering; and we should know that the Buddha-seed arises from conditional causation, that the commitment of many evil karmas is followed by the certain fall into the hells, and that the performance of many good karmas is rewarded with blessing ensuring our enjoyment of them. And so the ancients taught us this: 'Refrain from committing all evil actions (and) perform all good actions.' You have already read the causal circumstances of the killing of members of the Śākya clan by the Crystal King (Virūḍhaka) and know of this (law of causality).[6]

At present, all over the world, people are suffering from (all sorts of) calamity and are in the depth of the aeon (kalpa) of slaughter. This is the retribution (for evil actions). We (should) always exhort worldly men to refrain from taking life and to release living creatures, to take vegetarian food, to (think of the Buddha and) repeat his name, so that everybody can escape from the turning wheel of cause and effect.

All of you should believe and observe (this teaching) and sow now the good cause for reaping later the Buddha-fruit.

The Seventh Day

This ephemeral life is like a dream,
(And) this illusory substance is not stable.
If we rely not on the compassion of our Buddha
How can we ascend the transcendental Way?

In this life which is like a dream and an illusion, we pass our time in an upside-down manner. We do not realize the greatness of the Buddha

[1] Dharma nature, or Dharmatā in Sanskrit, is nature underlying all things.

[2] Bhūtatathatā is the real, 'as thus always', or 'certainly so'; i.e. reality as contrasted with unreality or appearance, and unchanging or immutable as contrasted with form or phenomena.

[3] The ten evils are: killing, stealing, adultery, lying, double-tongue, coarse language, filthy talk, covetousness, anger and perverted views.

[4] The ten good virtues are defined as the non-committal of the ten evils.

[5] That which sin does, its karma, producing subsequent suffering without interruption.

[6] See page 30.

and do not think of escaping from (the realm of) birth and death. We let our good and evil (actions) decide our rise and fall and we accept the retribution according to their karmic effects. This is why in this world, few accomplish good deeds but many commit evil actions, and few are rich and noble but many are poor and mean. In the six worlds of existence, there are all kinds of suffering. There are living beings who are born in the morning and die in the evening. There are those who live only a few years and others who live many years. They are not all masters of themselves. For this reason, we should rely on the Buddha's compassion if we want to find a way (out of this mess), because the Buddhas and Bodhisattvas possess the power of their vows of kindness, pity, joy and renunciation and can deliver us from the bitter ocean (of mortality) for our (safe) arrival at the bright 'other shore'. They are kind and compassionate and when they see living beings enduring suffering, they take pity on them and liberate them so that they can escape suffering and enjoy happiness. Their joy and renunciation consist in their rejoicing and praise for living beings who accomplish meritorious deeds or give rise to thoughts of kindness in the mind, and in granting all requests according to the latter's requirements.

When the World Honoured One practised His self-cultivation from the causal ground,[1] His deeds (in the successive Bodhisattva stages of His former lives) consisted in His renunciation of His own head, brain, bone and marrow. For this reason, He said:

> In the Universe, there is not a spot of land as small as a mustard-seed where I have not sacrificed my lives or have not buried my bones.

Today, all of you should endeavour to hold the hua t'ou firm (in your mind); be careful not to waste your time.

The Closing Day

Dear friends, I congratulate you all on the conclusion of this Ch'an week. You have completed your merit-(orious training) and in just a moment, the gathering will come to an end and I will have to congratulate you.

[1] Or cause-ground, the stage of self-cultivation which leads to the fruit-ground, or stage of attainment of Buddhahood.

According to the ancients, the opening and closing of a Ch'an week do not mean much, for it is (more) important to hold a hua t'ou continuously (in mind) until one's complete enlightenment. At present, no matter whether you have been awakened or not, we must follow the procedure set forth in the (standing) rules and regulations. During these (two) Ch'an weeks, you did not make any difference between day and night, because your (only) aim was your own awakening. The (ultimate) purpose of the meeting was, therefore, to produce men of ability for (spreading) the Buddhist doctrine. If you have wasted your time without achieving any result, you will indeed have missed a (great) opportunity.

Now, the (Venerable) Abbot and group leaders will follow the ancient rules and regulations and will examine the result of your training. I hope you will not talk wildly (when questioned); you should, in the presence of others, give in a sentence (a summary of) your achievement. If your replies are in order, the (Venerable) Abbot will confirm your realization. The ancients said:

> '(Self-) cultivation takes an unimaginable time[1]
> (While) enlightenment in an instant is attained.

If the training is efficient, enlightenment will be attained in one finger-snap.

In days gone by, Ch'an master Hui Chueh of Lang Yeh mountain, had a woman disciple who called on him for instruction. The master taught her to examine into the sentence: 'Take no notice.'[2] She followed his instruction strictly without backsliding. One day, her house caught fire, but she said: 'Take no notice.' Another day, her son fell into the water and when a bystander called her, she said: 'Take no notice.' She observed exactly her master's instruction by laying down all causal thoughts.[3]

One day, as her husband lit the fire to make fritters of twisted dough, she threw into the pan full of boiling (vegetable) oil a batter which made a noise. Upon hearing the noise, she was instantaneously enlightened.[4] Then she threw the pan of oil on the ground, clapped her hands and

[1] Lit. three great asaṅkhya: kalpas beyond number, the three timeless periods of a Bodhisattva's progress to Buddhahood.

[2] Lit. 'Let it go.'

[3] Thoughts productive of causes leading to effects.

[4] Her training was already very effective in disentangling her mind from the sense-organs, sense-data and perceptions, i.e. her mind was undisturbed at the time, and the noise had a tremendous effect on it. She did not hear it by means of her faculty of hearing which had ceased functioning, but through the very function of her self-nature which exposed her real 'face', hence her enlightenment.

laughed.[1] Thinking she was insane, her husband scolded her and said: 'Why do you do this? Are you mad?' She replied: 'Take no notice.' Then she went to master Hui Chueh and asked him to verify her achievement. The master confirmed that she had obtained the holy fruit.

Dear friends, those of you who have been awakened (to the truth), please come forward and say something about your realization.

(After a long while, as no one came forward, Master Hsu Yun left the hall. The (Venerable) Dharma master Ying Tz'u continued to hold the examination, and when it was over, Master Hsu Yun returned to the hall to instruct the assembly.)

Master Hsu Yun said:

In this tumultous world and (especially in this) bustling and disorderly city, how can one have spare time for, and thought of, coming here to sit in meditation and to hold a hua t'ou? (However), the deep good roots possessed by the people of Shanghai, in combination with the flourishing Buddha Dharma and the unsurpassed co-operating cause have made this great opportunity available for our gathering.

From olden time till now, we have had the Teaching, the Discipline (Vinaya), the Pure Land and the Esoteric (Yoga) Schools. A rigorous comparison between these schools and the Ch'an Sect proves the superiority of the latter. Earlier, I also spoke of this unsurpassed Sect, but owing to the present decline of Buddha Dharma, men of ability are not available. Formerly, in my long journeys on foot I went to and stayed at various monasteries but what I see now cannot be compared with what I saw then. I am really ashamed of my ignorance, but the (Venerable) Abbot who is very compassionate, and the group leaders who are very courteous, have pushed me forward (to preside over this meeting). This task should have been entrusted to the (venerable) old Dharma master Ying Tz'u who is an (acknowledged) authority on both Ch'an and the scriptures and is an (experienced) senior. I am now a useless man and cannot do anything, and I hope you will all follow him and push forward without backsliding.

Ancestor Kuei Shan said: 'It is regrettable that we were born at the end of the semblance period,[2] so long after the passing of the holy period,

[1] Usually after an awakening, or satori in Japanese, one is seized with a desire to cry' jump, dance or do something abnormal, like throwing down the pan of oil. If one fails to subdue this desire, one will catch the Ch'an illness described in Han Shan's autobiography.

[2] The three periods of Buddhism are: (1) the period of the holy, correct or real doctrine of the Buddha, lasting 500 years, followed by (2) the image, or semblance period of 1,000 years, and then by (3) the period of decay and termination, lasting 3,000, some say 10,000 years, after which Maitreya Buddha is to appear and restore all things.

when the Buddha Dharma is disregarded and when people pay little attention to it. I am (however) expressing my humble opinion to make the coming generation understand it.'

The Dharma name of (Master) Kuei Shan[1] was Ling Yu; he was a native of Fu Chien[2] province. He followed Ancestor Pai Chang and realized his (self-) mind (at the latter's monastery.) The ascetic[3] Szu Ma saw that Kuei Shan mountain in Hunan province was auspicious and would become the meeting place for an assembly of 1,500 learned monks. At the time Kuei Shan was a verger of Pai Chang monastery where, during a visit Dhūta Szu Ma met him, recognized him as the right owner of the mountain and invited him to go there to establish a monastery. Kuei Shan was a man of the T'ang dynasty (618–906) and the Buddha Dharma was already at the end of its semblance period. For this reason, he was sorry he was not born earlier, because at the time the Buddha Dharma was difficult to understand and worldly men, whose believing minds were retrograding, refused to make efforts in their study of the doctrine, with the result that there was no hope for their attainment of the Buddha fruit. Over a thousand years have elapsed since the time of Kuei Shan and not only has the semblance period passed, but over 900 years of the present period of termination have also elapsed. (Therefore), worldly men of good roots are now very much fewer. This is why men believing in the Buddha Dharma are many and men who actually realize the truth are very few.

I now compare my own case with that of those who are now studying the Buddha Dharma and who have the advantage of all kinds of convenience. In the reigns of Hsien Feng (1851–61) and Tung Chih (1862–74), all monasteries were destroyed in the region south of the three rivers, where only the T'ien T'ung monastery remained intact. During the Tai Ping rebellion (1850–64), monks of the Chung Nan mountains came (to the South) to rebuild (these monasteries) and at the time, they were equipped each with only a gourd and a basket, and did not possess as many things as you have now. Later, the Buddha Dharma gradually flourished again, and monks began to carry their loads (with a pole over the shoulder). At present, they even carry leather suitcases but they do not pay much attention to the correct practice of the doctrine. Formerly, Ch'an monks wishing to call at various monasteries for instruction, had to journey on foot. Now, they can travel by train, motor car, steamer and

[1] In deference to him, Master Ling Yu was called Kuei Shan, after the name of the mountain.

[2] The map version is Fukien province.

[3] Dhūta = a monk engaged in austerities: an ascetic.

aeroplane which relieve them of all (previous) hardships but intensify their enjoyment in indulgence and ease. At present, in spite of the increasing number of Buddhist institutions and Dharma masters, no one pays attention to the fundamental question, and from morning to evening everybody seeks only knowledge and interpretation with the least heed for (self-) cultivation and realization. At the same time, they do not know that (self-) cultivation and realization are the essentials of the doctrine.

(Ch'an master) Yung Chia said in his Song of Enlightenment:

> Get at the root. Do not worry about twigs.
> (Be) like pure crystal round the precious moon.[1]
> Alas! in this time of decay and in this evil world
> Living beings of ill fortune are hard to discipline.
> The holy period's long passed and perverted views are deep.
> With Demon strong and Dharma weak hatred and harm prevail.
> When they hear the Tathagata's Instantaneous Dharma door,
> They hate not having smashed it into pieces.
> While their minds so act their bodies will then suffer;
> They cannot accuse or blame their fellow-men.
>
> If you would avoid unintermittant karma,[2]
> Do not vilify the wheel of the Buddha's Law.[3]
> In my youth I amassed much learning,
> Sought sūtras, śāstras, and their commentaries
> Endlessly discriminating between name and form.[4]
> As one vainly counting sandgrains in the ocean
> I was severely reprimanded by the Buddha,
> Who asked what gain derived from counting others' gems.

Yung Chia called on the Sixth Patriarch for instruction and was completely enlightened. The Patriarch called him the 'Overnight Enlightened One'. For this reason, the ancients said: 'The search for truth in sūtras and śāstras is like entering the sea to count its sandgrains.'

[1] Enlightenment is the root and other details, such as supramundane powers and wonderful works are twigs. This is why enlightened masters never talked about miracles. All this is likened to the crystal which, if clung to, will hinder the attainment of enlightenment, symbolized by the moon.

[2] Karma which sends the sinner to the Avīci hell, the last of the eight hot hells in which punishment, pain, form, birth, death, continue without intermission.

[3] Dharma cakra in Sanskrit, Buddha truth which is able to crush all evil and all opposition, like Indra's wheel, and which rolls on from man to man, place to place, age to age.

[4] Name and form: everything has a name, e.g. sound, or has appearance, i.e. the visible; both are unreal and give rise to delusion.

The Ch'an Sect's device is likened to the precious Vajra king sword[1] which cuts all things touching it and destroys all that runs up against its (sharp) point. It is the highest Dharma door (through which) to attain Buddhahood at a stroke.[2] (To give you an example, I will tell you the story of) Ch'an master Shen Tsan who travelled on foot when he was young and who became enlightened after his stay with ancestor Pai Chang. After his enlightenment, he returned to his former master and the latter asked him: 'After you left me, what (new) acquisition did you make at other places?' Shen Tsan replied: 'I made no acquisition.' He was then ordered to serve his (former) master.

One day, as his (former) master took a bath and ordered him to scrub his dirty back, Shen Tsan patted him on the back and said: 'A good Buddha hall but the Buddha is not saintly.' His master did not understand what he meant, turned his head and looked at the disciple who said again: 'Although the Buddha is not saintly, he sends out illuminating rays.'

Another day, as his master was reading a sūtra under the window, a bee knocked against the window paper[3] trying to get out (of the room). Shen Tsan saw the struggling bee and said: 'The universe is so vast and you do not want to get out. If you want to pierce old paper, you will get away in the (non-existent) year of the donkey!'[4] After saying this, he sang the following poem:

'It refuses to get out through the empty door
And knocks against the window stupidly.
To pierce old paper will take a hundred years,
Oh when will it succeed in getting out?'

Thinking that Shen Tsan was insulting him, the (old) master put his sūtra aside and asked him: 'You went away for so long: whom did you meet, what did you learn and what makes you so talkative now?' Shen Tsan replied: 'After I left you, I joined the Pai Chang community where master Pai Chang gave me an indication as to how to halt (thinking and discriminating). As you are now old, I have returned to pay the debt of gratitude I owe you.' Thereupon, the master informed the assembly (of

[1] The royal diamond gem, or indestructible sword which destroys ignorance and delusion
[2] Lit. on the spot.
[3] In the East, thin sheets of white paper were, and are still, used instead of window glass.
[4] Old paper is old sūtras. The sentence means: If you want to search for the truth in old sūtras, you will never realize it, for it can only be experienced in the training. The meaning is: If you want to 'pierce' old sūtras in your quest of your self-nature, you will never succeed in experiencing it.

the incident), ordered a vegetarian banquet (in honour of Shen Tsan) and invited him to expound the Dharma. The latter ascended to the seat and expounded the Pai Chang doctrine, saying:

Spiritual light shines on in solitude[1]
Disentangling the sense organs from sense data.[2]
Experience of true eternity
Depends not just on books.[3]
Mind-nature being taintless
Fundamentally is perfect.
Freedom from falsehood-producing causes
Is the same as absolute Buddhahood.

After hearing this, his master became awakened to the truth and said: 'I never expected that in my old age I would hear about the supreme pattern.' Then he handed over the management of the monastery to Shen Tsan and respectfully invited him to become his own master.

You see how free and easy this all is! We sat in this Ch'an meeting for over ten days and yet why did we not experience the truth? This is because we were not seriously determined in our training, or we took it for child's play, or we thought it required sitting quiet in meditation in a Ch'an hall. None of this is correct and men who really apply their minds to this training, do not discriminate between the mutable and immutable, or against any kind of (daily) activity. They can do it while in the street, at the noisy market plaçe, or anywhere (they may happen to be).

Formerly, there was a butcher monk who called on learned masters for instruction. One day, he arrived at a market place and passed a butcher's shop where every buyer insisted on having 'pure meat'.[4] Suddenly, the butcher got angry and, putting down his chopper, asked them: 'Which piece of meat is not pure?' Upon hearing this, the butcher monk was instantaneously enlightened.[5]

[1] i.e. independent, not attached to and relying on anything.
[2] This disentanglement is followed by the state of Samādhi, with simultaneous functioning of Prajñā, or Wisdom.
[3] If one clings to names and terms, one will be held in bondage by them.
[4] Prime meat is called 'pure meat' in China.
[5] The butcher monk was so called because he attained enlightenement upon hearing the butcher's voice. He was undergoing intense training when he passed the butcher's shop and his mind was already still and free from all thinking and discerning. The butcher's loud voice made a great impact on the monk's mind and was heard, not by the ear's faculty of hearing, but by the very function of the self-nature. When the function of the self-nature manifested itself, the substance or essence of the self-nature, became apparent, hence his enlightenment.

This shows that the ancients did not require to sit in meditation in a Ch'an hall, when they underwent their training. Today, not one of you speaks about awakening. Is this not a waste of time? I now (respectfully) request the (Venerable) Master Ying Tzu and the other masters to hold the examination.

Master Hsu Yun's saying at the closing of the (two) Ch'an weeks.

After tea and cakes had been served, all the assembly stood up when the Venerable Master Hsu Yun, in formal robe (with large sleeves) entered the hall again and sat in front of the (jade) Buddha. With a strip of bamboo, he drew a circle[1] in the air, saying:

Convocation and meditation!
Opening and closing!
When will all this come to an end?[2]
When (productive) causes halt abruptly.
External objects will vanish.
Mahāprajñāpāramitā![3]

When mind is still, essence and function (of themselves) return to normal.[4]
Fundamentally there is nor day nor night but only complete brightness.[5]
Where's the dividing line 'twixt South and North, 'twixt East and West?[6]
Without hindrance things are seen to be the product of conditioning causes.[7]
While birds sing and flowers smile, the moon reaches the stream![8]

[1] The circle symbolizes the completeness of the Dharmakāya.

[2] These three lines show the illusory mundane activities which have nothing to do with the experiencing of the truth.

[3] When all causes productive of effects come to an end, the phenomenal also disappears, and this is the moment when one's 'great wisdom reaches the other shore', or Mahāprajñāpāramitā.

[4] When the mind is stripped of feelings and passions, it will be still; this is the moment the essence and function of the self-natured Buddha are restored to normal.

[5] Fundamentally, there is only the immutable bright wisdom which is unchanging.

[6] When the self-nature is under delusion, it is split into ego and dharma, or subject and object, hence all kinds of discrimination between East and West and North and South. Now that enlightenment is attained, where is all this division?

[7] The phenomenal is created only by conditioning causes but is devoid of real nature.

[8] Our delusion is caused by our attachment to things heard, seen, felt and known, but if the mind is disentangled from the hearing, seeing, feeling and knowing or discerning, we will attain the Complete Enlightenment of Avalokiteśvara Bodhisattva (see discourse on the second day of the second Ch'an week). The two faculties of hearing and seeing are mentioned here because they are constantly active, whereas the other four faculties are sometimes dormant. If one succeeds in disentangling the hearing from the birds' song and the seeing from the smiling flowers, the moon, symbol of enlightenment, will shine on the stream, for water is a symbol of the self-nature. This sentence means that one can attain enlightenment while in the midst of sound and sight which symbolize the illusory world.

Now, what shall I say to close the meeting?

> 'When the board is struck, the bowl springs up!
> Let us scrutinize the Prajñāpāramitā!'[1]

Now let us close the meeting.

[1] In a monastery, the board is struck for calling to meals. If the mind is efficiently stripped of all feelings and passions, all the eight vijñānas or consciousnesses will be frozen and inactive. This moment is referred to, in Ch'an parlance, as 'a temporary death followed by a resurrection', i.e. death of delusion and resurrection of self-nature. When the self-nature recovers its freedom, it will function and hear the sound of the board. As the phenomenal and noumenal are now an undivided whole, the self-natured Dharmakāya will pervade everywhere, including the bowl which reveals its presence. For this reason, the ancients said: 'The exuberant green bamboos are all Dharmakāya and luxuriant yellow flowers are nothing but Prajñā.' This attainment is made possible only by the Prajñāpāramitā which all seekers of the truth should put into practice.

4

The Master's Arrival At Ts'ao Ch'i

(From the Hsu Yun Ho Shang Fa Hui)

(In 1934) on the second day of the eighth moon, Master Hsu Yun arrived from Ku Shan and, followed by the district officials, literati and people, proceeded to Ts'ao Ch'i. It happened to be the day when people in the district were celebrating the anniversary of the Patriarch's birthday and about ten thousand of them were converging on the monastery to offer incense.

AT THE TS'AO CH'I GATE

On his arrival at the gate, the Master pointed his staff at it and chanted:

A dream has now come true at Ts'ao Ch'i[1]
From far away the poor man has returned.[2]
Let us no more think of what is and what is not,[3]
Even to call it a bright mirror is still wrong.[4]
Since the midnight transmission of robe and bowl at Huang Mei[5]
Imposingly the light for centuries has shone.
Who of the House descendants will carry on the line
So that the Lamps succeed each other to reveal Spiritual Majesty?[6]

AT THE GATE OF THE PAO LIN MONASTERY[7]

The Master pointed his staff at the gate and chanted:

Here clearly is the road to Ts'ao Ch'i:
Wide open is the Gate of Precious Wood

[1] A dream at Ku Shan came true at Ts'ao Ch'i.
[2] Lit: from the horizon: from distant Ku Shan. A monk calls himself a 'poor man' because he is really penniless.
[3] All expediencies of the teaching school should be put aside in this place where the mind is directly pointed at for instantaneous enlightenment.
[4] Even Shen Hsiu was wrong when he compared a bright mirror with the Mind which is indescribable. (See Shen Hsiu's gāthā in the *Altar Sūtra* of the Sixth Patriarch).
[5] Transmission from the 5th to the 6th Patriarch. (See *Altar Sūtra*).
[6] Lamps transmitted from one Patriarch to another to reveal the doctrine of the Mind.
[7] It was originally called 'The Pao Lin monastery'.

Where students of the Sect from the ten quarters
Come and go on their long journeyings.
When this place of Transcendental Bliss is reached,
The Pure Void is free from dust.[1]
The Dharma realm has nor centre nor circumference;[2]
This One Door holds the wonder (of all schools).[3]

IN THE MAITREYA HALL

The Master entered the Hall and chanted:

(When) the big belly thunders with loud roar of laughter[4]
Thousands of white lotus rain through all the worlds.[5]
With his bag of cloth vast is he as the Universe,[6]
He will succeed the Buddha, preaching in Dragon Flower Tree Park.[7]

Then the Master prostrated himself before the statue of Maitreya.

IN FRONT OF THE SHRINE OF WEI TO[8]

The Master chanted:

In answer to the needs (of all) as a youth you come
To conquer ghouls and demons with awe-inspiring majesty.

[1] The self-nature is essentially pure and free from all impurities.

[2] Dharma realm: Dharmadhātu in Sanskrit, the unifying underlying spiritual reality, regarded as the ground or cause of all things, the absolute from which all proceeds. It is neither within nor without nor between the two.

[3] The one door out of mortality into Nirvāṇa, i.e. the Ch'an Sect which contains all the wonders of the other schools.

[4] i.e. the Ch'an roar of laughter to reveal the Mind which actually laughs. In China, Maitreya is represented by a statue with a broad smile and a big belly, symbolizing his boundless benevolence.

[5] The white lotus is a symbol of the Pure Land of every Buddha. When the self-nature is realized, the six worlds of existence are transmuted into Pure Lands.

[6] In the Liang dynasty (907–921), there was a monk who carried a cloth bag everywhere he went and was called 'The cloth-bag monk'. When he was about to pass away, he sat on a rock and chanted a gāthā disclosing that he was an avatar of Maitreya. After his death, he reappeared in other places also carrying a cloth bag on his back. Maitreya had the power to appear everywhere because his spiritual body was as immense as space.

[7] Maitreya is the Buddhist Messiah, or next Buddha, now in the Tuṣita heaven, and is to come 5,000 years after the Nirvāṇa of Śākyamuni Buddha. He will attain enlightenment under a Bodhi tree called the 'Dragon Flower Tree' and will liberate all living beings.

[8] One of the generals under the Southern Deva king, guardian in a temple. His vow was to protect the Buddha Dharma in the eastern, western and southern worlds, i.e. Pūrvavideha, Aparagodānīya and Jambudvīpa (our earth) respectively.

Hey! The sermon on the Vulture Peak is still ringing in all ears,
O fiery General, O Protector of the Dharma![1]

Then the Master prostrated himself before the statue of Wei To.

IN THE HALL OF THE FIFTH PATRIARCH

The Master chanted:

The Transmission handed down in this Eastern Land
Produced a flower with petals five.[2]
From Hsiu in the North and in the South from Neng[3]
Shot leaves and branches spreading everywhere.

Then the Master prostrated himself before the Fifth Patriarch.

IN THE HALL OF THE SIXTH PATRIARCH

Holding incense sticks, the Master chanted:

Each year on this second day of the eighth and eighth day of
 the second month[4]
In the sky appear the tracks of birds.[5]
Although it never hid within the Universe,[6]
It could not be perceived e'en by Li Lou,[7]
How can it ever then be known?

Burning incense sticks, he continued:

Today clearly is it pointed out![8]

[1] i.e. the Buddha's injunction to all Protectors of the Dharma who were present when He expounded sūtras. The Western exclamation 'Hey' is used here instead of the text's 'I' which is unknown in the West. This cry was uttered by enlightened masters to reveal the presence of the self-mind which uttered it in their direct pointing at the Mind for realization of self-nature and attainment of Buddhahood.

[2] Bodhidharma came to the East and transmitted the robe which was handed down to five Chinese Patriarchs, hence five petals.

[3] Shen Hsiu and Hui Neng (the Sixth Patriarch) expounded the Ch'an Dharma in the North and South respectively, and handed it down to their succeeding descendants who spread it all over the country.

[4] The Patriarch's birthday fell on the second day of the eighth moon. The Master inverted day and month to wipe out all traces of *Time* which has no place in the absolute Wisdom.

[5] A bird leaves no tracks when flying in the air. Thus *Space* is also wiped out.

[6] The self-nature is omnipresent but is imperceptible to deluded men. It cannot be named and the word 'IT' is used to indicate the inexpressible.

[7] Li Lou, a man mentioned by Mencius—he was a contemporary of Huang Ti and could see even a hair at a hundred paces. The self-nature cannot be seen even by the cleverest deluded men.

[8] Today, thanks to the Patriarch, the self-nature can be perceived according to his method.

Holding incense sticks, the Master chanted:

In all the land there never was a rival.[1]
But now a rival comes by name Ku Shan.[2]
Occasionally a recollection
Makes one repent one's restlessness.[3]
What restlessness?[3]

Calling his followers, the Master continued:

Two clay oxen struggle to stride into the sea.[4]
Each time I offer incense sticks, my heart is full of sadness.[5]

After offering incense sticks, the Master continued:

Today this is Te Ch'ing,[6]
It was Te Ch'ing before.[7]
When past and present meet, there is change of form.[8]
The Dharma prospers and declines as good and bad prevail;[9]
(Yet) it has never ceased in wood and grass to dwell.[10]

Then the Master prostrated himself before Han Shan.

IN THE MAIN HALL

Holding incense sticks, the Master chanted:

O Lord-Teacher of Sahā![11]
The uncreate rightly taught by You

[1] Han Shan had no rival when he had the honour of rebuilding the monastery of the Sixth Patriarch in 1602. (See *Han Shan's Autobiography*.)

[2] Now master Hsu Yun also had the honour of rebuilding the same monastery; hence a competitor of Han Shan.

[3] Recollection of one's restlessness caused by delusion.

[4] The master called on his followers to wipe out their views of dualism, the cause of delusion. Two clay oxen: dualism which splits our undivided self-nature into 'ego' (self) and 'other'. One should cast away one's false views of dualism in order to realize one's undivided nature.

[5] Each time I offer incense sticks to Buddha, I think of deluded living beings who turn their backs on the Right Dharma and my heart is full of sadness.

[6] Te Ch'ing was the name Master Hsu Yun used when he was young.

[7] Te Ch'ing was also the name used by Han Shan before he called himself 'Han Shan' after the 'Silly Mountain'.

[8] So modern and ancient Te Ch'ing met at the same monastery which both found in the same deplorable condition and which both reconstructed although at different times. Han Shan had entered Nirvāṇa whereas Hsu Yun still appeared in human form.

[9] The Sect was revived by Han Shan and declined again after a period of prosperity. Now the master was doing the same thing.

[10] In spite of alternation of prosperity and decline, the self-nature is always the same whether in forests or meadows, i.e. it is everywhere and unchanging.

[11] Sahā, a Sanskrit word: our world. The Buddha was teacher of this world.

(Is) Dharma most profound and wonderful.[1]
(But) who is Buddha and who living being?[2]

Then the Master prostrated himself before the Buddha.

IN THE ABBOT'S ROOM

The Master entered the Abbot's room and chanted:

I enter now the room of the late Virtuous One
And climb up to the former Patriarch's seat.[3]
Holding firm the horizontal sword[4]
I give the Right Supreme Command.[5]
This is where the Patriarch and Ancestors
Taught the Dharma for the benefit of men.
Today, this unworthy man comes here.
What does he?

The Master snapped his fingers thrice and continued:[6]

These finger-snaps bring to perfection the 80,000 Dharma doors[7]
Ensuring 'straight entry' to the state of the Tathāgata.[8]

Then the Master prostrated himself (before the statue of Buddha).

IN THE DHARMA HALL

Pointing his staff at the Dharma seat, he chanted:

[1] The Buddha urged His disciples to strive to attain the 'endurance of the uncreate' in order to get out of this illusory Saṁsāra of birth and death.

[2] Buddha and sentient beings are of the same nature. Where is the difference? Cognizance of one's self-nature will, according to the Ch'an Sect ensure attainment of Buddhahood.

[3] Quotation from the Lotus Sūtra: the room or house and seat or throne are respectively the Tathāgata-House or Compassion and Tathāgata-Throne in the absolute vacuity, i.e. immutability.

[4] The indestructible sword of wisdom was held horizontally to bar the passage of falsehood, i.e. to arrest all false thinking.

[5] A Ch'an term meaning the correct command or order of the Supreme Vehicle, likened to an irrevocable order from the Commander-in-Chief.

[6] To reveal the mind which actually snapped the fingers. 'Thrice' is to reveal the presence of the threefold body (Tṛkāya) in one.

[7] The digit 8 symbolizes the eighth consciousness or Ālaya-vijñāna, or the self-nature under delusion. Many Dharmas were set up to deal with different kinds of delusion and constituted what was called the Teaching School of which the ultimate aim was enlightenment. The Chan Sect's finger-snap was also a Dharma which pointed direct at the mind for realization of self-nature and attainment of Buddhahood. Therefore, these finger-snaps would also bring about the complete perfection of all other Dharmas.

[8] Ch'an ensures the 'Straight Entry' into the Tathāgata-state, without the necessity of passing through successive stages of sainthood before final enlightenment. In Ch'an parlance, this is called the 'Straight or Direct Entry'.

The eminence of this Precious Seat
Has been handed down from Sage to Sage.[1]
(There is) no hindrance from all angles[2]
(And) all Dharmas are profound.[3]
When in the sun the head is raised,
The pressure of what can be grasped is cut off and turned away.[4]
Even eyes of iron with copper pupils
Though they look can never reach it.[5]
The coming of the mountain-monk
Is not peculiar in itself.
If long sight you want to penetrate all quarters,
To a higher storey must you climb.[6]

The Master pointed his staff (at the seat) and continued:

Let us ascend![7]

After ascending to the seat, he held incense sticks in his hand and chanted:

These incense sticks
Do not descend from heaven;
How can they come from Earth?[8]
They smoke in the (incense) burner
As a token of my offerings
To our Teacher Śākyamuni Buddha,
To all Buddhas and Bodhisattvas
To all Patriarchs and Sages from India and of this Eastern land,
To Ārya Jñānabhaiṣajya who founded first this monastery,[9]
To the great master the Sixth Patriarch,
And to all past Masters who revived and succeeded to this sect.
May the Buddha sun shine greater,
May the Wheel of the Law for ever turn.

[1] Sage to Sage. Literally Ancestor to Ancestor.
[2] Seen from all angles, Ch'an is free from all hindrances.
[3] From the Ch'an viewpoint, all Dharmas can be correctly interpreted and are very profound.
[4] When the mind wanders outside, the Ch'an method turns away and cuts off all discernings and graspings.
[5] The mind although disentangled from sense-organs, sense-data and consciousness, and even likened to iron eyes and copper pupils which are insensible to all externals, is still unable to perceive the self-nature. This is called a state one experiences when reaching the top of a hundred-foot pole. (See *Han Shan's Autobiography*, 'Song of the Board-bearer'.)
[6] From the top of a hundred-foot pole, one should take a step forward so that his self-nature will appear in full everywhere in the ten directions of space.
[7] Let us ascend to this Transcendental Path.
[8] Incense sticks are created by the mind only.
[9] See *The Altar Sūtra of the Sixth Patriarch*.

Then the Master arranged his robe and took the seat. Thereupon, the leading monk chanted:

> All elephants and dragons here assembled for the Dharma feast[1]
> Should look into the Supreme Meaning.[2]

Holding his staff, the Master said:

In this great affair,[3] it is clear that there exists not a single Dharma.[4] The causes, fundamental as well as secondary, are many and have not come to an end; after Han Shan's departure, I now come here. The restoration of this ancient monastery will depend on many (contributory) causes. It was set up by Ārya Jñānabhaiṣajya who predicted that some one hundred and seventy years later, a great Saint[5] would come here to expound the Dharma for the liberation of men and that those attaining sainthood would be as many as the trees in the wood. Hence, its name of 'Precious Wood'. Since the Sixth Patriarch came here to teach and convert people, one thousand and a few hundred years have passed and countless living beings have been liberated. There have been alternating periods of prosperity and decline, and in the Ming dynasty, ancestor Han Shan rebuilt this monastery and revived the Sect. Since then, over three hundred years have elapsed and during that period, the lack of a suitable successor has caused it to fall into disuse.

When I was at Ku Shan I saw in a dream the Patriarch who thrice called me here. At the same time, the high officials and upāsakas who sponsored the reconstruction of the monastery sent their representatives to Ku Shan to invite me to take charge of it. In view of their devotion, I have been obliged to accede to their requests and am now taking this seat. I feel ashamed of my poor virtues and shallow wisdom and also am not familiar with the management of the monastery. Therefore, I must rely on the support of all of you so that the withered branch will be sprinkled with Amṛta[6] and the house in flames[7] will be covered by the clouds of compassion. Together we will do our utmost to preserve the Patriarch's monastery.

[1] Dragons and Elephants: terms of respect applied to the whole assembly seeking enlightenment. Dharma feast: Sermon to satisfy the hunger of seekers of the truth.

[2] Supreme Meaning. In the Teaching School, this term means Supreme Reality; in a Ch'an hall, it means: 'Please look into the self-mind for attainment of enlightenment.' This sentence is always chanted by the leader of the assembly before a master gives a sermon.

[3] Revelation of mind for realization of self-nature and attainment of Buddhahood.

[4] Self-nature is fundamentally pure, and no Dharma is required to realize it. It will suffice to arrest false thinking and take cognizance of the self-mind.

[5] The Sixth Patriarch.

[6] Ambrosial drink.

[7] House in flames: Saṁsāra, our world. A quotation from the Lotus Sūtra.

About striving to preserve it,
What am I doing now?

With his two palms brought together, the Master turned to the right and to the left in salutation and said:

Under the corner of my robe stand the four deva kings.[1]

Then the Master got down from his seat.

[1] I can surely rely also on the four deva kings whose tall statues now stand at the entrance door of the monastery and who also appeared when the Patriarch unfolded his niṣīdana, or cloth for sitting on. (See Fa Hai's preface to *The Altar Sūtra of the Sixth Patriarch*.)

PART II

THE STORIES OF SIX CH'AN MASTERS

(*From The Imperial Collection of Ch'an Sayings—Yu Hsuan Yu Lu*)

Foreword

THIS Part II presents the following stories of six eminent Ch'an masters from 'The Imperial Selection of Ch'an Sayings' (Yu Hsuan Yu Lu):

Master Teh Ch'eng, the boat monk at Hua Ting,
Master Chi Hsien of Hsiang Yen,
Master Chu Ti of Chin Hua,
Master Hui Ts'ang of Shih Kung,
Master Wu Chu, alias Wen Hsi, of Hang Chou, and
Master Fu Ta Shih (Bodhisattva Fu, alias Shan Hui).

As said in the previous foreword, every man is endowed with an inner potentiality which can absorb the truth but cannot be activated so long as the mind is not disentangled from its attachments to the phenomenal. No amount of learning and knowledge of the sūtras can reach this potentiality the arousal of which is possible only when one succeeds in putting an end to one's chain of thoughts. After it has been aroused, any concurrent cause is sufficient to cause one's awakening.

We have also explained the meaning of kung an, and all the six stories of this Part II depict the concurrent causes producing the awakening of six masters whose inner potentialities had been activated to the full, ready for instantaneous union with the absolute. Two blows of a paddle caused Teh Ch'eng's enlightenment; the sound of a broken tile hitting a bamboo, that of Chi Hsien; the raising of a finger, that of Chu Ti; Ma Tsu's words, that of Hui Ts'ang the hunter; Yang Shan's instruction, that of Wu Chu; and a vision of three Buddhas, that of Fu Ta Shih.

When the human mind was more concerned with material than with spiritual values, men like the six masters became rare, and the ancients were compelled to devise the hua t'ou technique which is fully explained by Master Hsu Yun at the begining of this book.

As Master Hsu Yun said, the teaching has undergone several changes since the time the Buddha held up a flower and transmitted the Mind Dharma to Mahākāśyapa. The thirty-two Patriarchs were awakened after seeing or hearing something because of their high spirituality. After them, the ancients used what is known as the kung an to awake their disciples. In the present period of decline of the Dharma, the hua t'ou is considered the most effective device to isolate the mind from the seeing, hearing, feeling and discerning in order to arouse the potentiality inherent in every man. This does not mean that kung ans can be disregarded because the very purpose of the hua t'ou is also to enable students correctly to interpret all kung ans, thus enabling them to realize their minds and perceive their self-nature.

The Imperial Selection of Ch'an Sayings is a collection of fourteen volumes compiled by Yung Cheng, the third emperor (1723–1735) of the Ch'ing (Manchu) dynasty. He was well versed in the Mind Dharma and adopted the name 'Upāsaka Yuan Ming' before his ascension to the throne. The emperor used to hold in the imperial palace Ch'an weeks which produced enlightened masters and upāsakas.

Of the fourteen volumes of the collection, one volume is devoted to the emperor's works and Dharma words, and another, to those of his brothers and sons who were also adepts of Ch'an as well as of masters and upāsakas of his time, while the other twelve volumes are devoted to the stories and sayings of ancient masters.

The commentary on each of the six stories is mine.

UPĀSAKA LU K'UAN YÜ

Hongkong, 22 May, 1959.

I

Ch'an Master Teh Ch'eng The Boat Monk at Hua Ting

MASTER TEH CH'ENG arrived at Hua Ting in the Hsiu Chou district. He sailed a small boat, adjusted himself to circumstances and passed his days in receiving visitors from the four quarters. At the time, as no one knew of his erudition, he was called the Boat Monk.

One day, he stopped by the river bank and sat idle in his boat. An official (who was passing) asked him: 'What does the Venerable Sir do?' The master held up his paddle, saying: 'Do you understand this?' The official replied: 'I do not.' The master said: 'I have been rowing and stirring the clear water, but a golden fish is rarely found.'

When Chia Shan had dismissed his followers, he packed and went straight to Hua Ting. Master Teh Ch'eng saw him and asked: 'Virtuous One! At what temple do you stay?' Chia Shan replied: 'That which is like it does not stay (and) that which stays is not like it.' Master Teh Ch'eng asked: 'If there is no likeness, what is it like?' Chia Shan replied: 'It is not the dharma (thing) before the eyes.' Master Teh Ch'eng asked: 'Where have you learned all this?' Chia Shan replied: 'Neither the ear nor the eye can reach it.' Master Teh Ch'eng said: 'A good sentence is a stake to which a donkey can be tethered for ten thousand aeons.' He again asked: 'When a thousand feet of fishing line is let down, the quarry is deep in the pond. Three inches beyond the hook, why don't you speak?' Chia Shan (guessed and) was on the point of opening his mouth, when the master gave him, with the paddle, a blow that knocked him into the water. When Chia Shan was about to scramble back into the boat, the master said again: 'Speak! Speak!' Before Chia Shan could open his mouth, the master hit him again. Thereupon, Chia Shan was instantaneously enlightened and nodded thrice (in approval and gratitude).

The master said: 'You can play with the silken line at the end of the rod, but so long as you do not disturb the clear water, the meaning will be different.'

Chia Shan then asked: 'What is your idea about letting down the line and throwing in the hook?'

Master Teh Ch'eng said: 'The line dangling in the green water allows all ideas of existence and non-existence to float up to the surface until both become still.'

Chia Shan said: 'Your words lead to abstruseness but follow no paths; the tip of your tongue talks but is speechless.'

The master said: 'I have been letting my line down in every part of this river and only now have I found a golden fish.'

(Upon hearing this), Chia Shan closed his ears (with his hands). Master Teh Ch'eng said: 'It is so! It is so!' and then gave him the following instruction:

'In the future, your hiding place should have no traces and where there are no traces, you should not hide. I spent thirty years at master Yo Shan's monastery and understood nothing but this. You have got it now. From now on do not stay in towns and villages, but search deep in the mountains for one or two men with mattocks at their sides to continue (the transmission) and not allow it to be broken off.'

Chia Shan took leave of the master but turned back repeatedly to see (him). Master Teh Ch'eng called out: 'Venerable Sir!' When Chia Shan turned his head the master held up the paddle and said: 'Do you think that I still have something else?' Then he upset the boat and disappeared in the water.

The boat monk sailed a small boat, adjusted himself to circumstances and passed his days in receiving and enlightening men from all quarters for it is the duty of every Ch'an master to enlighten and liberate all living beings. He may use anything he can pick up, such as a paddle in this story, or a dust-whisk, a cup of tea, a staff, etc.

In reply to the official's question, the boat monk held up his paddle to show him that in one's daily activities, one should not stray from one's self-nature which was that which ordered his hand to raise the paddle. A man of high spirituality would understand the move and become awakened to the truth. However, the official was deluded and did not understand it.

When Chia Shan said to his disciples: 'The Dharma-kāya has no form and the Dharma eye has no flaws', Tao Wu, also an enlightened master, laughed. This laugh caused a doubt to arise in the mind of the speaker who asked Tao Wu about his error and was urged by the latter to go to Hua

Ting and call on the boat monk for instruction. What Chia Shan said to his disciples was not wrong but Tao Wu laughed because the speaker was merely repeating other people's sayings but did not himself have a personal experience of the teaching. Chia Shan was urged to go to the boat monk because there was an affinity between them which could ensure Chia Shan's enlightenment. (Literally—'for there existed between the two a co-operating cause'.)

The boat monk's first question was to probe Chia Shan's understanding of absolute wisdom (prajñā). Chia Shan who had read and probably learned by heart many sūtras, knew that 'staying at a temple' meant 'attachment to a place' and that such attachment to the phenomenal was wrong and could obstruct his wisdom. So he replied: 'That which is like the truth does not stay and that which stays is not like the truth for the truth is all-embracing and does not stay at a particular place.' The boat monk asked: 'If it is not like that, what is it like?' Chia Shan replied that what he meant was not the visible and could not be heard or seen. The boat monk said: 'If you cling to the words with which you have learned to interpret the truth, you will be held in bondage by them and will never realize the truth.'

As he was called 'boat monk' and since every boat—called sampan in China—contained a fishing rod, the master naturally mentioned the line to teach Chia Shan and said: 'When I let down a thousand feet of line, I expect to hook a dragon at the bottom of the deep pond but I do not want to catch a small fish.' This means that he expected to receive a pupil of high spirituality and not a man of dull disposition.

The sentence 'Three inches beyond the hook, why don't you talk?' is a literal translation of the text which can also mean 'Beyond the hook and three inches, why don't you talk?' According to ancient scholars, that which measures three inches is the tongue which is therefore called 'the three-inch tongue'. The Chinese language favours sentences with a double meaning and all masters availed themselves of this facility when probing their disciples. His idea was this: 'Why don't you throw away all that you have memorized and can be expressed by words and by means of the tongue? Why don't you talk about that which is beyond hook (i.e. word) and tongue?'

As Chia Shan was making use of his discriminating mind to find a reply and was about to open his mouth, the master gave him with the paddle a blow that knocked him into the water. The teacher gave the blow to cut off the pupil's chain of thought. When Chia Shan returned to the boat, the monk pressed him again: 'Speak! Speak!' and as Chia Shan was again thinking about a reply, the master hit him once more with the paddle. The master wanted to press the pupil hard, so that the latter's mind would have no time to discriminate and to think about an answer. This time, the boat monk succeeded in wiping out the pupil's last thoughts. As Chia Shan was stripped of thoughts, his real nature was exposed and could now function freely without further obstruction. It was now the self-nature which received the second blow, and when its function could operate without hindrance, his self-nature manifested itself simultaneously. Thereupon, Chia Shan realized instantaneous enlightenment and nodded thrice to thank the master.

Usually when one has no worries, one's discriminating mind gives rise to all kinds of thoughts, but in time of danger, one will try to save one's life first. When Chia Shan saw he was about to drown, he immediately applied the brake to his mind and thus realized singleness of thought, as taught by Ch'an masters who urged their disciples to hold firm a hua t'ou. Before receiving the first blow, it was a discriminating Chia Shan who merely repeated what he had learned to answer the boat monk's question. After the first blow, it was another Chia Shan who realized singleness of thought, that is he only thought of saving his own life, but he still clung to this single thought. The boat monk, who was a skilful teacher, gave the second blow to disentangle Chia Shan's mind from this last thought so that it became pure and free from this last bondage. After the second blow, Chia Shan, now free from discrimination, became instantly enlightened. It was not the discriminating Chia Shan but his real self-nature which received the second blow and clearly perceived the boat-monk's self-nature which struck his own nature. When the function of Chia Shan's self-nature could operate normally without obstruction, at that moment his self-nature manifested. This was the cause of his complete enlightenment.

From the above, we can see that the master was a very skilful teacher and that the disciple was also a man of very high potentiality. The whole training took less than ten minutes.

So far, only Chia Shan had been enlightened. What about the enlightenment of others? Every Ch'an practiser should develop a Bodhisattva mind before undergoing his training, and if he does not think of the welfare of others, he will never succeed in his self-cultivation.

Now the master gave his advice as to the disciple's future conduct. He said: 'You can play with any device or method you like, but if you do not disturb the clear water, that is if your mind does not give rise to discrimination, the result will transcend everything.' Chia Shan, who had only just been enlightened and had not fully recovered from his fright, asked the master: 'What do you mean by letting down the line and throwing in the hook?' He meant: 'If the teaching does not rely on words and phrases, how does one receive and enlighten others?' The boat monk replied: 'The angler dangles his line in the green water to find out whether a fish is feeding. If there is a (hungry) fish, it will certainly come to the baited hook. In future, when you receive disciples, you should use the same kind of words and phrases that I did a moment ago, to see if they still hold the dual conception of "existence" and "non-existence", that is if they still split their undivided self-nature into selfness and otherness, and teach them until they wipe out all dualisms so that their minds can become still.'

Chia Shan said: 'Your words lead to abstruseness but follow no paths and the tip of your tongue talks but is speechless.' Here the disciple praised the master for his marvellous way of teaching because the boat monk used, in illustration, only words and phrases which did not give rise to discrimination and could not be clung to by the disciple's mind. This was really an unsurpassed way of training a pupil.

In return, the boat monk praised Chia Shan's instantaneous enlightenment, saying: 'I have been letting my line down in every part of this river and only today have I caught a golden fish.'

Upon hearing his master's words of praise, Chia Shan closed his ears, for even these words of praise were basically wrong because self-nature can neither be praised nor censured. Instead of listening to these words, he found it better to close his ears as the best way to preserve the reality and brightness of his self-nature. The boat monk confirmed his pupil's correct conduct and said: 'It is so! It is so!' These words were the best praise a master could give to his enlightened disciple.

Then, the boat monk gave his disciple the following instruction: 'In future, your hiding place should have no traces, and where there are no traces, you should not hide.' In other words, 'You have now realized the Dharma-kāya which is immaterial and leaves no traces. However, you should refrain from giving rise to the idea of "no traces" or absolute voidness within which you should not abide, for in that case, you would give rise to the idea of "no traces", both "traces" and "no traces" being in the realm of dualism and having no place in absolute reality. I spent thirty years with my master Yo Shan and learned only this truth which you have now acquired.'

The master said further: 'From now on do not stay in towns and villages where you will not find men of high spirituality who can understand your teaching. You should go to places where men have no chance of seeking fame and wealth because there only can you look for disciples who are either wholly or at least half bent on the quest of truth. These are the people you should search for and receive to enlighten them so as to ensure the continuity of our Sect.'

Literally the sentence reads: 'But—you should—deep in the mountains search for one and a half (man) with a mattock by his side.' The Chinese idiom 'one or a half man' is equivalent to the Western saying, 'one or two men'. Therefore, another interpretation is: 'You cannot expect to enlighten more than one or two men for Ch'an is not so easy to understand. It will suffice to enlighten one or two people to continue our sect.'

Chia Shan left the boat monk but repeatedly turned his head to see him. The master called him and held up the paddle, saying: 'I have only this (paddle) and do not think that I still have something else.' This means: 'I have only this, that is that which held up the paddle and I have taught it to you. I have nothing else to teach you and do not give rise to any further suspicion about it.'

Then the master overturned his boat and disappeared in the water to show that when one is enlightened, one is free to come and free to go. This is only possible after one has obtained enlightenment. This was also to show Chia Shan that the transmission was actually handed down to him and that he should take over the master's mission which was now ended on this earth, but would begin in another world where other living beings were waiting for him.

2

Ch'an Master Chi Hsien of Hsiang Yen

WHEN master Chi Hsien called on Kuei Shan, the latter asked him: 'I heard that when you were with my late master Pai Chang, you were able to give ten replies to each question and a hundred replies to every ten questions. This was possible because of your high intelligence and of the power of your (discriminating) mind's understanding and thinking, but all this is the cause of birth and death. (Now try to) tell me (in) a sentence about (your real face) before you were born.'

Master Chi Hsien was dumbfounded by the question and returned to his hut where he took out all the books he had read before but failed to find an appropriate sentence for his reply. He sighed and said to himself: 'A cake drawn on paper can never satisfy hunger.' He repeatedly asked Kuei Shan (to disclose the truth to him but) the latter said: 'If I tell you about it now, you will curse me afterwards. Whatever I tell you will always be mine and will never concern you.'

Master Chi Hsien (was disappointed and) burned all his books. He said to himself: 'I will not study the Buddha Dharma any more in my present life. I will be a wandering gruel-and-rice monk, in order not to weary my mind.' Then he wept and left Kuei Shan. He passed through Nan Yang where he saw the ruins (of the ancient monastery of) the late state master Hui Chung. He stopped and stayed at the site.

One day, as he was collecting grass, he picked up a broken tile which he threw away and which hit a bamboo with a ping. Upon hearing it, he was instantly awakened. Returning to his hut, he took a bath, burned incense sticks and from the distance, paid reverence to Kuei Shan, praising him:

> O Venerable Master! You (indeed) have great compassion.
> Your grace exceeds that of my parents.
> Had you then disclosed to me (the truth),
> How could this today have happened to me?

Then he composed the following gāthā:

The sound of a blow causes all knowledge to cease,
Gone is my need of further practice and observance.
Casting away old habits, I tread the Ancient Path
To avoid falling back into (a state of) dull potentiality.
That path leaves no traces anywhere
Being beyond both sound and form.
Those who on it achieve success
Say that this is the highest (state of) potentiality.

Kuei Shan heard of the poem and said to Yang Shan: 'The lad is awakened.' Yang Shan replied: 'This may be the product of his mental potentiality and knowledge or the result of his habit of reading and writing. Please wait until I have myself probed into all this.' Later, Yang Shan visited Master Chi Hsien and said to him: 'The (venerable) monk praised you for your discovery of the "great affair". Please say something about it so that I too can see.' Master Chi Hsien sang the (above) hymn, and Yang Shan said: 'This comes from your former habit of memorizing and if it is correct awakening, please say something else.'

Master Chi Hsien sang a gāthā:

Last year my poverty was not poor enough,
But this year it is real.
Last year, though poor, I still had ground in which to stick an awl,
This year, my poverty is real for I do not even own an awl.

Yang Shan said: 'I concede that you understand the Tathāgata's Ch'an but you have not even dreamt of the Patriarch's Ch'an.' Master Chi Hsien sang another gāthā:

I possess potentiality;
It is seen in a blink.
He who does not understand
Cannot be called a monk.

Yang Shan then returned and said to Kuei Shan: 'I am glad younger brother (Chi) Hsien understands the Patriarch's Ch'an (as well).

In the hall, master Chi Hsien said (to the assembly): 'If I have to discuss this matter, it is like a man who climbs a tree; with his mouth, he bites a branch while his feet do not tread on and his hands do not hold the (other) branches. Suddenly someone under the tree asks him this question: "What was the Patriarch's meaning when he came from the West?" If no reply is given, the question will remain unanswered. If a reply is given, the man on the tree will (fall down and) lose his life. Under the circumstances, what should one do?'

The leading monk Chao of Hu T'ou monastery who was in the assembly, came forward and said to Master Chi Hsien: 'I do not ask this question when the man is on the tree but I ask it before he climbs up. Will the Venerable Master say (something about it)?'

Thereupon, master Chi Hsien gave a loud roar of laughter.

Kuei Shan was an eminant Ch'an master and founded with his disciple *Yang* Shan the Kuei Yang Sect (Ikyō in Japanese), one of the five Ch'an Sects in China.

Before his enlightenment, master Chi Hsien appeared to be well versed in the Buddha Dharma as taught in the sūtras and could reply to all questions according to the Scriptures. But his knowledge was useless without a personal experience of the truth. Kuei Shan said to Chi Hsien: 'If you rely on your discriminating mind for your understanding and interpretation of the Buddha's teaching, you will not escape from the round of births and deaths. Now tell me something about your "fundamental face" before you were born.' The master could not reply to this question, the purpose of which was the direct pointing at the self-nature, and realized the futility of sticking to names and terms which he could memorize and which were completely useless. So he requested Kuei Shan to disclose the truth to him. The latter replied that whatever he might say would be useless if Chi Hsien did not experience it personally. Moreover, master Chi Hsien would stick to it, would again use his discriminating mind to interpret it, would never experience the truth and would blame Kuei Shan later for his (Chi Hsien's) failure to attain enlightenment.

Master Chi Hsien was disappointed and burned all his books. He was determined no longer to study the Buddha Dharma but to wander from place to place and to refrain from making further use of his discriminating mind. A gruel-and-rice monk was one who was lazy and did not practise the Buddha Dharma.

In spite of his disappointment and helplessness, master Chi Hsien was, however, undergoing the Ch'an training without being aware of it. Since he had put an end to all feelings and discriminations, he succeeded in disentangling his mind from all disturbances. So when he heard the sound of the broken tile hitting a bamboo, it was not his faculty of hearing which heard it because that faculty had ceased functioning, for all notions of subject and object which split his undivided whole were already wiped out. His self-nature was now free from bondage and was able by means of its function, to hear the sound. When its function could operate without hindrance, the self-nature revealed itself simultaneously. Hence his enlighenment.

He now recalled that Kuei Shan was right when he rejected his request to disclose the truth, and sang a gāthā to praise Kuei Shan's great compassion.

The first poem means this: When the mind was disentangled from the illusion of subject and object, the self-nature revealed itself when coming into contact with the sound of the tile hitting a bamboo. When the self-nature was revealed, there was no further need of observance and practice. Former habits were shaken off to reveal the ancient Path—that is, the very self-nature which every man possesses—so that he might get out of his former quiet and dull state. The self-nature had no traces and its dignity was inexpressible for it was immaterial and beyond all sound and form. Those who had achieved the same success agreed that this was the unsurpassed potentiality which exposed the self-nature without difficulty.

Yang Shan, a disciple of Kuei Shan, thought master Chi Hsien's poem might be the result of his reading and recollection of sūtras and sayings. So he wanted to probe all this.

The second gāthā described master Chi Hsien's gradual elimination of all feelings and discriminations. Last year, he had wiped out all coarse conceptions but still clung to the subtle ones symbolized by the awl and the clod of earth holding the awl, the two subtle views of the subject who stuck the awl in the ground and the object, that is the awl which was planted in the ground. This year, he was really poor for his mind was completely disentangled from both subject and object, with the elimination of the awl which he no longer had.

However, Yang Shan conceded that that was only the Tathāgata's Ch'an, or Ch'an realized according to the teaching school. The Tathāgata's Ch'an would not be perfect until the Patriarch's Ch'an had also been achieved.

Now master Chi Hsien sang the third gāthā which means this: 'I possess a lively potentiality which enables me to attain enlightenment. As my mind is now free from all disturbances, the act of closing the eyelids and of opening them again is the very function of the self-nature which is thus exposed by its function. A monk who does not understand this cannot be called a true monk.' This was the Patriarch's Ch'an as taught by Bodhidharma whose aim was the direct pointing at the mind for realization of self-nature and attainment of Buddhahood. This was the transmission of Dharma outside Scriptures.

Both master Chi Hsien and Yang Shan were disciples of Kuei Shan. Chi Hsien was younger than Yang Shan and was, therefore, called his younger brother.

Now after his own enlightenment, master Chi Hsien taught his own disciples. In order to probe their ability to understand the truth, he set, as all Ch'an masters used to do, a trap well camouflaged by the man on the tree, with his teeth clenched in a branch and his hands and feet in the air, to conceal the most important thing, that is Bodhidharma's meaning when he came from India. It was Bodhidharma's aim to point direct at the mind for realization of the self-nature and attainment of Buddhahood. The leading monk, Chao, who knew of the trap, asked the master not to talk about the man on the tree; that is, not to use unnecessary camouflage which had nothing to do with the main meaning. Obviously, it was impossible to express in words that which was inexpressible.

In reply to the monk-leader's question, master Chi Hsien gave a loud roar of laughter to reveal the presence of that which laughed but could not be described in words. That is exactly what Bodhidharma meant when he came from the West.

3

Ch'an Master Chu Ti of Chin Hua

A NUN named Shih Chi came (one day) to (Chu Ti's) temple, carrying a basket on her head and holding a staff in her hand. She circumambulated the master thrice, saying also thrice: 'If you can say (something), I will take down the basket.' As the master could not say (anything), the nun left. The master said to her: 'It is already late; why do you not stay (for a night)?' The nun replied: 'If you can say (something), I will stay.' Again the master could not say (anything).

After the nun had left, the master sighed and said to himself: 'Although I am a man, I am lacking in manliness. It is better to leave this temple and go elsewhere in search of enlightened masters.' That night, the god of the mountain said to him: 'You should not leave this place; a real flesh-and-blood Bodhisattva is coming.'

Later, when T'ien Lung arrived at the temple, the master received him with reverence. To teach him, T'ien Lung raised a finger and the master was instantly awakened. Since then, when students came for instruction, the master only raised a finger and did not give any other instruction.

There was a boy who had previously come to the master, and when people asked him questions, the lad also raised a finger in reply. Someone said to the master: 'Your boy also understands the Buddha Dharma and in reply to visitors' questions, like you he also raises a finger.'

One day, concealing a (sharp) knife in his long sleeve, the master asked the boy: 'I hear that you understand the Buddha Dharma; is it true?' The boy replied: 'Yes, Sir.' The master asked him: 'What is Buddha?' The boy raised a finger which the master immediately cut off with the knife. As the lad cried and ran out, the master called him and the boy turned back his head. (Again), the master asked him: 'What is Buddha?' The boy raised his hand but did not see the finger; thereupon, he was greatly enlightened.

When the master was about to pass away, he said to the assembly:

The Ch'an of T'ien Lung's finger
E'er was used throughout my life.

'To say something' is in Ch'an terminology to say something to reveal the mind. The nun came to probe the master's ability to understand the truth and since he was still deluded, he could not say anything to satisfy the caller. The nun was not an ordinary person for her idea was to encourage the master in his self-cultivation. In those days there were in China many enlightened nuns.

The master felt ashamed of his ignorance and intended to journey to other places to call on enlightened masters. T'ien Lung was a learned master and his raising of a finger revealed that which raised it. The master's potentiality was already aroused to the full but required only someone to provoke its union with the absolute. A concurrent cause in a former life was responsible for the two men meeting and for the master's attainment of the truth. The master only used his teacher's method of revealing the mind for it was a direct pointing, very simple and easy to understand by his disciples.

It was now the master's turn to enlighten the boy who boasted of his understanding of the Buddha Dharma. Before, the lad clung to the finger which he took for the real, but when he did not see it again, he perceived that which raised the hand, hence his great awakening. For this reason, most Ch'an masters forbade their students to read sūtras during the time of their Ch'an training, for the latter would cling to names and terms which really obstructed their perception of the reality. For the same reason, in the special meetings, specific names were never used and those unaccustomed to reading Ch'an texts, are always puzzled as to why the ancients like to use terms such as 'that one', 'this one', '*it*', 'the fundamental', etc. which seem very strange to them. The Buddha also urged His disciples never to look at the finger which pointed at the moon, but at the moon which was actually pointed at.

4

Ch'an Master Hui Ts'ang of Shih Kung

THE master was formerly a hunter by profession and disliked the sight of Buddhist monks. (One day), while chasing deer, he passed before the temple where Ma Tsu stayed. As the latter (who was at the door) greeted him, he asked Ma Tsu: 'Have you seen any deer pass by?' Ma Tsu asked back: 'Who are you?' The master replied: 'I am a hunter.' Ma Tsu asked: 'Do you know how to shoot?' He replied: 'Yes, I do.' Ma Tsu asked: 'How many deer can you shoot with one arrow?' He replied: 'I can shoot one animal with an arrow.' Ma Tsu said: '(Then) you do not know how to shoot.' He asked Ma Tsu: 'Does the Venerable Sir know how to shoot?' Ma Tsu replied: 'Yes, I do.' He asked: 'How many animals can you shoot with one arrow?' Ma Tsu replied: 'I can shoot the whole herd with one arrow.' He said: 'They possess life, why do you shoot the whole herd?' Ma Tsu asked: 'If you know this, why do not you shoot yourself?' The master replied: 'If you want me to shoot myself, I really do not know how to do it.' Ma Tsu said: 'The whole aeon of this fellow's troubles (kleśa) caused by ignorance is now dissipating.' Thereupon, the master threw away his bow (and arrows) and followed Ma Tsu to become a monk.

One day, as the master was working in the kitchen, Ma Tsu asked him: 'What are you doing?' The master replied: 'I am tending an ox.' Ma Tsu asked: 'How do you tend it?' The master replied: 'As soon as it goes back to grass, I drag and pull it back by its nostrils.' Ma Tsu said: 'You are really tending an ox.' Thereupon, the master stopped talking and withdrew.

After he had become abbot, Hui Ts'ang used (to hold) his bow and arrows when receiving students of various potentialities. One day, he asked a guest monk: 'Do you know how to catch the void?' The monk replied: 'Yes, I do.' The master asked: 'How do you catch it?' The monk then (tried to) catch the air with his hand. The master said: 'You really do not know how to catch the void.' The monk asked the master: 'How does the venerable Dharma brother catch it?' Thereupon, the master grasped the monk's nose and pulled it with force, and the guest cried with pain, saying: 'You pull my nose as if you want to tear it off.' The master said: 'To see successfully, the void should be caught in this manner.'

(The following is omitted in 'The Imperial Selection of Ch'an Sayings' and quoted from 'The Transmission of the Lamp'.)

One day, as the monks gathered in the hall, Hui Ts'ang asked them: 'Where did you go just now?' One of the monks replied: 'I was here.' The master asked him: 'Where are you?' The monk made a sound by snapping his fingers once.

Another day, a monk came to pay reverence to the master who asked the visitor: 'Do you also bring that one along with you?' The visitor replied: 'Yes, I do.' The master asked: 'Where is it?' The visitor made three sounds with three finger-snaps. When asked: 'How can one escape from birth and death?' the master replied: 'What is the use of escaping?' The questioner insisted: 'How can one succeed in escaping from them?' The master replied: 'That one does not have birth and death.'

Ma Tsu, or Ancestor Horse, was a famous Ch'an master whose coming was predicted by the Sixth Patriarch when he said to Huai Jang: 'The twenty-seventh Patriarch Prajñātāra predicted that a colt would rush out from under your feet, trampling on and killing people all over the world. The answer will be found in your mind but do not talk about it too soon.' (See *The Sūtra of the Sixth Patriarch*, Chapter VII.) Huai Jang was Dharma successor of Hui Neng and teacher of Ma Tsu whose successor was Pai Chang. Pai Chang's first and second successors were Kuei Shan and Huang Po. Ma Tsu was, therefore, the ancestor of both the Kuei Yang (Ikyō Zen) and Lin Chi Sects (Rinzai Zen).

Ma Tsu knew that the time was ripe to liberate the hunter monk and purposely waited for his arrival at the door of the temple. In spite of his previous hatred of Buddhist monks, the hunter joined the order after his interesting conversation with Ma Tsu who had managed skilfully to develop the caller's potentiality hitherto concealed by his love of hunting.

An ox symbolizes the stubborn mind which is always prone to wander outside in quest of external objects, symbolized by the grass. To pull back the ox by its nose is to subdue the mind so that it can return to the self-natured stillness. Ma Tsu praised Hui Ts'ang for his correct way of taming the wandering mind. When the absolute has been reached, it cannot be spoken of any further. Therefore, the master stopped the chat and withdrew to reveal the return of all mental activities to the immutable.

The bow and arrows were used by the master who would hold them up or hang them on the wall to reveal the function of that which did so. To catch the void is to reveal the absolute voidness, or Dharma-kāya. The master wanted to take advantage of the moment to enlighten the guest monk by posing the question. The monk was deluded and thought of the air which was only the relative void but not the absolute. The master's act of grasping and pulling the monk's nose revealed the absolute Dharma-kāya which actually did it. Likewise, the monk's cry of pain also revealed that which uttered it, although he did not notice it.

The master asked the monks: 'Where did you go just now?' to see if they understood that the Dharma-kāya was beyond coming and going. The monk's reply: 'I was always here' was correct for his self-nature was omnipresent, and to reveal its presence, he snapped his fingers once to make a sound, the act of snapping being its function and the sound meaning all things returnable to the One Mind.

In special meetings, Ch'an masters never used specific names lest they should give rise to grasping and attachment by their disciples. 'That One' here is a Ch'an term meaning the One Mind. 'Do you bring that one along with you?' means: 'Do you also bring your mind along with you?' In other words, are you straying from your mind? If you do so, you will never realize it. The three sounds made by snapping the fingers thrice mean the threefold body (Trikāya) in one. Since the self-nature is beyond creation and annihilation, why should one think of escaping from birth and death which are illusory transformations having no real nature of their own?

5

Ch'an Master Wu Chu (alias) Wen Hsi, of Hang Chou

MASTER WEN HSI was on his way to Hua Yen (Avataṁsaka) monastery on Wu T'ai (Five-Peaked) mountain and visited the Diamond Cave to pay his reverence there. He met an old man who was walking, leading an ox. The latter invited the master to the temple and, on arrival at the door, called: 'Chun Ti!' A boy answered and came out. The old man released the ox and led the master to the hall. The entire building was of a brilliant golden colour. The old man sat down and pointing to an embroidered cushion, told the master to sit.

The old man asked the master: 'Where do you come from?' The master replied: 'From the South.' The old man asked: 'How is the Buddha Dharma upheld in the South?' The master replied: 'In this period of degeneration and extinction (of the Buddha law), few bhikṣus observe the rules.' The old man asked: 'How many monks in each community?' The master replied: 'Some three hundred, some five hundred.'

The master asked: 'How is the Buddha Dharma upheld here?' The old man replied: 'Dragons and snakes are mixed up; saints and sinners live together.' The master asked: 'How many monks are there in your community?' The old man replied: 'Front three three, rear three three.'

The old man called the boy to serve tea and also koumiss. After taking tea and koumiss, the master's mind and thoughts were opened up and became brisk. The old man held up his glass (cup) and asked: 'Do you have this in the South?' The master replied: 'No.' The monk asked: 'What do you normally use to take tea?' The master did not reply.

When the master left, the old man ordered the boy to escort the visitor to the door. (When outside), the master asked the boy: 'How many (persons) does the sentence "Front three three, rear three three" mean?' The boy called the master: 'Most Virtuous One!' and the master replied: 'Yes.' The boy asked him: 'How many?'

The master asked again: 'What is this place?' The boy replied: 'This is the temple of the Diamond Cave.' (Thereupon), the master realized that the old man was Wen Shu (Chinese name of Mañjuśrī); he became sad for he knew that he could not meet Mañjuśrī again. He bowed to the boy and implored him to say a few words before he left the place. Thereupon the boy chanted the following gāthā:

> Without anger on the face, the offering is complete,
> Without anger in the mouth, it's fragrance is superb.
> Without anger in the mind, it is a precious jewel,
> Whate'er is nor impure nor soiled is true eternity.

After the gāthā had been chanted, both Chun Ti and the temple disappeared. (Above in the sky), Mañjuśrī was seen riding on a lion with golden hair to and fro in the five-coloured clouds. Suddenly the view was hidden by white clouds coming from the east.

Because of this, the master stayed on Wu T'ai mountain. Later, he called on Yang Shan for instruction and obtained the instantaneous awakening. He was ordered to be verger of the monastery. As Mañjuśrī appeared frequently above the cauldron of rice congee, the master struck him with the bamboo stick used for churning the porridge, saying 'Wen Shu is Wen Shu whereas Wen Hsi is Wen Hsi.' Mañjuśrī chanted the following gāthā:

> The roots of bitter cucumber are bitter,
> The stalk of a sweet melon too is sweet.
> I spent three long aeons in self-cultivation,
> Yet am I still disliked by the old monk.

One day a strange monk came and begged for food. The master gave his own share to the beggar. Yang Shan who knew of this beforehand, asked the master: 'A man who has reached the stage of attainment has just come here; did you give him any food?' The master replied: 'I gave him my share.' Yang Shan said: 'You have got a great benefit (blessing).'

Ox symbolizes the stubborn mind and Mañjuśrī is the symbol of wisdom inherent in every man, which alone can tame the mad mind.

When asked by the old man, the master talked about illusory bhikṣus who did not observe the rules and of non-existent communities of three hundred and five hundred monks. These bhikṣus and communities were created by his own mind and had nothing to do with his self-cultivation for attainment of Buddhahood.

The old man's reply means that although dragons or the saintly and snakes or the profane, that is all good and evil conceptions respectively, are mixed up in one's mind, all this is caused by one's delusion produced by one's entanglement with 'three three' in front of self and 'three three' behind self. Three plus three makes six, or six sense-organs in front of the mind. Another three plus three makes six, or six consciousnesses at the back, which use the six sense-organs in front and indulge in feelings and discriminations. Another interpretation of 'three three' is: three by three equals nine and another three by three also equals nine, and nine plus nine makes eighteen, that is the eighteen realms of senses (dhātus).

The old man wanted to teach the master when he held up his glass and asked two questions to reveal that which held up the glass and that which asked the questions. The second question: 'Usually what do you normally use to take tea?' insisted that the master should recognize that which used any object to take tea and that which took tea in the South. The old man directly pointed at the mind but the master was still deluded and did not understand his instruction.

When the boy called: 'Most Virtuous One!' and when the master replied: 'Yes', there was also direct pointing at that which asked and that which replied. That which asked and that which replied were, in fact, the minds. Thus the boy's reply to the master's question: 'How many persons does the sentence "Front three three, rear three three" mean?' is the One Mind which without impurities and taints, is the eternal reality. The boy's gāthā was his instruction to the master concerning the purification of mind for attainment of Buddhahood.

Chinese devotees going to the Five Peaked mountain to worship Mañjuśrī sometimes met on their way either an old man, or a beggar, or an old lady selling tea and cakes along the mountain tracks. Even nowadays, tales of Mañjuśrī's apparition and transformation with meaningful talks are still circulated and believed all over the country. Readers interested in these tales are urged to read the book *Sous Des Nuées d'Orage*, by Madame Alexandra David-Neel, who relates some very interesting experiences during her visit to the mountain during the last war.

In a monastery, the verger indicates the order of sitting and is also in charge of cooking rice porridge for the morning meal as well as other petty jobs.

Mañjuśrī's gāthā means: When the cucumber is bitter, even its roots are also bitter, that is when the master was deluded, his delusion was complete. When the melon is sweet, even its stalk is sweet, that is when the master was enlightened, his enlightenment was complete. The third and fourth lines mean that after the master's awakening, he remained immutable and unperturbed by the visions of Mañjuśrī. This is in contrast with the time when he was sad because of his hopelessness of meeting Mañjuśrī again. Thus the master set a good example to all Buddhists who should pay no attention to visions appearing in their meditations, for all visions are but flowers in the sky, as the Buddha himself put it.

The strange monk came to test the master and Yang Shan who was the latter's teacher and was already enlightened, knew of the visit beforehand.

There are two stages: the cause-stage, i.e. that of a Buddhist, for he has accepted a cause, or enlightenment, that produces a changed outlook, and the fruit-stage or stage of attainment, or reward. A man of the stage of attainment is one who has attained the fruit, i.e. escaped the chain of transmigrations, a Buddha or Bodhisattva.

A great aeon, or Mahākalpa in Sanskrit, is a great kalpa from the beginning of a universe till it is destroyed when another begins in its place. It has four periods known as (1) the creation period, (2) period of abiding, or existence, (3) period of destruction, when fire, water and wind destroy everything except the fourth dhyāna and (4) period of annihilation.

6

Master Fu Ta Shih

(Literally) Bodhisattva Fu, (alias) SHAN HUI

(ONE day), the emperor Liang Wu Ti invited master (Fu Ta Shih) to expound the Diamond Sūtra. As soon as he had ascended to his seat, the master knocked the table once with a ruler and descended from his seat. As the emperor was startled, the master asked him: 'Does Your Majesty understand?' 'I do not,' replied the emperor. The saintly master said: 'The Bodhisattva has finished expounding the sūtra.'

(Another day), wearing a robe, a hat and a pair of shoes, the Bodhisattva came to the palace where the emperor asked him: 'Are you a monk?' In reply, the Bodhisattva pointed a finger at his hat. 'Are you a Taoist?' asked the emperor. In reply, the Bodhisattva pointed his finger at his shoes. 'Are you a lay man?' asked the emperor. In reply, the Bodhisattva pointed his finger at his monk's robe.

His gāthā read:

> The handless hold the hoe.
> A pedestrian walks, riding on a water buffalo.
> A man passes over the bridge;
> The bridge (but) not the water flows.

The following is quoted from 'The Stories of Eminent Upāsakas' (Ch'u Shih Ch'uan):

'Fu Ta Shi (literally Bodhisattva Fu) was born in the fourth year of Chien Wu's reign (A.D. 497) in the Nan Ch'i dynasty. He was a native of Tung Yang district and his lay surname was Fu. Married at sixteen, he had two sons. At twenty-four, he met one day an Indian ascetic who said to him: 'You and I took the same vow at Vipaśyin Buddha's (the first of the seven Buddhas of Antiquity) place and your robe and bowl still remain in the palace of Tuṣita Heaven. When will you return there?'

The ascetic pointed to a peak and urged him to stay on it to meditate. One day, the master had a vision of three Buddhas, Śākyamuni, Vimalakīrti (also called 'The Golden Grain Tathāgata) and Dīpaṁkara, sending out rays of light to shine on his body. After his realization of Śūraṅgama-samādhi in which all things are perceived in their ultimate imperturbability, he knew he had attained the ninth Bodhisattva stage, hence his alias 'Shan Hui'.

Fu Ta Shih was a contemporary of Bodhidharma but both he and the Indian Patriarch failed to liberate emperor Liang Wu Ti.

The master's acts of ascending to the seat, knocking the table once and descending from the seat, were to reveal the Supreme Reality expounded in the Diamond Sūtra. His was the best way of revealing the pure and clean mind inherent in every man, which is responsible for all common acts of daily life.

One day he presented himself at the palace to enlighten the emperor In olden times as well as in our modern age, people attach great importance to the outward appearance of a man as well as to his academic titles and social standing. All this having no value in relation to the Buddha Dharma, Fu wore a hat, a monk's robe and a pair of shoes, to wipe out all conceptions of form, appearance, aspect and characteristic as taught in the Diamond Sūtra. A monk usually wears no hat, a Taoist no shoes and a layman no monk's robe.

The first gāthā which the Bodhisattva composed to enlighten his disciples was:

> Each night, (one) embraces a Buddha while sleeping,
> Each morning, (one) gets up again with him.
> When rising or sitting, both watch and follow one another,
> Whether speaking or not, both are in the same place,
> They never even for a moment part,
> (But) are like the body and its shadow.
> If you wish to know the Buddha's whereabouts,
> In the sound of (your own) voice, there is he.

This gāthā reveals that the self-natured Buddha is inherent in every man and never leaves him. Fu Ta Shih's teaching was in line with that of Buddhas and Patriarchs and his first gāthā directly pointed at everybody's mind. Its simplicity, however, soon gave rise to doubts and suspicions in the minds of his disciples who wanted something more abstruse. He was, therefore, compelled to compose his second gāthā which read:

There is a thing preceding heaven and earth,
It has no form and is in essence still and void.
It can master all things in this world
(And) follows not the four changing seasons.

This second gāthā is not so clear and simple as the first one. The thing that precedes heaven and earth is the eternal nature which is immaterial and imperceptible. It produces all appearances but does not change in the midst of the changing phenomenal. This gāthā especially pleases scholars who like its poetic form, but soon people, whose minds would wander outside in constant search of something new and sensational, began to cast it aside and looked for something extraordinary to satisfy their desires for emotional things. Hence, the third gāthā presented in the above text.

The first line of the gāthā means: the handless mind uses its phenomenal human form which is endowed with two hands, to hold the hoe.

The second line means: the phenomenal man has a mind inherent in him, which directs his two feet to walk.

The man's act of passing over the bridge reveals that which enters his body at birth and leaves it at death.

In the fourth line, the bridge, or human body, is always changing whereas the water, or the self-nature, is immutable and never changes.

It is very regrettable that this gāthā has given rise to discrimination in the minds of some modern commentators who like to link it with Albert Einstein's Theory of Relativity which has no place in the Mind Dharma.

PART III

THE DIAMOND CUTTER OF DOUBTS

A Commentary on The Diamond Sūtra
Vajracchedikā-prajñā-pāramitā Sūtra

By Ch'an Master Han Shan
(*from the Chin Kang Chueh I*)

Foreword

THE *Vajracchedika-prajñā-pāramitā Sūtra*, widely known as the Diamond Sūtra, is of very profound and subtle meaning, and few really understand it. It has been wrongly divided into thirty-two chapters which seem to be unconnected random sayings, and the sub-title of each chapter creates more confusion in the mind of readers who usually rely on it for their interpretation of the text. The chapter divisions and sub-titles have therefore been omitted in this version.

A correct interpretation of the sūtra is difficult because as soon as a doubt or question arose in Subhūti's mind, the Buddha, who knew it perfectly, gave an immediate reply without waiting for the mental query to be expressed in words. Therefore, all these mental questions were not recorded by Ānanda who only noted down the questions and answers actually heard by him, to be in accord with the first sentence of the sūtra: 'Thus have I heard'.

In China many commentaries have been written on this sūtra but most of them have failed to satisfy readers who have not seen the continuity of the Buddha's teaching which began by wiping out Subhūti's coarse conceptions and ended with destroying his subtle ideas, until all his wrong views were eliminated one by one, resulting in the exposure of his fundamental nature. It was thus a continuous string of the disciple's wrong conceptions, from the coarse to the finest, which the Buddha broke up successively in His teaching of Wisdom (prajñā), for prajñā had no room for the smallest particle of dust, or impurity caused by ignorance.

Master Han Shan wrote this commentary after he had attained enlightenment, had read the whole Tripiṭaka and had apprehended the deep meaning of all the sūtras. According to his commentary, the Diamond Sūtra has only two parts, Part I dealing with the coarse views held by Subhūti and in fact by all students of Mahāyāna Buddhism, and Part II dealing with the subtle views still held by but imperceptible to them.

A student who succeeds in ridding his mind of coarse concepts, will reach a stage described in master Han Shan's 'The Song of the Board-bearer' which warns against 'sitting on the clean white ground' and of 'hankering after attractive side-lines'. (See Han Shan's autobiography—

Han Shan Ta Shih Nien P'u.) Once he has reached this stage, the student should advance a step further to get rid of all subtle and imperceptible views which continue to split his undivided whole into subject and object. Only when these subtle views are completely uprooted, can he perceive the Tathāgata of his fundamental nature.

The correct interpretation of this sūtra is, therefore, of paramount importance to students of Mahāyāna for if they fail to grasp its meaning they will have difficulty in studying the Supreme Vehicle. This sūtra is of special importance to followers of the Ch'an Sect, and the Fifth and Sixth Patriarchs used it to seal the mind in their 'Transmission of the Dharma'. Students of the doctrine of the Mind who understand the Diamond Sūtra, are able to interpret correctly the instructions of the Patriarchs which consisted solely in driving out all wrong feelings and passions for the purpose of quieting the mind and revealing the real fundamental face of each living being.

As the Sixth Patriarch Hui Neng urged his listeners to purify their minds before he expounded the prajñā, the adherents of Ch'an should abandon all dual conceptions of the subjective and objective during their spiritual training. In this respect, the Diamond Sūtra is a precious guide for cleansing the mind for the purpose of attaining samādhi without which prajñā cannot manifest itself.

In this presentation, I have used the Sanskrit word *Dharma* instead of its equivalent 'Law' and 'thing'. By 'thing', it should be understood as all things or anything small or great, visible or invisible, real or unreal, concrete things or abstract ideas.

All brackets are mine.

The commentator on this sūtra and the Heart Sūtra was Ch'an master Han Shan of the Ming dynasty. Born in 1546, he left his home at the age of twelve and went to a monastery where he was taught literature and sūtras. Urged by an eminent master to practise Ch'an, he read 'The Sayings of Chung Feng' (Chung Feng Kuang Lu) which completely changed the young novice who then joined the Saṅgha order. After listening to the Avataṁsaka Sūtra, he obtained a clear understanding of the unobstructed integration of all things into the Dharma-dhātu. His monastery was destroyed by a disastrous fire and he vowed to rebuild it but realized that he could not do so before his own enlightenment without which he would not win support for the purpose. He went North and in the vicinity of the capital, he climbed a mountain and stayed on its peak where he lived with a hermit. There he experienced the samādhi of voidness. This experience is usually the first one every serious Ch'an meditator has after he has successfully put a stop to his thinking. When he read the work of Seng Chao, he suddenly realized the fundamental immutability of the phenomenal. During his stay on the Five Peaked mountain, he realized Avalokiteśvara Bodhisattva's complete enlightenment which is described in the Śūraṅgama Sūtra. He had many more other experiences among which two were the most important; in each of them, he sat, cross-legged and face to face with another enlightened monk, immobile and speechless, for forty successive days and nights, obviously without sleeping. At seventy-eight, he announced his death to his disciples and passed away peacefully. His body still remains intact at the monastery of the Sixth Patriarch.

UPĀSAKA LU K'UAN YÜ.

Hongkong, 21 March, 1959.

Preface

PRAJÑĀ is a true cause (hetu) of all Buddha Mothers[1] and Bodhisattvas, the Buddha nature of all living beings and the great fundamental of the mind. The individual attitude towards it, either concurrent or contradictory, will determine the difference between the saintly (ārya) and the worldly.

It is, therefore, clear that the daily activities of all living beings, such as their seeing, hearing, knowing and feeling, are really prajñā's bright (manifestations), the (essential) point being belief or disbelief in it. For this reason, it is said: 'Belief alone makes possible an entry into the wisdom-ocean of all the Buddhas.'

At the Vulture Peak assembly, the Buddha's disciples who had already been ferried across the (ocean) of life and death, had no share in the attainment of Buddhahood, solely because of their disbelief in this Dharma. The World Honoured One was, therefore, obliged to use many means to weed out (their disbelief) and all kinds of abuse (to awaken them), but those who were dull of apprehension, doubted and doubted again as if their knowledge was not qualified for it. As their doubts were not uprooted, their fundamental wisdom could not manifest itself. Finally, at the prajñā assembly, the Tathāgata[2] used his diamond wisdom to cut off (their doubts) to ensure the complete removal of their conceptions of both the holy and worldly and the elimination of their (perverted) views of birth and death, so that the fundamental light of wisdom could be revealed to them. (Only then) did they begin to believe that their minds were pure and clean and did not contain a single thing that could hinder them.

This prajñā diamond pulled up the roots of all doubts and this sūtra was expounded for the benefit of initiates of the Supreme Way and not for those of shallow knowledge and poor virtue who could not understand it. For this reason, (the Fifth Patriarch at) Huang Mei used it to seal the mind,[3] for the Ch'an sect did not establish a single Dharma.

[1] Buddha Mothers: begetters of all Buddhas.

[2] Tathāgata: He who came as did all Buddhas; who took the absolute way of cause and effect, and attained to perfect wisdom, one of the highest titles of a Buddha.

[3] Mental impression, intuitive certainty; the mind is the Buddha mind in all, which can seal or assure the truth; the term indicates the intuitive method of the Ch'an School which is independent of the spoken or written word.

Formerly, Vasubandhu (the Twenty-First Patriarch of the Ch'an Sect) listed twenty-seven doubts to explain this sūtra. Since these doubts lay hid in the written words (of the sūtra), in this country many missed its real meaning by clinging to its words, and very few indeed gathered the real ideas behind them.

When I was a child, I could already recite this sūtra by heart, but when I attained to manhood, I could not understand its meaning. When I thought of the Sixth Patriarch who, upon hearing a sentence of the sūtra, achieved the instantaneous realization of his mind, I could not help feeling why no one in this world could apprehend and enter it. This was due to the fact that the right eye was not opened, thence the real hindrance to the (realization of one's own) nature.

During my stay in (the monastery of the Sixth Patriarch at) Ts'ao Ch'i, once by chance, while explaining the sūtra to my followers, I obtained a sudden understanding of it, although I was unready for the experience, and all doubts which lay beyond the words of the sūtra became evident to my mind's eye. It is true that this Dharma is outside words and letters and cannot be understood by reasoning and discriminating.

I, therefore, took up this sūtra to explain it for the almsgiving of Buddha truth. The wood-blocks from which to print it were first cut in Ling Nan, next at Wu Yun, and later at Nan Yo. My disciple Fang Yu who saw the sūtra, believed and received it, undertook also the carving of wood-blocks at Wu Men.

It is hoped that the four vargas[4] will all open up their correct Dharma eye and really believe in their own minds. Thus the cause of their attainment of Buddhahood will begin with this sūtra.

Written in the month of the summer solstice in the year Ping Ch'en (1616). Śramaṅa Te Ch'ing, (alias) Han Shan, of the Ts'ao Ch'i monastery in the Ming dynasty.

[4] The four vargas: monks, nuns, male and female devotees.

The Diamond Cutter of Doubts

Part I

All those who explain the word 'Diamond' agree that it means something hard and sharp that can cut. This is a vague explanation. In fact, there exists in India a precious stone called diamond, which is very hard and cannot be broken but can cut all other objects. If it is compared with prajñā which can cut off all troubles (kleśa), this comparison, although valid in theory, is not the Buddha's. It is only the usual view originating from inherited habits.

Prajñā which means wisdom in our language, is the Buddha Mind, also called Buddha Wisdom.

Pāramitā means 'reaching the other shore'. It points to the ultimate extremity of this Mind.

The full title *Diamond Prajñā-pāramitā* indicates the teaching expounded in this sūtra which aims at revealing the Buddha's Diamond Mind. Moreover, this Diamond Mind was the fundamental mind of the Buddha in His practice, as a cause, resulting in His enlightenment, as an effect. Now He appeared in this world to teach and convert living beings by using solely this mind. He taught Bodhisattvas to use this Diamond Mind as a cause in their practice so that they could enter the initial door of Mahāyāna. This is why He purposely taught them to cut off their doubts (about it). As this mind had nothing in common with the realm of feeling of living beings, people in this world did not know the Buddha. Moreover, the Buddha did not, in fact, belong to this world. When He came to the world, those who saw Him harboured doubts about Him. Since His daily activities did not conform with those of others, His talking being different, and all His practice and Dharma being in contrast with the world, these disparities aroused their doubts about Him. No wonder that the demon kings of the heavens wished to harm Him, Devadatta and Ajātaśatru wanted to kill Him and all men slandered Him. For this reason He said: 'When I appeared in this world, gods (devas), men, spirits (asuras), heretics and demon kings doubted with apprehension.' Not only did men and devas suspect Him, but even His elder disciples, such as Mahākāśyapa, were suspicious of Him, for when He expounded the Dharma, the Buddha used to mention now the non-existent, now the existing; now the right, now the wrong; either He praised or blamed; either He exhorted or scolded; and He never used words on a fixed basis. The disciples who listened to His teaching, harboured doubts and did not believe Him. They said: 'Is He not Māra who feigns to be a Buddha to annoy us and disturb our minds?' With the elder disciples' attitude being such, one can guess that of beginners, for it was difficult to believe and understand the Dharma expounded by the Buddha. Since He had appeared in this world, He had now expounded the Dharma for thirty years. As His disciples were still suspicious and unbelieving, they had done Him an injustice for a long time.

Fortunately, it was a happy day when Subhūti perceived something (extraordinary) in the World Honoured One and suddenly praised Him. The World Honoured One (took advantage of) His disciple's doubts to cut them off, and revealed his real Diamond Mind to him so that he could be thoroughly awakened to it and would not have any more doubt about it, thus enabling all those present to wipe out theirs as well. Therefore, this sūtra (tells how) the Buddha clearly revealed His own mind in order to cut off His disciples' doubts in their studies of the truth. It does not expound Prajñā which can cut out the troubles (kleśa) of living beings. Those who do not agree to this can read the sūtra in which (they will find that) Subhūti's doubts about the Buddha Mind were cut off one by one after the Buddha had exposed this mind. Is there (in the sūtra) any reference to the wisdom which cuts out the troubles of living beings? For this reason, the title of this sūtra points direct to the Dharma and is not used as an allegory. Obviously, when the disciple's doubts were cut off, their troubles would disappear also. The sūtra's only aim was the cutting out of doubts and the awakening of faith. For students of the truth, faith is fundamental and doubts are their obstacles. There are three kinds of doubt: about the man (who expounds the Dharma), about the Dharma and about oneself (the student).

The (first) doubt about the expounder is because he is not recognized as right. For instance, when the disciples heard the Buddha speaking of the physical body (rūpa-kāya) the spiritual body (dharma-kāya), and the great and small bodies, they did not know which body was the true Buddha. This was doubt about the expounder of Dharma.

When the Buddha expounded the Dharma, as soon as He had spoken of the existing, He mentioned the non-existent; as soon as He had spoken of the void, He mentioned the not-void (amogha). His sermons were not consistent and caused a great deal of doubt. This was doubt about the Dharma.

There might be those who listened to His sermons, could believe Him, and had no doubt about the Dharma, but they found it (too) extensive and doubted whether their inferior roots were qualified for it and whether they could observe it. This was doubt about oneself.

This sūtra contained three kinds of doubt. As soon as one of them arose in Subhūti's mind, the Buddha drove it out (until) they were all cut off completely. It was said: 'When all one's doubts and repentance (for them) are wiped out for ever, one will abide in the wisdom of reality.' This was the aim of the sūtra.

In our country, there are many commentaries on this sūtra, but they are not in accord with the Buddha's idea. Only the commentary by Bodhisattva Vasubhandu who listed the twenty-seven doubts which occur in the sūtra, is correct. When his commentary was brought to this country, it was translated into Chinese, but since the work was done by men whose ability (to understand it) differed greatly, in spite of the fact that the commentator was a sage, the translation could not convey the exact meaning and became a hindrance for students who could not comprehend it. Its subtle, profound and hidden meaning cannot be taught by word of mouth, and if expressed in words, it becomes as worthless as leavings. Thus, how could coarse and unstable words and phrases penetrate its abstruseness? In a commentary, it is difficult to describe the Buddha Mind. For example, when writing a biography, facts can be narrated but the painting of its spiritual aspects is impossible.

When interpreting this sūtra as a cutter of doubts, the most important and wonderful thing is to discover first those doubts which Subhūti had in his mind. If they are uncovered, the Buddha's sermon on 'the cutting of doubts' automatically becomes clear and does not require any explanation. Therefore, these doubts should be searched out (even) before attempting to interpret the text, and their traces ferreted out in each chapter so as to tackle them one by one, thus forgetting all about the written words in order to comprehend the deep meaning. Only then can the aim of the teaching automatically be found.

Thus have I heard. Once upon a time, the Buddha sojourned in the Jetavana park[1] near Sravasti with an assembly of twelve hundred and fifty bhiksus.

[1] Jetavana, a park near Śrāvastī, said to have been obtained from Prince Jeta by the elder Anāthapiṇḍada, in which monastic buildings were erected. It was the favourite resort of the Buddha.

This describes the assembly where the Buddha expounded the Dharma. It would be superfluous to deal with it here as other commentaries have already been written about it.

One day, at mealtime, the World Honoured One put on His robe, took His bowl, and entered the great town of Śrāvastī to beg for His food. After He had begged from door to door, He returned to His place. When He had taken His meal, He put away His robe and bowl, washed His feet, arranged His seat and sat down.

This shows the Buddha's ordinary life and daily activities which were similar to those of others and had nothing special about them. There is here, however, something which is uncommon, but very few know it.

At the time, the elder Subhūti who was in the assembly, rose from his seat, uncovered his right shoulder, knelt upon his right knee, respectfully joined the palms of his hands and said to the Buddha: 'It is very rare, O World Honoured One! . . .'

The Tathāgata's daily activities were similar to those of other men (but) there was here one thing which was different and those who sat face to face with Him did not see it. That day, suddenly Subhūti uncovered it, praised it and said: 'Very rare. . . .' Alas! the Tathāgata had been thirty years with His disciples and they still did not know anything about His common acts of daily life. As they did not know, they thought these acts were ordinary and let them pass (unnoticed). They thought only that He was similar to others and were, therefore, suspicious of and did not believe what He said. Had Subhūti not seen clearly, no one would really know the Buddha.

'. . . how well the Tathāgata protects and thinks of all Bodhisattvas; how well He instructs all the Bodhisattvas.'

Subhūti praised the Buddha for this rare quality of His, for he saw His kindly heart (i.e. mind). The Bodhisattvas referred to were disciples who were studying His doctrine. They were precisely those who were previously of the Hīnayāna (mind) and began to develop the Mahāyāna mind; they were all Bodhisattvas whose minds were disturbed by the conception of the void. The Buddha always protected and thought of these Bodhisattvas. He had no other idea than that of enjoining upon them (the realization of) the Buddha Mind. The Buddha protected and thought of them, because when He appeared in this world, His fundamental vow was to guide all living beings so that they could become similar to Him. This mind (of His) would reach its extremity only when every living being had obtained Buddhahood. However, living beings were of little virtue and saturated with impurity, and since they were of weak purpose, they were incapable of carrying it out. Thus they were like babies and the Buddha was like a kind mother who protects and thinks of her children without a moment's respite. The Buddha knew perfectly all living beings whom He protected and for whom He had only kind thoughts, just as a kind mother cares for her babes. By protection and kind thoughts, it should be understood that His sole aim would be fulfilled only after all living beings had attained Buddhahood. This is why he instructed the Bodhisattvas so well. He did not dare to say it plainly, but used convenient and close methods to teach them. This is why the adjective 'well' was used. The sūtra says: 'I use unlimited and numberless (expedient) methods to guide living beings so that every one of them will attain all-knowledge (sarvajña).'[1] This is the meaning of the words 'protected', 'thought of' and 'instructed'.

'O World Honoured One, when virtuous men or women develop the supreme-enlightenment mind,[2] how should their minds abide and how should they be subdued?'

Subhūti asked for the means to quiet the mind. When the disciples' minds abided in Hīnayāna, they consented to save only themselves but did not think of saving all living beings. Therefore, their minds were narrow. Now that they had for over twenty years listened to the teaching of the Buddha who had used all means to sweep away (their false ideas) and to urge them to save all beings, they were called living beings of broad mind and were Bodhisattvas. They were enjoined to convert all beings here below, in order to seek the Buddha fruit from above. They now consented to save all beings and were determined to develop the Bodhi mind.

Subhūti had already believed in the Buddha Mind, but he saw new Bodhisattvas who had just begun to develop the broad mind of a Bodhisattva and were not yet awakened to the absolute voidness of reality which they could not distinguish from the relative voidness as previously conceived by them. Formerly the Hīnayāna's nirvāṇa could be clung to for their minds' tranquil dwelling. Now they had relinquished the former (conception of one-sided) voidness, but had not yet attained the true voidness. Thus, when advancing further, they did not gain any

[1] Sarvajña: all-knowledge or Buddha-wisdom.

[2] Anuttara-samyak-saṁbodhi, or Anubodhi: unexcelled complete enlightenment, an attribute of every Buddha. Translated into Chinese: the highest, correct and complete, or universal knowledge or awareness, the perfect wisdom of a Buddha, Omniscience.

new experience, and when turning back, they lost their old abode. They were called Bodhisattvas whose minds were disturbed by the conception of voidness. As they used to cling to names and words, they were still bound by habit. They still held the false view that there was a real abiding place and that there was really a Buddha fruit to seek. Thus, they thought that they should search for a Buddha fruit in which to abide. As they were required to convert living beings here below in order to obtain the Buddha fruit from above, they had to save all living beings before they could become Buddhas themselves. Now they saw uncountable and limitless numbers of living beings in the universe[1] and wondered when all these beings could be saved and how they could obtain the Buddha fruit since the universe would never be emptied of these beings. As they were impatient in their efforts to seek a tranquil dwelling, their minds were not at rest and they could not subdue them. Therefore, Subhūti purposely solicited for them the (appropriate) means so that their minds could abide in tranquillity and could be subdued. Why, then, did Subhūti, who had seen and praised the so-rare Buddha Mind, ask only about these two things? The whole assembly had agreed that the World Honoured One had already obtained (the fruit of) enlightenment. Subhūti had seen that His mind was quiet and comfortable whereas the minds of those who were now determined to seek the Buddha fruit were (still) disturbed. He wanted to know where these minds should abide and how they should be subdued.

As regards how to quiet the mind, (an example can be found in the dialogue between Bodhidharma and the Second Ch'an Patriarch) who was his attendant and solicited from him the means to quiet his mind. Bodhidharma replied: 'Bring me your mind so that I can quiet it.' The Second Patriarch said: 'I cannot find my mind.' And Bodhidharma replied: 'I have now quieted your mind.' In the Ch'an School, just a word was sufficient and this was the Ch'an doctrine. Now the World Honoured One spoke of so many methods to quiet the mind because of His compassionate heart. This was the Teaching School. After all, it was only the quest of the mind which could not be found. This is why before the Fourth Patriarch, the Laṇkāvatāra Sūtra was used to seal (and prove) the mind, and why, afterwards, (the Fifth Patriarch at) Huang Mei and the Sixth Patriarch used the Diamond Sūtra to seal it. The (Diamond) Sūtra is, therefore, not a sūtra of spoken and written words and should not be regarded as such. Its wonder(ful meaning) is outside of words. In it, the question 'What do you think?' is asked to probe (the disciple's) doubts.

[1] Literally 'the great trichiliocosm'. See footnote 4, p. 169.

The whole assembly gave rise to (new) doubts upon hearing the Buddha's words, and although these doubts were not disclosed, their minds were already on the move. This was discrimination by mental words and originated in habitual (conceptions) of names and words.

The Buddha said: 'Excellent, excellent, Subhūti! As you say, the Tathāgata protects, cherishes and instructs Bodhisattvas so well. Now listen attentively and I will tell you how the minds of virtuous men and women, who develop the supreme enlightenment mind, should thus abide and be subdued.

Subhūti's question referred to Bodhisattvas in quest of supreme enlightenment (anubodhi) who could not be like the Buddha whose mind was so quiet and comfortable. He thought that if they wished to become Buddhas, they should perform the same daily activities as the Buddha did, and only then could they become Buddhas. He saw the Buddha's mind which was at ease and the Bodhisattvas' minds which could not abide in stillness. Hence his question: 'How should they be subdued in order to abide in tranquility?'

In His reply, the Buddha's idea was that Bodhisattvas who wished to quiet their minds in order to become Buddhas themselves should not seek anything other than that mind of His which, as understood by Subhūti, protected, cherished and instructed (the Bodhisattvas). Thus their minds would be quieted, and there would be no need to subdue them. Therefore, He said: 'As you say.' It would suffice to set their minds at rest and (then), what else would they seek to subdue? They ought to do 'thus', hence the word 'thus' in His reply.

(Subhūti replied:) 'Oh yes, World Honoured One, I shall be glad to hear (your instruction).'

Subhūti said: 'Oh yes,' because he now believed in the Buddha Mind about which he had no more doubt. As he had already seen the Buddha Mind, it seemed that there was no need for further teaching (about it). But since the other Bodhisattvas did not know it, he was glad to hear about it (so that these Bodhisattvas should have a chance to know it also).

The Buddha said: 'Subhūti, all Bodhisattvas and Mahāsattvas should subdue their minds as follows . . .'

Here the Buddha points out the means to quiet the mind which is indicated in the following paragraph of the sūtra. Subhūti asked about two things: How the mind should abide and how to subdue it? Now the

Buddha talked only about subduing the mind and did not say anything about how it should abide.

Since worldly men, Śrāvakas[1] and Pratyekas[2] clung to an abiding place because of their (false) habits (through the use) of names and terms, and as they were now resolved upon entering Mahāyāna, it was important first to eliminate these (false) habits, for neither living beings nor nirvāṇa are real, both being non-existent, with only names and terms as their substances. Once names and terms were wiped out, their (false) habits would disappear completely, and the mind would become automatically calm and comfortable and would thus not require to be subdued. Therefore, the Buddha taught them only how to subdue their minds and did not say anything about their abiding in stillness in order not to bring these (false) habits to life again. It is said: 'The mad mind never stops; if it does, it will become enlightened (bodhi). It will suffice to empty the mind of all worldly feelings; there should be no interpretation of the holy.' As the Buddha did not bind others with a firm Dharma,[3] He did not talk about abiding (in stillness).

'... All living beings born from eggs, wombs, humidity or by transformation, with or without form, either thoughtful or thoughtless, and neither thoughtful nor thoughtless[4] are all led by me to the final nirvāṇa for the extinction of reincarnation. Although immeasurable, uncountable and unlimitable numbers of living beings are thus led to (the final nirvāṇa for) the extinction of reincarnation, it is true that not a living being is led there. Why so, Subhūti? (Because) if a Bodhisattva (still) clings to the false notion (lakṣaṇa)[5] of an ego, a personality, a being and a life,[6] he is not (a true) Bodhisattva.'

[1] Śrāvaka: a hearer, disciple of Buddha who understands the Four Noble Truths, rids himself of the unreality of the phenomenal, and enters the incomplete nirvāṇa.

[2] Pratyeka: one who lives apart from others and attains enlightenment alone, or for himself, in contrast with the altruism of the Bodhisattva principle.

[3] The Buddha did not teach any fixed Dharma, but only stripped His disciples of their erroneous tenets so that their self-possessed prajñā could manifest itself.

[4] Nāivasaṁjñānāsaṁjñāyatana: the heaven or place where there is neither thinking nor not thinking; the fourth of the four immaterial heavens, known as Akaniṣṭha, the highest heaven of form.

[5] Lakṣaṇa: form, appearance, indication, sign, aspect and characteristic.

[6] The four lakṣaṇas of an ego, a personality, a being and a life are explained by Han Shan on page 187. The Hinayana definition of these four false notions is: (*a*) the illusion that there is a real ego or self in the five skandhas; (*b*) that this ego is a man or personality and different from the beings on other paths; (*c*) that all beings have an ego born of the five skandhas; (*d*) that the ego has a determined or fated period of life.

In Mahāyāna and Ch'an Buddhism this is taught by means of a meditation in four stages: (1) Meditate on the ego or self as owner of the physical body and as the subject who is meditating, another man or personality being the counterpart of that ego as object. The mind which seeks wisdom is the ego or subject and the wisdom sought is the object. When it realizes that the ego is non-existent and rejects it, it is called personality. (2) Meditate on this personality which from being object becomes subject and understand that this too is an illusion. When the mind realizes that personality is also an empty name without real nature, it is called

Here the World Honoured One indicated a method of meditation for quieting the mind. Since a Bodhisattva is resolved on only two things, namely the quest of Buddha fruit and the conversion of all living beings, his mind is not quiet because he sees that living beings are always unchanged and exist everywhere, and wonders when all of them can be delivered. If all living beings cannot be saved, it will be difficult indeed to obtain the Buddha fruit which will not be within reach. Therefore, his mind is not quiet and he is constantly anxious about this and seeks to subdue this mind. Now the Buddha taught the method of saving living beings, which consisted of looking into the non-existence of an ego as the main point. However, a Bodhisattva sees such a great number of living beings whom he cannot save solely because he clings to the false notion of an ego which leads to that of a personality, and if everybody had a counterpart in this manner, the number of living beings in the universe would have no limit. Furthermore, the circle of rebirths being endless, he is scared when thinking of the difficulty in delivering all of them. He does not realize that (all) living beings are fundamentally in the Bhūtatathatā condition.[1]

In spite of the uncountable number of living beings, there were only twelve categories of them. A (close) examination of these twelve leads to their classification in four groups, namely beings born of eggs, wombs, humidity and by transformation. These four groups of births comprise only two dharmas, namely Form (or the material) and Mind (or the immaterial). The form dharma comprises the realms of Form and No-Form, the mind dharma of the thoughtful and the thoughtless. If extended further, these dharmas also comprise the realms of neither Form nor No-Form and of neither the thoughtful nor the thoughtless. Thus, these

---

being. (3) Meditate on being, which is a state of relative voidness, until that too disappears, but something hangs on. (4) Meditate on that which remains, a determined or fated period of life. This is incomplete awareness as the element of time is still present. Eliminate that element.

An analysis of these four stages in the meditation reveals: (1) Subject and its elimination. Disentanglement from sense organs (or sense data). (2) Object and its elimination. Disentanglement from sense data (or sense organs). (3) Relative voidness (of subject and object) and its elimination. Disentanglement from the relative voidness of (1) and (2). (4) Incomplete awareness (of relative voidness).

The fourth stage is called 'sitting on the top of a pole one hundred feet high' from which one should take a step forward over the sea of suffering and then reach the other shore. This stage can only be reached when one's potentiality has been aroused to the full and so is ready for awakening.

Thus the meditator passes through all four lakṣaṇas from the coarse to the subtle, before wiping out all of them for his attainment of prajñā, which is free from all dual concepts of object and subject including the subtle view of ego and dharma which is the hardest nut to crack.

[1] Bhūtatathatā: the real, suchness or reality, the ultimate or all.

twelve categories contain the whole realm of all living beings and their number is not great. Moreover, they are called living beings whose forms and minds move in the world of phenomena.[1] Since they are phenomena, these living beings fundamentally are non-existent. As such they are falsely viewed as existing.[2] If they are regarded as non-existent, they are fundamentally in the condition of suchness (Bhūtatathatā). As they are in the state of Bhūtatathatā, they are all in the condition of nirvāṇa. Thus they were all led (by the Buddha) to the Final Nirvāṅa. Was this a difficult thing?

Vimalakīrti said: 'All living beings are fundamentally (in the state of) calmness and extinction (of reincarnation, that is in nirvāṇa) and cannot be calmed or become further extinct.' Thus when immeasurable, uncountable and unlimitable numbers of living beings were delivered, not one was really delivered. Why is this? Because fundamentally there is no ego. The idea of an ego leads to that of a personality and the idea of a personality to that of a being and a life. One who holds these four false notions cannot be called a Bodhisattva, and how can he talk about saving living beings? Therefore, a Bodhisattva should look into the non-existence of an ego, and the non-existence of an ego will lead to the non-existence of a personality. When ego and personality have no existence, the realm of living beings is bound automatically to be calm and extinct. When living beings are calm and extinct, the Buddha fruit is within the reach of all. Then why be scared about it being far distant? Therefore, a Bodhisattva should look into the non-existence of an ego.

In one of the following paragraphs of the sutra (see page 200), the Buddha said that if a man realized that all dharmas were egoless and achieved the (perfection) of patience (kṣānti), he would be a true Bodhisattva.

Doubt.—The Buddha taught Bodhisattvas to save living beings, mainly by charity or the giving of alms (dāna).[3] Those who received the alms were all living beings. Now (according to His teaching), all living beings are non-existent; then, if alms are given, who will receive them? In the following paragraph of the sūtra, the Buddha says that a Bodhisattva giving alms, should not cling to the false notion of living beings.

'Furthermore, Subhūti, a Bodhisattva's mind should not abide anywhere when giving alms; that is to say, he should give without a mind abiding in form, or he should give without a mind abiding in sound, or in smell, or in taste, or in touch

[1] They are empirical combinations without permanent reality.
[2] Taking the seeming as real.
[3] Dāna. Charity: almsgiving (of goods or the doctrine).

or in things.[1] Subhūti, thus a Bodhisattva should give alms without a mind abiding in false notions of form (lakṣaṇa).'

The Buddha wiped out a doubt originating from the disciple's grasp of appearances (lakṣaṇa). Subhūti doubted when he heard that living beings were non-existent and thought that if they were, no one would receive alms when a Bodhisattva practised giving them. As the six objects of sense (guṇas)[2] are unreal (being caused by illusion) and since living beings are fundamentally non-existent, the Buddha said: 'The mind should not abide anywhere.' This was to teach (a Bodhisattva) not to cling to the appearances of living beings and the objects of sense (guṇas).

Doubt.—Again another hidden doubt: 'If the mind does not abide in forms (lakṣaṇas), how can there be merits?' In the next paragraph of the sūtra, the reply is given that merits are the greater when attachment to forms is eliminated.

'Why? (Because) if a Bodhisattva's mind does not abide in forms (lakṣaṇas) when practising charity (dāna), his merit will be inconceivable and immeasurable. Subhūti, what do you think? Can you think of and measure the extent of space in the East?'

'I cannot, World Honoured One!'

'Subhūti, can you think of and measure (all) the extent of space in the South, West and North, as well as in the intermediate directions, including the zenith and nadir?'

'I cannot, World Honoured One!'

'Subhūti, (when) a Bodhisattva practises charity without a mind abiding in forms, his merit is equally inconceivable and immeasurable.'

The Buddha wiped out a doubt about attachment to forms (lakṣaṇas) and pointed out the 'profound' act of rejecting them. A Bodhisattva seeks merit when practising charity (dāna). If his mind then clings to forms, his merit will not be great. Therefore, the World Honoured One expediently pointed out the greater merit derived from the practice of charity without attachment to forms in order to quiet Subhūti's mind. If charity is practised while the mind clings to forms, this (act) will be conditioned by them and since the forms of living beings are just as insignificant as a particle of dust, even if some merit is reaped, how great will it be? Now when charity is practised for the welfare of living beings, neither the

[1] Though this reads somewhat clumsily, it is correct, for it is impossible and would be unnecessary deliberately to give up all six objects of sense at the same time. But if any one of them is wiped out the other five simultaneously disappear. Avolakiteśvara wiped out sound only and attained enlightenment.

[2] The six guṇas are: sight, sound, smell, taste, touch and dharma.

giver, the receiver nor the gift are seen, thus the three-fold condition does not obtain[1] and there are no forms for the mind to grasp. The merit thus obtained without attachment to forms, is inestimable and is likened to the immense space.

'Subhūti, a Bodhisattva's mind should THUS abide as taught.'

In conclusion, the Buddha taught the mind quieting Dharma. The previous question asked for (means) to subdue the mind which does not abide in stillness. The World Honoured One taught the method, which consists in looking into the non-existence of an ego as the main point. If ego does not exist, personality also disappears. When the conception of an ego and a personality is eliminated, the self-mind is in the state of nirvāṇa. Thus all living beings become calm and free (from reincarnation, or are in nirvāṇa). As soon as all living beings are still, there is no necessity to seek Buddhahood. Thus the mind which used to seek (something) is set at rest; all wish to grasp and to reject will disappear; the internal (organs) and external (objects) being void, the One Mind remains immutable. This is the method to quiet the mind. Therefore, the Buddha used the word 'THUS' as above.

Doubt.—The giving of alms, the performance of virtuous actions and the conversion of living beings here below have only one aim, that is the quest for the Buddha fruit from above. Now if living beings are non-existent and the three-fold condition is extinct, the cause will be fictitious. Therefore, how can a formless cause lead to a fruit which has form? Moreover, the Tathāgata's body was distinctly visible and was (certainly) not obtained from a formless cause. This being tantamount to perceiving the Tathāgata by means of forms, the Buddha wiped out this (new) doubt (in the following paragraph).

'Subhūti, what do you think? Can the Tathāgata be seen by means of His bodily form?'

'No, World Honoured One, the Tathāgata cannot be seen by means of His bodily form. Why? Because when the Tathāgata speaks of bodily form, it is not (real) form.[2]

The Buddha said to Subhūti: 'Everything with form is unreal; if all forms are seen as unreal, the Tathāgata will be perceived.'

The Buddha pointed out directly the profound act of perceiving the nothingness (of phenomena). As Subhūti heard of a cause which had no

[1] Literally the three wheel condition: giver, receiver and gift.
[2] The lakṣaṇa of the physical body is not real but is so called for convenience sake.

form (lakṣaṇa), he harboured a doubt about a formless cause by means of which one could not obtain the Buddha fruit which had form. He was thus seeing the Tathāgata by means of form and clinging to the form of the Buddha's Transformation Body (Nirmāṇa-kāya).[1] This was the cause of his inability to perceive the Dharma-kāya's real substance. The Buddha broke up Subhūti's notion of form and the disciple understood His idea. This is why the Buddha pointed out the necessity of not perceiving the Tathāgata by means of form, since the body the Buddha spoke of was actually His Dharma-kāya. Therefore, Subhūti said: 'It is not a (real) bodily form. Moreover, the Dharma-kāya has no form. If, in the midst of the forms of all things, one can see that they are unreal, one perceives the Tathāgata. This does not mean that the Tathāgata's Dharma-kāya has a special form outside that of all things. It is thus clear that a formless cause tallies exactly with a formless fruit.'

Doubt.—Another doubt surged in Subhūti's mind: As the meaning of (the doctrine of) a formless cause tallying with a formless fruit is most profound, it is very difficult to believe it and expound it.

Subhūti said to the Buddha: 'World Honoured One, will there be living beings who can develop a true belief in these words, sentences and chapters when they are expounded to them?'

The Buddha said: 'Subhūti, do not speak like that. In the last 500 years, after the final passing of the Tathāgata, there will be those who will observe the rules of morality and perform good actions which will result in blessing. These people will be able to develop a faith in these sentences (which they will consider as) embodying the Truth. You should know that they will not have planted good roots in just one, two, three, four, or five Buddha lands. They will have planted them in countless thousands and tens of thousands of Buddha lands. Upon hearing these sentences, there will arise in them a single thought of pure faith. Subhūti, the Tathāgata knows and sees all; these living beings will thus acquire immeasurable merits. Why? (Because) they will have wiped out false notions of an ego, a personality, a being and a life, of Dharma and Not-Dharma. Why? (Because) if their minds grasp form (lakṣaṇa), they will (still) cling to the notion of an ego, a personality, a being and a life. If their minds grasp the Dharma, they will (still) cling to the notion of an ego, a personality, a being and a life. Why? (Because) if their minds grasp the Not-Dharma, they will (still) cling to the notion of an ego, a personality, a being and a life. Therefore, one should not grasp and hold on to

[1] The Buddha possessed three bodies (trikāya) which are essentially one, each in the other; (1) Dharma-kāya, the embodiment of the Law, shining everywhere and enlightening all; (2) Sambhoga-kāya, the embodiment of purity and bliss; and (3) Nirmāṇa-kāya, the body of transformation, by which He appeared in any form.

the notion of Dharma as well as that of Not-Dharma.[1] This is why, the Tathāgata always said: "Ye Bhikṣus, should know that the Dharma I expound is likened to a raft."[2] Even the Dharma should be cast aside; how much more so the Not-Dharma?'

The World Honoured One gave a direct indication of the penetrating power of Buddha wisdom (or vision). First, Subhūti clung to things having form as the cause and the Buddha broke up his (false) view with (the doctrine of) giving alms without attachment to forms. Next Subhūti doubted about a formless cause which could not tally with a fruit which had forms, thus grasping the notion that the Buddha had form. The Buddha broke up this (wrong) view by pointing out that the Dharmakāya has no form. It was, therefore, clear that a formless cause tallied exactly with a formless fruit. Thus cause and fruit were all void and both ego and Dharma[3] were eliminated. As this meaning was too profound to be believed and explained, Subhūti, still doubtful, asked the Buddha if there would be people who could believe this doctrine. The 'words', 'sentences' and 'chapters' referred to what had just been said about formless cause and formless fruit. The Buddha replied: 'Why will there be no such people? Those who believe in this doctrine, will not be vulgar men, as (only) those who will observe commandments and perform good actions (resulting in blessings) will be able to believe it. These people will not have planted good roots just in one, two, three, four, or five Buddha lands, but they will have planted them in countless thousands and tens of thousands of Buddha lands.' This means that those who long ago planted deep roots, will be able to have such a faith. These living beings with deep roots will, in a single thought, have faith (in this doctrine) and 'I know and see that the merits they will gain will be immeasurable.'

It was thus clear that this formless merit would far exceed that sought while (the mind) clung to the forms of things. Why does the non-attachment to forms reap more merits? Because these living beings will have no more attachment to the form of an ego, a personality, a being and a life. Not only will there be no attachment to these four forms, but also all notions of things having form and things having no form will be completely eliminated. Therefore, the Buddha said that there would

[1] Dharma and Not-Dharma, are a pair of positive and negative, i.e. a pair of opposites which has no room in the absolute prajñā. Moreover, one who clings to Dharma, or Not-Dharma, still holds the view of an ego (the subject) and a thing held (the object). Subject and object are also a pair of extremes which should be wiped out so that prajñā can manifest itself.

[2] The Dharma or method expounded by the Buddha was likened to a raft which His disciples should leave behind after reaching 'the other shore'.

[3] Ego and Dharma. The Buddha here is expounding the Dharma. Elsewhere it means 'ego and things'.

be no more notions of Dharma and Not-Dharma. As these living beings would not cling to forms, they would relinquish everything. If in a single thought, the mind still grasped the Dharma and Not-Dharma, it would cling to the four forms (of an ego, a personality, a being and a life). As they had no attachment to forms, their minds and objects would be void and the merits (thus reaped) would be unsurpassable. This was the Tathāgata's power of true knowing and true seeing. (He said:) 'This is why I teach Bodhisattvas not to grasp Dharma and Not-Dharma. Why? Because when one "enters" this doctrine, (for him) the notion of ego and Dharma will be void, and instantaneously all attachments will be thrown away, thus rising above all that exists. Is it a small matter? Therefore, I teach my disciples to relinquish the Dharma. Moreover, the relinquishment of Dharma is relinquishment of all feelings. When all feelings are relinquished, wisdom will be complete.' For this reason, He said: 'Even the Dharma must be cast aside, how much more so (that which is) not Dharma!'

Doubt.—As Subhūti heard that the Buddha had no physical form (i.e. was not visible) and that the Dharma should be relinquished, another doubt surged in his mind: If both Buddha and Dharma had no form, there would exist no Buddha and no Dharma, but why was the Buddha actually seen to have attained enlightenment and to be expounding the Dharma? How could it be said that there was neither Buddha nor Dharma? Thus he thought that there was contradiction in His sayings. In the next paragraph, the Buddha wipes out this doubt.

'Subhūti, what do you think? Has the Tathāgata (in fact) obtained Supreme Enlightenment (Anubodhi)? Does the Tathāgata (in fact) expound the Dharma?'

Subhūti replied: 'As I understand the meaning of the Buddha's teaching, there is no fixed Dharma called Supreme Enlightenment and there is also no fixed Dharma the Tathāgata can expound. Why? (Because) the Dharma the Tathāgata expounds cannot be clung to and cannot be expressed (in words); it is neither Dharma nor Not-Dharma. Why is this?[1] All Bhadras and Āryas[2] differ on account of the Eternal (Asaṁskṛta) Dharma.'[3]

The above wiped out the knowing and seeing of both Buddha and Dharma. As there arose in Subhūti's mind the unspoken conception of Buddha and Dharma, the Buddha, in order to break up this false con-

[1] Why should the two extremes 'Dharma' and 'Not-Dharma' not be retained?

[2] Bhadras are those who are noted for goodness but are still of ordinary human standard and Āryas are those who are noted for wisdom or insight and transcend the Bhadras in wisdom and character.

[3] Asaṁskrta: anything not subject to cause, condition, or dependence; out of time, eternal, inactive, supra-mundane. Wu wei in Chinese.

ception, called and asked him: 'What do you think?' This meant: 'What is your mind discriminating about? Now, can the Buddha-bodhi actually be obtained? Does the Tathāgata actually expound the Dharma?' These questions were posed to test Subhūti who understood the Buddha's teaching and confirmed his awakening by stating that he understood His statement that there was fundamentally no fixed Dharma called enlightenment (bodhi) or for the Tathāgata to expound. This was Subhūti's deep comprehension of the Buddha's doctrine of non-attachment (to things). All Bhadras and Āryas, including the Tathāgata Himself, differed on account of the Eternal (Asaṁskṛta) Dharma. Therefore, there should be no grasping. The expounding of the temporal[1] to reveal the absolute[2] had already begun (in the above paragraph of the sūtra).

Doubt.—Subhūti had understood the doctrine of the non-existence of Buddha and Dharma but did not understand why unsurpassed merits could be reaped (when the mind was in unison with) the Eternal Dharma. In the following paragraph of the sūtra, the Tathāgata wipes out this doubt by teaching the (doctrine of) forsaking all forms.[3]

'Subhūti, what do you think? If someone filled the Universe[4] with the seven treasures[5] and gave them all as alms, would his merit be great?'

Subhūti replied: 'Very great, World Honoured One. Why? Because this merit is not the nature of merit, the Tathāgata says it is great.'[6]

'Subhūti, if on the other hand, someone received and kept even a four line stanza of this sūtra and expounded it to others, his merit would surpass that (of the giver of treasures). Why? (Because), Subhūti, all Buddhas and their Supreme-Enlightenment-Dharma originate from this sūtra. Subhūti, the so-called Buddhas and Dharmas are not real Buddhas and Dharmas.'[7]

The above by expounding the formless merit revealed the formless Dharma which was unsurpassable. Subhūti had already understood the

[1] The temporal: referring to the conditional, functional, differential or temporary; the expedient teaching, preparatory to the perfect teaching.

[2] The absolute: the fundamental, or real; the perfect teaching.

[3] This doctrine consisted in abandoning all attachment to form, appearance, aspects and characteristics of all things either visible or invisible.

[4] Tri-sahasra-mahā-sahasra-loka-dhātu = a great trichiliocosm. Mt. Sumeru and its seven surrounding continents, eight seas and ring of iron mountains form one small world; 1,000 of these form a small chiliocosm; 1,000 of these small chiliocosms form a medium chiliocosm; 1,000 of these form a great chiliocosm, which consists of 1,000,000,000 small worlds. The word 'universe' is used for convenience sake.

[5] The seven treasures or precious things (sapta ratna): they are gold, silver, lapis lazuli, crystal, agate, rubies or red pearls and cornelian.

[6] The merit was great, because it was 'conditioned' and could be estimated. However, in the case of the nature of merit, i.e. the fundamental nature, it was as immense as space and was, therefore, inexpressible and inestimable.

[7] Buddhas and Dharmas are only empty names, have no nature, and are, therefore, not the real.

doctrine of formlessness[1] but did not know how to enter into union with it. (He was puzzled as to) how formless merits could surpass merits reaped while one still grasped and held on to forms. Therefore, the Buddha pointed out first that charity (dāna) practised with attachment to forms, reaped a (limited) merit which cannot be compared with the unsurpassed merit resulting from the keeping of even a four line stanza for the reason that all Buddhas originated from this prajñā. For this reason, He said: 'Prajñā is the mother of all Buddhas.' Therefore, the (corresponding) merit is the greater. It is just like the common saying: 'The mother is held in honour because of her (distinguished) sons.' Prajñā can produce Buddhas and Dharmas, but is (actually) neither Buddha nor Dharma. For this reason, He said: 'The so-called Buddhas and Dharmas are not real Buddhas and Dharmas.'

Doubt.—As there was no Dharma to expound and no Buddha to become, both were thus unobtainable. However, in former days, when His disciples were Śrāvakas, the Buddha expounded the Four Noble Truths which were Dharma. They followed His teaching and obtained the fruit. They dwelled in the Nirvāṇa which was their abode. But why did the World Honoured One contradict all (His previous) teaching by saying that nothing existed?

These were discriminating thoughts of those in the assembly and the World Honoured One poses (in the next paragraph) questions about the small fruits (of Hīnayāna) for the purpose of cutting their doubts.

'Subhūti, what do you think? Can one who has entered the stream (śrota-āpanna) have this thought (in his mind): I have obtained the fruit of entering the stream?[2]

Subhūti replied: 'No, World Honoured One. Why? Because śrota-āpanna means 'entering the stream', but actually there is no entry into either form, sound, smell, taste, touch or dharma. Therefore, he is called śrota-āpanna.'

'Subhūti, what do you think? Can a Sakṛdāgāmin have this thought (in his mind): I have obtained the fruit of a Sakṛdāgāmin?'[3]

Subhūti replied: 'No, World Honoured One. Why? Because sakṛdāgāmin means "once more to come", but actually there is neither coming nor going. Therefore, he is called a Sakṛdāgāmin.'

'Subhūti, what do you think? Can an Anāgāmin have this thought (in his mind): I have obtained the fruit of an Anāgāmin?'[4]

[1] The doctrine of formlessness consisted in the abandonment of all form (lakṣaṇa).

[2] Śrota-āpanna: one who has entered the stream of holy living, the first stage of the path.

[3] Sakṛdāgāmin: once more to come, or be born, the second stage of the path involving only one rebirth.

[4] Anāgāmin: a no-coming or non-returning Arhat who will not be reborn, the third stage of the path.

Subhūti replied: 'No, World Honoured One. Why? Because anāgāmin means "no-coming" but actually there is no such a thing as no-coming. Therefore, he is called an Anāgāmin.'

'Subhūti, what do you think? Can an Arhat have this thought (in his mind): I have obtained the enlightenment of an Arhat?'[1]

Subhūti replied: 'No, World Honoured One. Why? Because there is no Dharma which is called Arhatship. World Honoured One, if an Arhat thinks "I have obtained the enlightenment of an Arhat", he will still grasp and hold on to the notion of an ego, a personality, a being and a life. World Honoured One, the Buddha has declared that I have obtained the Passionless Samādhi[2] and that I surpass all men. I am, therefore, the highest passionless Arhat. World Honoured One, I do not think "I am a passionless Arhat" for, World Honoured One, if I had thought "I have attained Arhatship", the World Honoured One would not have said: "Subhūti takes delight in the calm and quiet, free from temptation and distress."[3] The fact that Subhūti does not act (mentally) is called the calm and quiet in which Subhūti takes delight.'

The above pointed out the true doctrine of non-abiding (or non-attachment). Now the assembly had heard that Buddhahood could not be sought and that Dharma could not be grasped and held on to, which meant that when advancing further, there would be no abiding anywhere. Why then in former days, had the World Honoured One taught his disciples who were then śrāvakas to get out of birth and death and to abide in Nirvāṇa, thus proving that there was an abiding place in the Dharma and in the fruit? Why had the World Honoured One said that neither Buddha nor Dharma were the real? This suspicion was due to the fact that those of the Hīnayāna did not forget their old habits in respect of names and terms and still clung to the existence of a true Dharma. Thus, they encountered difficulty in entering the Prajñā and had many doubts arising in their minds. The World Honoured One took advantage of Subhūti's understanding to awaken the whole assembly. Therefore, He listed the four fruits obtained in former days and asked him: 'What do you think?' This meant: 'What is your opinion (about these four fruits)?'

Śrota-āpanna means 'entering the stream'. To enter (the stream of holy living) is to go against the current of life and death. But 'to go against the current', really means not to enter (or abide) in the six sense data (guṇas), as there is actually nothing to go against and nothing in which to abide.

[1] Arhat: a saintly man, the highest type or ideal saint in Hīnayāna in contrast with a Bodhisattva as the saint in Mahāyāna.

[2] Passionless Samādhi: in which there is absence of debate, disputation, or distinction of self and other.

[3] An equivalent of Passionless Samādhi.

Sakṛdāgāmin means 'once more to come (or be reborn)'. It means that just one remnant of thought remains linked with the world of desires, necessitating one more rebirth to cut it off so that there will be no more return afterwards. It does not mean that there is coming and going or a place of abode.

Anāgāmin means simply 'no-coming'; there will be no more rebirth in the world of desires. It does not mean that there will be a place of abode from which 'no-coming' will take place.

Arhat means 'not to be born'. For an arhat, all dharmas are (already) non-existent. In reality, there are no dharmas, and there should be only the non-arising of a single thought in the mind. He does not think that he is an arhat and that there is an arhat-land where he can abide. If an arhat thinks like that, he will not differ from (other) living beings holding wrong views, as he is clinging to the four forms (of an ego, a personality, a being and a life). Subhūti told of his own experience, saying: 'The World Honoured One has always declared that I have obtained the Passionless Samādhi. He has also praised me and said that I was the foremost among men. He has again said that I was the highest passionless arhat. Although I have received so much praise, I have examined my mind and have found in it not a single thought that I am a passionless arhat. Had I so thought, the World Honoured One would not have said that I took delight in calm and quiet, free from temptations and distress. As I see it now, the Nirvāṇa referred to in former days, is not a place of abode. (From the foregoing), the Tathāgata's enlightenment (Bodhi) is also not a place in which the mind can abide. For this reason, there should be no doubt about all this.' This cut off a doubt about the Buddha fruit as a place of abode (for the mind). In the next paragraph, another doubt about the actual attainment of Buddhahood is wiped out.

Doubt.—According to the Buddha's teaching, it was clear that there was no place of abode called Buddha fruit. If a fruit could not be acquired, why was the Tathāgata seen to have received (from Dīpaṁkara Buddha) the prophecy of His future Buddhahood? Since there was a Buddha to become, why should there be no fruit which provided a place for dwelling? In the next paragraph (of the sūtra Subhūti) replied that there was no acquisition at all.

The Buddha said to Subhūti: 'What do you think? Did the Tathāgata obtain anything from the Dharma, when in the past He was with Dīpaṁkara Buddha?'

'No, World Honoured One. When the Tathāgata was with Dīpaṁkara, He did not obtain anything from the Dharma.'

In the above text, the Buddha taught the doctrine of non-attainment. After hearing the teaching about (the mind which did) not abide anywhere, Subhūti had understood the non-abiding enlightenment (Bodhi), but he doubted and thought that although Bodhi did not abide anywhere, there should be an acquisition of the Buddha fruit. If there was no Buddhahood to attain, how could the (teaching) be transmitted and handed down. For this reason, the World Honoured One asked (the above question) to cut off his doubt. Although Dīpaṁkara Buddha gave the prophecy, it was only to seal the realization of this mind, but nothing was acquired. If there was something obtainable, Dīpaṁkara would not have prophesied (to the Tathāgata).

Doubt.—As Bodhi did not abide anywhere and since Buddha fruit was unobtainable, there would be no need to adorn Buddha lands (with morality and wisdom). But why did the World Honoured One teach us to perform Bodhisattvas' (moral) actions to adorn Buddha lands?

'Subhūti, what do you think? Do Bodhisattvas adorn Buddha lands (by their moral actions)?'

'No. World Honoured One. Why? Because this is not real adornment; it is (merely) called the adornment of Buddha lands.'[1]

'Subhūti, this is why all Bodhisattvas and Mahāsattvas[2] should thus develop a pure and clean mind which should not abide in form, sound, smell, taste, touch and dharma. They should develop a mind which does not abide in anything.'[3]

The above is the method to quiet the mind. Subhūti doubted and thought that since there was no Buddha to become and no Nirvāṇa in which to abide, what then was the use of adorning Buddha lands? As he had this doubt, he thought that in the work of salvation of living beings, it was necessary to adorn Buddha lands, by repairing temples, and so on. This was stupid grasping of and attachment to forms. The Tathāgata therefore asked: 'Do Bodhisattvas actually adorn Buddha lands?' Subhūti understood His idea and replied: 'It is not real adornment but is (merely) called the adornment of Buddha lands.' What does this mean? Buddha lands are pure. How can pure lands be adorned with the seven treasures piled up in heaps as ornaments? What living beings see (around them) are unclean lands adorned with evil karmas and all kinds of suffering. In

[1] It is expediently called adornment for convenience's sake only.

[2] A Bodhisattva is a Mahāyānist seeking Buddhahood, but seeking it altruistically; whether monk or layman, he seeks enlightenment to enlighten others, and he will sacrifice himself to save others; he is devoid of egoism and devoted to helping others. A Mahāsattva is the perfect Bodhisattva, greater than any other being except a Buddha.

[3] Hui Neng obtained complete enlightenment upon hearing this sentence read by the Fifth Patriarch.

the pure Buddha lands, all impurities have been cleansed by the pure and clean mind. As all impurities have been swept away, these lands have automatically become pure. Therefore, this adornment consists solely of pure and clean minds. This kind of true adornment is not the same as that thought of (by the disciple). For this reason, it is said in the text that it is not real adornment but is (merely) so called. From the foregoing, it is clear that when Bodhisattvas adorn Buddha lands, they do not seek anything from without but simply purify their own minds, and when their minds become, the lands will (automatically) be, pure. Therefore, it is said that a pure and clean mind should be developed and no other adornment sought.

Another doubt: As the mind should be pure and clean, how can it be developed? The Buddha said that the mind should be pure and clean. To bring this about it is enough not to develop a mind soiled by the six sense objects (guṇas), for there is nothing which is pure and clean in which one can abide in order to develop such a mind. It was said that when both grasping and feeling had ceased, the pure mind would appear. Therefore, the Buddha said: 'They should develop a mind which does not abide in anything.' The Third Patriarch said: 'Do not pursue the (co-operating) causes of that which exists and do not abide in void-patience.'[1] This is the doctrine (or method) of developing a mind which does not abide anywhere. No other method to quiet the mind can surpass it. This is why the Sixth Patriarch attained instantaneous enlightenment upon hearing this sentence.

Doubt.—If there is no adornment of Buddha lands, there will be no such lands. If so, where did the ten-thousand-foot Buddha dwell? His doubt was about the Buddha's Sambhoga-kāya which must dwell in the real land (or the reality).

'Subhūti, supposing a man has a body as great as mount Sumeru, what do you think? Would such a body be great?'

Subhūti replied: 'Very great, World Honoured One. Why? Because the Buddha says it is not the real body but is (merely) called a great body.'[2]

The above sentences pointed out the Dharma-kāya's real land. As he heard that the Buddha land could not be adorned, Subhūti doubted and thought that the Sambhoga-kāya must abide in the real land. If the land was not adorned, where would the Sambhoga-kāya abide? The Buddha cut off this doubt by declaring that the Dharma-kāya was not a

[1] Void-patience: patience or endurance attained by regarding all things as void or unreal.

[2] It was expediently called 'great body' for convenience sake only as the Dharma-kāya is beyond name and measure.

body. His idea was that the land of no-land was permanently calm and illuminating[1] and that the body of no-body was the Dharma-kāya. The Dharma-kāya had no form and the real land had no form. As the body could not be perceived by means of form, how then could the land be adorned? He now cut off all doubts (which had arisen) from His teaching that the objects of sense (guṇas) should be relinquished and that the mental cognition of environment[2] should cease until (the conception of) both body and land had vanished. When (the conception of) mind and (external) world is wiped out, the absolute prajñā is reached, in order to reveal the (doctrine of) the non-abiding Dharma-kāya. As a result, the Truth does not require words to express it.[3] He who believes in this teaching, will reap therefrom merits which will be immeasurable. In the next (paragraph of the sūtra), a comparison is made between these and other kinds of merit.

'Subhūti, if there were as many rivers like the Ganges as there are grains of sand in the Ganges, would the total of grains of sand in all these rivers be very great?'

Subhūti replied: 'Very great, World Honoured One! These rivers would be innumerable; how much more so would be their sand-grains.'

'Subhūti, I now tell you truly. If a virtuous man or woman filled a number of universes, as great as the number of sand-grains in all these rivers, with the seven treasures, and gave them all away in alms (dāna), would his or her merit be great?'

Subhūti replied: 'Very great, World Honoured One!'

The Buddha said to Subhūti: 'If a virtuous man or woman receives and holds (in mind) even a four-line stanza of this sūtra and expounds it to others, his or her merit will surpass that of the almsgiver. Furthermore, Subhūti, wheresoever this sūtra or even one of its four-line stanzas is expounded, you should know that all devas, men and asuras[4] should make their offerings there as if the place was a Buddha stūpa or a Buddha temple. How much more so if someone is able to receive, hold (in mind), read and recite the whole sūtra! Subhūti, you should know that such a person will achieve the highest and rarest Dharma. Wheresoever this sūtra may be found, the Buddha and His respected disciples will be there also.'

The above text reveals the unsurpassed Dharma with the aid of a parable. The merit from the expounding of four lines surpasses that derived from the gift of the seven treasures with which were filled as many universes as the sand-grains of innumerable rivers like the Ganges, because this Dharma is the highest and rarest one. Since a four-line

[1] As were Truth and knowledge.
[2] To lay hold of external things by means of the mind.
[3] Because it cannot be expressed in words.
[4] They belong to the three high realms of the six worlds of existence which are those of: (1) devas; (2) humans; (3) asuras or malevolent nature spirits; (4) animals; (5) hungry ghosts; and (6) the hells.

quotation represents the whole body of the Dharma-kāya, it is exactly the same as if the Buddha is present and as if His great disciples are expounding it. As the revelation of the Dharma-kāya is complete, all doubts are cut off. From the words now falling into oblivion, emerges the absolute Truth. As Subhūti understood all this, he asked what the sūtra should be called.

Subhūti then asked the Buddha: 'World Honoured One, what name should be given to this sūtra and how should we receive and hold it (in mind)?'

The Buddha said: 'This sūtra should be called "The Diamond Prajñā-pāramitā" under which name you should receive and hold it. Why? Because, Subhūti, the Prajña-paramita as expounded by the Buddha, is not Prajña-paramita but is (merely) so called.'[1]

The above points out the return to the actual reality of prajñā. Subhūti had received the teaching and had been awakened to it. The whole body of prajñā was exposed and there was no further Dharma (to be revealed). Therefore, he asked for the name of the sūtra. The World Honoured One said to him: 'This sūtra should be named "Diamond Prajñā-pāramitā".' He meant that this Dharma had no name and was just the mind. When further asked how to receive and hold it (in mind), He told Subhūti that the mind should receive and hold this Dharma, since mind was fundamentally not-mind and since Dharma was also Not-Dharma.[2] Therefore, He said: 'Prajñā-pāramitā is not Prajñā-pāramitā.'

His mind before hearing this Dharma, was not quiet, hence his request for the method to subdue it. What he knew and saw were external objects. There was a great distance between living beings and the Buddha, between the clean and the unclean, and there was a difference of tendency between attachment and renunciation. Therefore, his mind was not quiet and it was difficult to subdue it, with the result that all kinds of doubt surged therein.

At first, his doubt was about the difficulty of saving (all) living beings and he was taught that fundamentally they were non-existent.

Next he doubted about the Buddha fruit which it was hard to find and was taught that the search for it was unnecessary.

Next he doubted about alms-giving (dāna) which would be incomplete and was taught that the threefold condition was non-existent.

[1] Pāramitā = to cross over from this shore of births and deaths to the other shore, or nirvāṇa. The six pāramitās or means of so doing are: dāna, almsgiving; śīla, moral conduct; kṣānti, patience or endurance; vīrya, energy, or devotion; dhyāna, meditation, or abstraction and prajñā, wisdom or knowledge.

[2] This is elimination of mind or subject which receives and keeps the teaching, and Dharma or object which is received and kept, for both subject and object have no room in the prajñā which is absolute.

Next he doubted about the Buddha land which it was difficult to adorn and was taught that (only) clean minds would provide ornaments for it.

Next he doubted about the Sambhoga-kāya which had no place of abode, and was taught that the Dharma-kāya (which was the real body) did not depend on anything.

The moment had come when Subhūti's ingenuity was exhausted and all his doubts were solved. The Buddha Mind was completely exposed, and not a single thing was hidden. All those who listened to (the teaching) had their minds calmed and self-subdued. Therefore, Subhūti asked for a name to be given to this sūtra. As the World Honoured One did not give any firm Dharma to others, he named only this mind to sum up the sūtra.

In the next paragraph, only the absolute Dharma-kāya is pointed out. It is said: 'When one has reached the top of a hundred-foot pole, one should take a step forward.' It is only necessary to have a diamond-eye to be in communion with the absolute (reality). This is why Subhūti who was now awakened (to the truth), was moved to tears and praised the unfathomable (doctrine) like a man returning home after a long residence in a foreign land. It was quite natural for him to shed tears when meeting his dear mother again. (The meaning could be understood) only when there was no more room for thinking and discriminating.

'Subhūti, what do you think? Does the Tathāgata expound the Dharma?'

Subhūti said: 'World Honoured One, the Tathāgata does not expound anything.'

Subhūti had understood the teaching on the Dharma-kāya but he (still) doubted: Who expounds the Dharma if the Dharma-kāya has no form? He thought that there was some actual expounding of Dharma. For this reason, the Buddha asked him the above question. (Thereupon), Subhūti realized that since the Dharma-kāya has no body, there is also no (actual) expounding of Dharma.[1]

Doubt.—If the Dharma-kāya had no form, the conception of a Dharma-kāya without form would fall into the (notion of) annihilation. If the Dharma-kāya thus had no form, where could it be perceived? As the whole assembly had this doubt, the Buddha wiped it out (in the next paragraph).[2]

[1] Body is an empty term and cannot describe the Dharma-kāya which is beyond description. The Nirmana-kaya Buddha used only expediences to wipe out Subhuti's wrong and discriminatory thoughts so as to reveal his fundamental nature with its self-possessed Dharma, for Dharma and Dharma-kāya are inexpressible in human language.

[2] Only deluded minds imagine that the Dharma-kāya has form. Since there was no creation of form, it follows that there is also no annihilation of it, for creation and annihilation are a pair of opposites which exist only in deluded minds.

'Subhūti, what do you think? Are there many particles of dust in the universe?'

Subhūti replied: 'Many, World Honoured One!'

'Subhūti, the Tathāgata says these particles of dust are not (real), (but) are (merely) called particles of dust. The Tathāgata says the universe is not (real), (but) it is (merely) called the universe.'

The above pointed out that although all dharmas are (perceived as) non-existent, there is no fall into (the false conception of) annihilation. As he heard that the Dharma-kāya had no form, Subhūti thought of the fall into (the false notion of) annihilation. If there were actual annihilation, there would be no place where the Dharma-kāya could be found. The World Honoured One pointed out that (both) particles of dust and universe are actually Dharma-kāya. For this reason, He asked Subhūti: 'Are there many particles of dust in the universe?' Subhūti replied: 'Many.' If they are looked at as particles of dust and a universe, the realm of the six sense data (guṇas) will be everywhere with the appearance of phenomena. (On the other hand) if they are not so looked at, there will be in empty space only the profound and still absolute voidness which is called the calm and extinct nothingness which uses the universe to reveal its symbol, with interweaving illusory patterns melting into the reality within a single nature. Therefore, it was said: 'Green bamboos are the Bhūtatathatā (the thatness, suchness) and yellow flowers are prajñā.' Mountains, rivers and the great earth, all disclose the body of the King of the Law (Dharma-rāja).[1] If one wishes to perceive the Dharma-kāya, one should be provided with the right Diamond-eye. This was why He said: 'The universe is not real but is merely called a universe.'

Doubt.—Subhūti had heard that the Dharma-kāya can have no form if it is to be the (real) Buddha. (Now) assuming that the formless is Buddha, was the Buddha who had thirty-two characteristics (lakṣaṇas)[2] and was present here, not a (true) Buddha? Subhūti mistook the Nirmāṇa-

[1] That is Buddha.

[2] The thirty-two lakṣaṇas or physical characteristics of a Buddha are: (1) level feet, (2) a thousand-spoke wheel-sign on feet, (3) long slender fingers, (4) pliant hands and feet, (5) toes and fingers finely webbed, (6) full-sized heels, (7) arched insteps, (8) thighs like those of a royal stag, (9) hands reaching below the knees, (10) well-retracted male organ, (11) height and width of body in proportion, (12) dark blue coloured hair, (13) body hair graceful and curly, (14) golden-hued body, (15) a ten-foot halo, (16) soft smooth skin, (17) the seven parts (two soles, two palms, two shoulders and crown) well rounded, (18) below the armpits well-filled, (19) lion-shaped body, (20) erect body, (21) full shoulders, (22) forty teeth, (23) teeth white, even and close, (24) the four canine teeth pure white, (25) lion-jawed, (26) saliva improving the taste of all food, (27) tongue long and broad, (28) voice deep and resonant, (29) eyes deep blue, (30) eye-lashes like those of a royal bull, (31) a white curl between the eyebrows emitting light, (32) a fleshly protuberance on the crown. Cakravartī, or the wheel-king, a world ruler, also possessed the same thirty-two physical characteristics.

kāya for the (true) Buddha. To remove his doubt the next paragraph points out that the Dharma-kāya and the Nirmāṇa-kāya are of the same substance.

'Subhūti, what do you think? Can the Tathāgata be perceived by means of His thirty-two physical characteristics (lakṣaṇas)?'

'No, World Honoured One. The Tathāgata cannot be perceived by them. Why? Because the Tathāgata says they are not real but are (merely) called the thirty-two physical characteristics.'

This points out the sameness of Dharma-kāya and Nirmāṇa-kāya. (Therefore), one should not say that the Buddha with these characteristics is not Buddha. Even these thirty-two physical marks were essentially formless. If marks (lakṣaṇas) are perceived as unreal, the Nirmāṇa-kāya will be Dharma-kāya. The three Bodies (Trikāya) are of the same substance. Now that the body and land are void, the absolute is reached, and all feelings have sunk into oblivion. Since there is no room for words and speech, those (who) agree with this doctrine are praised. The resultant merit from their expounding it to others will be immeasurable.

'Subhūti, if on the one hand, a virtuous man or woman, in giving alms (dāna), sacrifices as many lives as there are sand-grains in the Ganges, and on the other hand, someone receives and holds (in mind) even a four-line stanza of this sūtra, and expounds it to others, the merit resulting from the latter will be greater.

The above shows the unsurpassed benefit derived from the (doctrine of) Dharma-voidness.[1] The World Honoured One had revealed the Absolute, all doubts had been cut off and the four (false notions of) form were wiped out completely. When the conception of an ego (atmagraha) is eliminated, the Dharma-kāya is exposed. Therefore, the World Honoured One compared the (conditioned) merit resulting from giving alms in the form of the sacrifice of as many lives as sand-grains in the Ganges with the immeasurable merit derived from receiving and holding even a four-line stanza of the sūtra and expounding it to others.

Now that Subhūti understood the teaching, he was moved to tears and praised the rare (doctrine) which he had not heard before. It was the World Honoured One's aim which was praised (by Subhūti) because of His excellent protection and enjoinment mentioned at the beginning of the sūtra.

Hitherto, Subhūti had received and understood (the teaching). In the next paragraph, he states his feelings (about it).

[1] Dharma-voidness: the emptiness or unreality of things; the illusory nature of all things as being composed of elements and not possessing reality.

At that time, after listening to this sūtra, Subhūti had understood its profound meaning and was moved to tears.[1] He said to the Buddha: 'How rare, O World Honoured One! The Buddha has expounded such a very profound sūtra. Since I have acquired the wisdom eye, I have not heard of such a sūtra. World Honoured One, if someone after listening to this sūtra believes that his mind is clean and pure, he will realize reality. We should know that such a person will achieve the highest and rarest merit. World Honoured One, this Reality is not Reality but the Tathāgata calls it Reality.[2] World Honoured One, as I now listen to this sūtra I have no difficulty in believing, understanding, receiving and holding it, but in the last epoch, the last five hundred year period[3] if there be a man who (happens to) listen to this sūtra, believes, understands, receives and holds it, he will be most rare. Why? Because he will no longer (think in terms of) an ego, a personality, a being and a life. Why? Because the forms of an ego, a personality, a being and a life are not forms. Why? Because when he has rejected all forms he is called a Buddha.'

The Buddha said: 'Just so! Subhūti, just so! If on the one hand, there be a man who listens to this sūtra and is not filled with alarm, fear, or dread, you should know that such a person is most rare. Why? Because, Subhūti, as the Tathāgata says, the first perfection (pāramitā) is not so (but) is (merely) called the first perfection (pāramitā).'[4]

This is union with the Buddha Mind and entry into the Buddha Wisdom. Like Subhūti, the followers of Hīnayāna and all living beings clung to forms. Over twenty years had passed since the Buddha appeared in the world. When He expounded the Dharma he used formal thoughts in order not to alarm (His disciples). When he taught them, He used many expedient methods to sweep away their false ideas and waited until then to disclose the real mind. Why? Because His original vow was to lead all living beings to the supreme height of Mahāyāna. As he was about to show the followers of Hīnayāna how to develop the Mahāyāna mind, He purposely used this Diamond Mind as a cultivating cause[5] and to cut off all doubts, so that a true faith could be developed (in them). Therefore, this prajñā was the first gate to Mahāyāna. It was the essential mind which

[1] It is not unnatural that those who have understood the deep meaning of the sūtra and realized their past errors are moved to tears, for their sufferings are caused by their ignorance and are only self-inflicted.

[2] This Reality cannot be named but the Tathāgata expediently called it Reality for convenience sake only, because Reality and Unreality are two extremes which have no place in the absolute.

[3] Pratirūpaka: symbol or image period, to begin five hundred years after the nirvāṇa of Buddha; also the last of the periods of five hundred years when strife will prevail.

[4] The first pāramitā was so called for convenience sake only. If there was a first pāramitā, there would also be a last pāramitā, and both first and last are extremes which must be discarded before the absolute can be attained.

[5] Cultivating cause: a cause to cultivate oneself in the practice of Mahāyāna.

these Bodhisattvas discovered. It was precisely this mind which was so well protected and so well enjoined upon (by the Tathāgata). Those disciples of Hīnayāna now heard of it for the first time. They had not understood it before and were only now awakened to it, like hungry babes suddenly given suck by their mothers. It was quite natural that Subhūti was moved to tears when he heard of it. Therefore, he praised the Buddha, saying: 'How rare!' Previously he had also praised the Buddha and said: 'It is very rare!' when he suddenly perceived the Tathāgata's kind mind but he had not as yet heard His teaching about it. Now that the World Honoured One had exposed it and had cut off all doubts, one after the other, this mind was really a very wonderful thing indeed. For what he had never heard of in former days was really a very rare Dharma. Subhūti spoke of his (personal) awakening and (endeavoured to) stimulate his comrades, saying: 'I have heard of it, have been awakened to it and have found it very rare. If there be another man who, upon hearing it, can believe that his own mind is also as pure and clean, Reality will appear before him, with the dissipation of all false conceptions. This man will really be rare. Why? Because it is very difficult to believe and understand this Dharma which consists in forsaking all idea of forms. Furthermore, we personally see the Tathāgata and although it is difficult to believe it, after we have heard His wonderful voice, we have no difficulty in believing and understanding it. If after the passing of the Buddha, long after the Ārya era, in the last five hundred-year period, when the five signs of degeneration (kaṣāya)[1] will worsen and when Māra (the demon) will be powerful and when the Dharma will be weak, it will be very difficult to believe this Dharma. If someone is able to believe it, he will be a very rare person. Why? Because he will be able to discard the four forms (of an ego, a personality, a being and a life). However, these four forms are themselves fundamentally the absolute and if this can be understood, the Dharma-kāya can be perceived. Therefore, it was said: 'He who has rejected all forms is called a Buddha. This person will be very rare.'

The World Honoured One listened to Subhūti and gave the seal of His approval by saying: 'Just so, just so!' As said in the sūtra, those who hear this (Dharma) are filled with alarm, fear and dread, because of the vastness of the Dharma and the narrowness of (our) capacity to receive it. One who listens to it free from alarm, fear and dread, will be very rare,

[1] The five kaṣāya: the five periods of impurity and turbidity: (1) the kalpa in decay, when it suffers deterioration and gives rise to the ensuing form; (2) deterioration of view, egoism, etc., arises; (3) the passions and delusions of desire, anger, stupidity, pride and doubt prevail; (4) in consequence human miseries increase and happiness decreases; (5) the span of a human life is gradually reduced to ten years.

because what the Buddha expounded is beyond words and speech.[1] Therefore, He said: 'The first pāramitā is not (but) is (merely) called the first pāramitā.'

Subhūti's doubt: when (Buddha) spoke of almsgiving (dāna) He referred to things which would benefit the six objects of sense (guṇas). This was an external gift.[2] Things difficult to give up were offered to gain merit. The World Honoured One had taught them not to be attached to forms and had talked about the formless merit which was the greater. He also said that merits resulting from gifts of the seven treasures and also from the sacrifice of as many lives as sand-grains in the Ganges, could not be compared with formless merit (which was unsurpassable). As the dāna of lives was practised by sacrificing one's own life, Subhūti harboured this suspicion: To offer external objects could be forgotten, but one's own life was something most difficult to sacrifice; how could it be forsaken? The World Honoured One knew of his doubt and talked purposely about patience (kṣānti) to cut it off. When the body was mutilated, the absence of feelings of anger and hatred proved that the conception of an ego was non-existent. This was Subhūti's doubt (which the Buddha cut off) but in the sūtra, the meaning goes deeper. The World Honoured One broke up the Bodhisattvas' attachment to the twin view of an ego and a dharma (i.e. self and things). The idea of an ego covers the body and mind of the five aggregates (skandhas). Moreover, this five skandha body has its false name and seeming dharma. The (conception of) its false name was previously wiped out. Now mutilation of the body is (mentioned) to break up (the conception of) the seeming dharma of the five skandhas.

'Subhūti, the Tathāgata speaks of the Perfection of Patience (kṣānti-pāramitā) which is not but is called the Perfection of Patience.[3] Why? Because, Subhūti, in (a) past (life) when my body was mutilated by Kalirāja, I had at that time no notion of an ego, a personality, a being and a life. Why? Because, in the past, when my body was dismembered, if I (still) held the conception of an ego, a personality, a being and a life, I would have been stirred by feelings of anger and hatred. Subhūti, I also remember that in the past, during my former five hundred lives, I was a Kṣāntyṛṣi[4] and held no conception of an ego, a personality, a being and a life. Therefore, Subhūti, Bodhisattvas should forsake all conceptions of form and resolve to develop the Supreme Enlightenment Mind (Anuttara-samyak-saṁbodhi). Their minds should not abide in form, sound, smell, taste, touch and

[1] The noumenal cannot be expressed and described by words.
[2] Dāna practised by means of external objects.
[3] Kṣānti-pāramitā: perfection attained through boundless patience or endurance.
[4] Kṣāntyṛṣi: a Ṛṣi, also wrongly called an immortal, who patiently suffered insult, i.e. Śākyamuni, in a former life, suffering mutilation to convert Kalirāja.

dharma. Their minds should abide nowhere. If minds abide somewhere, it will be in falsehood. This is why the Buddha says that Bodhisattvas' minds should not abide in form when practising charity (dāna). Subhūti, all Bodhisattvas should thus make offerings for the welfare of all living beings.[1] The Tathāgata speaks of forms which are not forms and of living beings who are not living beings.'[2]

The above destroyed the (conception of the) five skandhas, in final answer to the question: 'How should the mind abide?' (see page 158). When Subhūti heard of the sacrifice of lives in the practice of dāna, he did not realize that the five skandhas were fundamentally non-existent. Therefore, he doubted and did not believe it and found it impossible to practise. It was possible for him to offer the seven external treasures without attachment to form (lakṣaṇa). As to the sacrifice of lives, this simply could not be done. If a man cannot sacrifice his life, the conception of an ego is still there, and because of his attachment to form it will be impossible for him to realize union with absolute voidness. Therefore, the World Honoured One spoke purposely of (His former) acts of endurance. Had He still clung to false notions of form when Kalirāja mutilated His body, feelings of anger and hatred would have been aroused in Him. He did not hate because He had already realized the non-existence of the five skandhas. This mutilation of His (formless) body only had the effect of a futile attempt to cut water (with a knife) and to blow out the (day) light. If He remained serene and unmoved, it was because He had forsaken all form. This is why He taught Bodhisattvas to relinquish all form when they developed the Bodhi mind, for their minds should not abide in the six objects of sense (guṇas). They should develop a mind which abides nowhere. This concludes the doctrine of relinquishment of forms and serves to answer the question: 'How should the mind abide?' (see page 158) He further pointed out that if the mind had a place in which to abide, it would be in falsehood because both mind and (outside) objects are false. This was so when the Buddha taught the Bodhisattvas that the mind should not abide in forms when practising charity (dāna). Moreover, for the welfare of all living beings, all Bodhisattvas should thus practise dāna which would then be a wonderful act. They should not be attached to anything in order not to develop other false notions and views. The Tathagata said that all forms as well as all living beings were (essentially) in the Bhūtatathatā condition (of suchness). This is why He had said previously: 'If all forms are seen as unreal, the Tathāgata will be perceived.'

[1] By so doing, they would attain enlightenment quickly and would also be able to save living beings quickly.

[2] Because forms and living beings were only empty names having no real nature.

(See page 165). Therefore, He said in conclusion: 'Forms are not forms and living beings are not living beings.'

Doubt.—If, then, the mind does not abide in forms, all things will be void. If (all things are) void, the wisdom which can be realized, will also be void and will have no substance. How can a Dharma which has no substance be used as a cause to obtain fruit? The (Buddha's) reply is that he should truly believe the Buddha's words as the stage the Tathāgata had experienced could not be unreal and false.

'Subhūti, the Tathāgata's words are true and correspond to reality. They are ultimate words, neither deceitful nor heterodox. Subhūti, the Dharma the Tathāgata has obtained is neither real nor unreal.'[1]

Subhūti was urged to have faith in the Buddha's words. He had heard from Him that both cause and fruit were void. He doubted and thought that if the fruit was void, there would be no necessity of using a cause and that if a cause was void, it would not produce fruit. When practising charity (dāna) as a cause, if the mind did not abide anywhere, no real fruit would be obtainable. The World Honoured One urged him to have faith in the Buddha's words and not to harbour further doubts, for the Dharma attained by the Tathāgata was neither real nor unreal, and should not be sought while the mind grasped and held on to (false) feelings. This was to wipe out the disciple's doubt.

Doubt.—If almsgiving (dāna) is practised with a mind which does not abide in form, how can this mind which does not abide anywhere, obtain prajñā? This doubt is cut off in the following reply:

'Subhūti, if a Bodhisattva practises charity (dāna) with a mind abiding in things (dharma), he is like a man entering the darkness where he cannot see anything; (but) if a Bodhisattva practises dāna with a mind not abiding in dharma, he is like a man with open eyes, who can see everything in the sunshine.'

The Buddha pointed out the advantage of having a mind which does not abide anywhere. A mind which abides somewhere, associates itself with ignorance and because of the obstruction (caused by) a subjective mind and its objective environment, it is likened to a man entering the darkness in which he cannot see anything.[2] The mind which does not abide anywhere, is free from all obstructions and since the twin view of ego and personality is forsaken, it is likened to a rising sun illuminating everything. Therefore, the non-abiding mind is nothing but the prajñā of

[1] The real and unreal are a pair of extremes which have no room in the absolute reality.
[2] The deluded mind is divided between subject and object and remains in the dark.

reality. What the Buddha had experienced himself was precisely this mind.

Doubt.—Supposing that a mind which does not abide anywhere is prajñā, how can it be in unison with the Buddha Mind. This doubt is cut off in the next paragraph.

'Subhūti, in future ages, if a virtuous man or woman is able to receive, hold (in mind), read and recite this sūtra, the Tathāgata, by means of His Buddha Wisdom, will know and see clearly that such a person will achieve immeasurable and unlimitable merits. Subhūti, if (on the one hand) a virtuous man or woman sacrifices in the practice of charity (dāna), as many lives as the sand-grains of the Ganges in the morning, at midday and again in the evening, and continues so doing throughout numberless aeons; and if (on the other hand) a person after listening to this sūtra believes in his own mind without (further) contradiction, the latter's merit will surpass that of the former. How much more so if this sūtra is written, received, held, read, recited and expounded to others!'

The above shows the sameness of mind and Buddha. Subhūti's doubt was whether his wisdom could unite with the Buddha Wisdom. The Buddha's meaning was that prajñā has no written words (but that) written words are prajñā. This sūtra which he was expounding is prajñā in its entirety. If someone believes and receives it, (his mind) will be in wonderful unison with the Buddha Wisdom, and the Buddha, by means of His own Wisdom, knew that his merits would be immeasurable. These merits derive from a moment's thought uniting with the Buddha Mind. Although the sacrifice in dāna of as many lives as the sand-grains of the Ganges, three times a day, can result in many merits, these cannot, however, be compared to those deriving from a moment's thought of faith in the mind. The compliance with prajñā without any contradiction, is the excellent entry into the Buddha Wisdom, with much greater merits. How much more so if this sūtra is written, held (in mind), read, recited and expounded to others! The unsurpassed prajñā is praised in the following paragraph.

'Subhūti, to sum up, the merits resulting from this sūtra are inconceivable, inestimable and without limit. The Tathāgata expounds it to those initiated into the Mahāyāna and the Supreme Yāna. If they are able to receive, hold (in mind), read and recite it and expound it widely to others, the Tathāgata will know and will see that they will achieve inexpressible and inconceivable merits that are without measure or limit. They will bear (responsibility for) the Tathāgata's Supreme Enlightenment (Anuttara-samyak-saṁbodhi). Why? Because, Subhūti, those who take delight in the Hīnayāna and hold the view of an ego, a personality, a being and a life, cannot listen to, receive, hold (in mind), read and recite this sūtra and explain it to others.'

The Buddha praised this prajñā which benefits only those with roots of highest quality. Previously, frequent mention was made of the '*four forms*' (of an ego, a personality, a being and a life) which are of a COARSE nature. Now mention is made of '*four views*' (of an ego, a personality, a being and a life) which are of a SUBTLE nature.[1]

'Subhūti, wheresoever this sūtra may be found, all worlds of devas, men and asuras should make offerings, for you should know that such a place is just a stūpa which should be revered, worshipped and circumambulated, with offerings of flowers and incense.'

The Buddha praised the eternity of the prajñā's Dharma-kāya.

'Furthermore, Subhūti, if a virtuous man or woman receives, holds (in mind), reads and recites this sūtra and is despised by others, this person who is bound to suffer from evil destinies in retribution for his past sins, and whose karmic sins are now eradicated by the others' contempt, will attain Supreme Enlightenment (Anuttara-samyak-saṁbodhi).'

The Buddha praised the prajñā which gives the advantage of getting rid of all obstruction and bondage; it enables one not only to eliminate sins, but also to attain the unsurpassed fruit.

'Subhūti, I remember that in the past countless aeons before the advent of Dīpaṁkara Buddha, I met 84,000 milliards[2] of Buddhas to whom I made offerings and whom I served faultlessly. Now if in the last period (of 500 years) in the Buddha kalpa someone is able to receive, hold (in mind), read and recite this sūtra, his merits will far exceed mine which resulted from my offerings made to Buddhas, for mine cannot be reckoned as one hundredth, one thousandth, one ten thousandth or one hundred thousandth part thereof; in fact no computation or comparison is possible. Subhūti, in the last period of the Buddha kalpa, if a virtuous man or woman is able to receive, hold (in mind), read and recite this sūtra, my full statement of this person's merits will create derangement, doubt and disbelief in the minds of all listeners. Subhūti, you should know that as the meaning of this sūtra is inconceivable, so is the fruit of its reward.'

The Buddha praised those who were awakened to prajñā and who, in a moment's thought, were instantaneously born in the family of Buddhas

[1] From coarse *forms* to subtle *views* until the complete elimination of all concepts.

[2] Literally 840,000,000 times 100,000 Nayutas. The number 8 is a symbol of the Eighth Consciousness or ālaya-vijñāna and 4 of the four forms (lakṣaṇa) of ego, being, personality and life. Together they imply the Eighth Consciousness held in bondage by the four forms, i.e. *Space*. The long line of zeros is a symbol of *Time*, and so long as one remains deluded it is immaterial to add 10 or 1,000 more zeros at the end of the line. The Buddha was still under delusion when he met Dīpaṁkara Buddha, but when he attained enlightenment, the digits 8 and 4 were instantly transmuted into the Great Mirror Wisdom and the Dharma-kāya respectively, and the long line of zeros became meaningless. Thus, space and time were wiped out in an instant (kṣaṇa).

and would never again be separated from the Buddhas. Their merits were, therefore, unsurpassable. In the last period (cf. the Buddha kalpa) the merits of those who can believe (this sūtra) will be the greater, since the virtue of prajñā and the fruit of its reward are both inconceivable.

Since the first question 'How should the mind abide and how should it be subdued?' was asked, all doubts in the minds of common men who were determined to develop a great mind and to act like a Bodhisattva, have been completely cut off, one by one. However, the twin view of the reality of ego and of the reality of dharma (things) has its *coarse* and *subtle* natures.

Previously, two *coarse* views were broken up in the search for enlightenment (Bodhi): (1) that of the reality of ego in the five skandhas of body and mind, and (2) that of the reality of dharma, in the performance of the six perfections (pāramitās) linked with circumstantial guṇas. These two (coarse) views originated from attachment to forms, and the Buddha wiped out the doubts about prajñā, held by newly initiated Bodhisattvas. His revelation was (only) about the unperceiving of living beings who could be saved.

From now on, the two '*subtle*' views of reality of ego and of dharma, are wiped out. These Bodhisattvas who had been awakened to prajñā (still) clung to the (view that) the wisdom which can manifest, is an ego; that real Suchness (Bhūtatathatā) which is manifested, is a personality; that that which can manifest and be awakened, is a being; and that the manifesting and awakening which are not relinquished but are still hanging on continuously as a life, are a life-time. These two views are subtle because the four forms are fine. This is called the preservation and awareness of ego.

For this reason, the word 'I' occurs frequently in the next part (of the sūtra). If this view of the reality of ego is broken up, there will be no seeing of the Buddha fruit which may be sought.

In the next paragraph, the same question posed at the beginning of the sūtra, is asked again by Subhūti, but its new meaning is different from the previous one. Readers should note this.

The Diamond Cutter of Doubts

Part II

At the time, Subhūti asked the Buddha: 'World Honoured One, if a virtuous man or woman is determined to develop the Supreme Enlightened Mind, how should his or her mind abide and how should it be subdued?'

The Buddha said to Subhūti: 'A virtuous man or woman who is determined to develop the Supreme Enlightened Mind, should thus develop it: I have to lead all living beings to put a stop to (reincarnation) and escape (suffering), and when they have been so led, not one of them in fact stops (reincarnating) or escapes suffering. Why? Because, Subhūti, if a Bodhisattva clings to the notion of an ego, a personality, a being and a life, he is not a (true) Bodhisattva. Why? Because, Subhūti, there is not really a Dharma which can develop the Supreme-Enlightenment-Mind.

From now on, the two subtle views of the reality of ego and of dharma are broken up. In the sūtra, at the beginning, the question: 'How should the mind abide? How should it be subdued?' was asked because newly initiated Bodhisattvas were ordinary broad-minded men, who were determined to develop a mind for the liberation of all living beings. Therefore, they had every kind of attachment to the forms (of things). In their self-cultivation, they relied on their physical bodies of the five aggregates (skandhas) and in their practice of almsgiving (dāna) in quest of merits, they clung to the six coarse objects of sense (guṇas). In their quest of enlightenment, they grasped the external appearance of the Buddha's Nirmāṇa-kāya. For them, the Buddha land was adorned with treasures. Therefore, they still had attachment to forms in their deeds and were too far away from prajñā.

The Buddha successively cut off all doubts which arose in Subhūti's mind until all his concepts of material appearance were eliminated and the true wisdom of the real suchness of wisdom (Bhūtatathatā-prajñā) could be realized, resulting in Subhūti's awakening and in the dissipation of the whole assembly's doubts. The first part of the sūtra covers these points, which cannot be understood at first sight, (dealing with) the elimination of ego caused by the ordinary man's conception of it in the visible form of the five aggregates (skandhas). The four forms thus perceived were all *coarse.*

From now on, the (second half of the sūtra) deals with the elimination of doubts harboured by Bodhisattvas who are already awakened to the prajñā but who do not as yet relinquish the idea of the wisdom which could realize (prajñā). They grasp this wisdom as an ego. This is the self-preservation and self-awareness of ego. These are the two subtle tenets (of the reality of ego and dharma) and the four forms are now fine. For this reason, the word 'I' (now) occurs often in the sūtra which says: 'I have to lead all living beings to destroy reincarnation' and does not mention the practice of dāna. This shows that although the meritorious performance is complete, the conception of Buddha and living beings is still not relinquished. Their conceptions were coarse before, but are *subtle* now.

Question.—(About this erroneous fine view that) this subtle wisdom is an ego, why does the question 'How should the mind abide and how should it be subdued?' not have the same meaning as when it was asked previously (at the beginning of the sūtra?)

Answer.—In this second question 'How should the mind abide?' the Bodhisattva has already relinquished (the conception of) the five aggregates (skandhas), but since he has not abandoned his old habits, he still seeks a place of quiet abode in the Bhūtatathatā Wisdom. Moreover, he is also impatient in his quest of enlightenment (Bodhi) and clings to the idea that Bodhi should have a place of abode. Since he cannot seek it, his mind is ill at ease and he asks: 'How should the mind be subdued?' It was the mind which sought Buddhahood which was not at ease, because he still clung to his views of Buddha and living beings and because he failed to perceive the sameness of the two. The question is the same but its meaning is now different. For this reason, the World Honoured One wipes out (this doubt) by saying that those who develop the Bodhi Mind, should look into the fact that not a single living being is actually liberated, after they have delivered all living beings, for the latter are fundamentally Bhūtatathatā and should not be subjected to further extinction (of reincarnation). If these Bodhisattvas still hold the view of the end (of reincarnation) and an escape (from suffering), they cannot rid themselves of the (false idea of the) four forms and cannot be true Bodhisattvas. This was the (doctrine of) the non-seeing of living beings who could be delivered. However, Buddhas and living beings were fundamentally one, and if there be no end to (reincarnation for) living beings, there would be no Dharma enabling Bodhisattvas to develop a mind in quest of Bodhi. Why? Because living beings are fundamentally calm, do not reincarnate and are identical with Bodhi itself. What more then should be sought? This is the (doctrine of) not-seeing the Buddha fruit.

Doubt.—If there is no Dharma which can enable one to attain enlightenment (Bodhi), is the Bodhi which we now apprehend, not a Dharma? Did not the World Honoured One who became Buddha because he had obtained this Dharma with Dīpaṁkara Buddha, really obtain the Bodhi? How can it be said that no Dharma is obtained? This doubt is dealt with in the following paragraph.

'Subhūti, what do you think? When the Tathāgata was with Dīpaṁkara Buddha, did He have any Dharma by means of which He attained Supreme Enlightenment (Anuttara-samyak-saṁbodhi)?'

'No, World Honoured One. As I understand the meaning of the Buddha's teaching, when He was with Dīpaṁkara Buddha, He had no Dharma by means of which He attained "Supreme Enlightenment".'

The Buddha said: 'Just so! Subhūti, just so! There was really no Dharma by means of which the Tathāgata attained Supreme Enlightenment. Subhūti, if there had been, Dīpaṁkara Buddha would not have predicted: "In your next life, you will be a Buddha named Śākyamuni".'

The Buddha pointed out that Bodhi cannot be obtained to destroy a doubt caused by attachment to (the idea of) Buddha. Subhūti was suspicious and thought that the Buddha had obtained a Dharma when He was with Dīpaṁkara Buddha. The World Honoured One successively broke up Subhūti's wrong conjectures again and again to reveal the non-acquisition of a single Dharma.

Doubt.—The Prajñā-dharma was the real cause of the attainment of Buddhahood. If, as now said, there is no Dharma, there will be no cause. If there is no cause, how can one obtain the Bodhi fruit? In the following text, this doubt is wiped out by the teaching that Dharma-kāya does not belong to either cause or fruit (or effect).

'. . . Why is it? Because "Tathāgata" means the suchness of all Dharmas.[1] If someone still says: "The Tathāgata obtained Supreme Enlightenment," (I tell you), Subhūti, there is no Dharma by means of which the Buddha did so, (because), Subhūti, that Enlightenment was by itself neither real nor unreal. This is why the Tathāgata says that all Dharmas are Buddha's Dharmas. Subhūti, these so-called Dharmas are not but are (expediently) called all Dharmas.[2] Subhūti, supposing there is a man whose body is great. . . .'[3]

[1] The undifferentiated whole of all dharmas, or things.

[2] The words 'all Dharmas' are two meaningless terms having no real nature, but are expediently so-called for convenience sake.

[3] Here Subhūti who already understood what the Buddha wanted to say, replies without waiting for Him to finish His question. The great body is the Sambhoga-kāya which cannot be compared to the essential one, the Dharma-kāya.

Subhūti said: 'World Honoured One, the great body of which the Tathāgata speaks is not great, but is (expediently) called a great body.'

The above shows that Dharma-kāya does not belong to either cause or fruit. Subhūti, who did not realize that Dharma-kāya was beyond both, clung to the idea that the Tathāgata had practised and had gained. The Buddha wiped out this concept by saying that He had not obtained anything.[1] As He was apprehensive that Subhūti was not sufficiently awakened to this, He said to him: 'Why do I say that Bodhi does not gain anything? Because the word Tathāgata cannot be applied to material things. It is the absolute in the very substance of all things (dharmas). Moreover, all dharmas are fundamentally absolute. How then can this be realized by practice? Therefore, I say there is no Dharma which enables the Buddha to obtain Bodhi.'

In the Ch'an Sect, this is the Transcendental Path which all Buddhas of the past, present and future forbid one to look at. If you do you go blind,[2] because in it there is no room for searching and grasping. The Tathāgata-bodhi has no positive (characteristic to grasp). It is enough not to hold inverted views of annihilation or of permanence in relation to all things (dharmas).[3] Therefore, the Buddha said: It is neither real nor unreal,' because all dharmas were not dharmas. If one realizes that the great body has no body, one will readily understand that all dharmas are not in fact dharmas.

Doubt.—As Subhūti heard that there is no Dharma which enables one to develop his mind, he doubted: 'A Bodhisattva is so-called because he has a Dharma to save living beings. Now if there is no Dharma, where did the name of Bodhisattva come from?' In the following text, this doubt is cut off by the (teaching on the) unreality of things (dharmas) and of ego.

'Subhūti, in like manner, if a Bodhisattva says: "I should lead uncountable living beings to put a stop to (reincarnation) and escape (from suffering)", he cannot be called a Bodhisattva. Why? Because there is really no dharma called the Bodhisattva (stage). Therefore, the Buddha says: "Of all dharmas, there is not a

[1] The self-natured prajñā is immanent in every living being who, because of ignorance, thinks that he can acquire it by means of self-cultivation. The Buddha taught that prajñā is self-possessed by man and can manifest itself only after he has been stripped of all feelings and passions. Therefore, there is no gain whatsoever when one attains enlightenment. A Ch'an master said: 'Just strip yourselves of worldly feelings but don't interpret anything as saintly.'

[2] The word 'blind' should not be interpreted literally. It means that he who uses his discriminating mind to look at the Transcendental Path will never perceive it, for it only appears after one has put an end to all worldly feelings and discerning and can be equated with a pure and clean mind.

[3] Bodhi is free from all dual concepts of permanence and of annihilation or impermanence which are a pair of opposites produced by the deluded mind.

single one which possesses an ego, a personality, a being and a life." Subhūti, if a Bodhisattva says: "I should adorn Buddha lands", he cannot be called a Bodhisattva. Why? Because when the Tathāgata speaks of such adornment it is not, but is (expediently), called adornment. Subhūti, if a Bodhisattva is thoroughly versed in (the doctrine of) the unreality of ego and of things (dharma), the Tathāgata will call him a true Bodhisattva.'

The above shows that Dharma-kāya has no ego with which to break up the Bodhisattva's two fine (erroneous) views of the reality of ego and of things (dharmas). Subhūti grasped the idea that a Bodhisattva was so called because of the existence of a Dharma which enabled the latter to liberate all living beings. The World Honoured One told him that there was no real Dharma to kill the idea of the reality of things (dharmas). He was apprehensive that Subhūti might have a doubt about the unreality of Dharma, without which Dharma a Buddha land could not be adorned. Therefore, the World Honoured One pointed out that the land (or realm) of permanent peace and enlightenment did not need adornment, in order to kill the idea of a mind abiding there and of the reality of an ego. If one is not thoroughly versed in this doctrine, one will not be a true Bodhisattva. Therefore, He declared: 'If one is thoroughly versed in the unreality of ego and things (dharmas), the Tathāgata will call him a true Bodhisattva.'

Doubt.—If a Bodhisattva cannot see any living beings to liberate or realms to purify, how is it that the Tathāgata has five kinds of vision? To kill this doubt, the sūtra points out that he uses the minds of living beings for eyes and has not Himself five kinds of vision.

'Subhūti, what do you think? Does the Tathāgata possess human eyes?
'Yes, World Honoured One, the Tathāgata possesses human eyes.'
'Sūbhāti, what do you think? Does the Tathāgata possess deva eyes?'[1]
'Yes, World Honoured One, the Tathāgata possesses deva-eyes.'
'Subhūti, what do you think? Does the Tathāgata possess wisdom eyes?'[2]
'Yes, World Honoured One, the Tathāgata possesses wisdom eyes.'
'Subhūti, what do you think? Does the Tathāgata possess Dharma eyes?[3]
'Yes, World Honoured One. The Tathāgata possesses Dharma eyes?'
'Subhūti, What do you think? Does the Tathāgata possess Buddha eyes?'[4]
'Yes, World Honoured One, the Tathāgata possesses Buddha eyes.'
'Subhuti, what do you think? Does the Tathagata say that the sand-grains in the Ganges are sand-grains?'

[1] Deva eye: divine sight, unlimited vision.
[2] Wisdom eye: eye of wisdom that sees all things as unreal.
[3] Dharma eye: because it is able to penetrate all things, to see the truth that releases us from reincarnation.
[4] Buddha eye, the eye of the Buddha, the enlightened one who sees all and is omniscient.

'Yes, World Honoured One, the Tathāgata says they are sand-grains.'

'Subhūti, what do you think? If there were as many Ganges rivers as sand-grains in the Ganges, and if there were as many Buddha realms as sand-grains of all these Ganges rivers, would there be many world systems?'

'Many, World Honoured One!'

The Buddha said: 'The living beings in all these world systems have many different minds which are all known to the Tathāgata. Why? Because the minds the Tathāgata speaks of are not minds but are (expediently) called minds. And why? Because, Subhūti, neither the past, the present nor the future mind can be found.'[1]

This shows that mind, Buddha and living beings do not differ from one another.[2] Subhūti doubted and thought that since the Buddha possesses the five kinds of eye, there should be things (dharmas) which He can see, and worlds and living beings to match (these eyes). The World Honoured One said that His five kinds of eye are not really eyes and that He sees by using the minds of living beings. Moreover, there are uncountable living beings in the worlds which are as many as the sand-grains of the Ganges rivers, and the Tathāgata knows them all and sees all their different minds because these beings are (inside) His own mind. Therefore, when the mind of a being is stirred by a thought, it is the Tathāgata's own mind which is moved. How then can this be unknown to and unseen by Him?

Subhūti doubted again and thought that since the mind of a being is born and dies, did the Tathāgata's mind also have birth and death? For this reason, the World Honoured One said that in all this, the mind of a being is fundamentally the absolute and has neither birth nor death, the same as the Tathāgata's mind which is in the universal condition of Nirvāṇa. The Tathāgata and living beings are clearly immutable and free from birth and death as well as from coming and going. This is called the sameness of Mind, Buddha and living being. For this reason, the mind cannot be found in the past, present or future.

Doubt.—Hitherto the Tathāgata had wiped out all attachments by saying that there are no (Buddha) lands to adorn and no beings to liberate. He was apprehensive that Subhūti might turn his thoughts to the non-existence of lands and living beings, and might think that since almsgiving (dāna) did not reap any merit, it would be useless to practise it. Therefore, the World Honoured One wiped out this doubt by declaring that the merit of no-merit is the greatest merit.[3]

[1] This is elimination of the conception of time.
[2] Mind, Buddha and being are intrinsically the same.
[3] A merit not conditioned by the deluded mind is the greatest merit.

'Subhūti, what do you think? If someone filled the universe with the seven treasures and gave all away in his practice of dāna, would this (good) cause enable the giver to gain a great merit?'

'Yes, World Honoured One, because of this (good) cause the giver would gain a great merit.'

'Subhūti, if the merit was real, the Tathāgata would not say it was great.[1] He says so because there is no merit.'

The above shows the formless merit. Subhūti clung to form in the practice of dāna which, he thought, would reap merits. He did not realize that the giver and the six objects of sense (guṇas) are fundamentally non-existent, so that any merit gained is (equally) non-existent. Therefore, the World Honoured One wiped out this (wrong) view by declaring that the merit is great because of the non-existence of merit. When He said: 'There is no merit', He did not mean that there was no merit at all. As the capacity of the mind (when freed from delusion) is as great as space, the merit will be very great.

Doubt.—As Subhūti heard that the mind should not be attached to form when liberating living beings and adorning Buddha lands, he doubted and thought: Liberation of living beings and adornment of (Buddha) lands are the causes of attaining Buddhahood, with the resultant fruit adorned with myriads of good virtues. Now, if there are no living beings to liberate and no (Buddha) lands to adorn, this means that there is no cause whatsoever. He also thought that, if there is no enlightenment (Bodhi) to attain, there will be no fruit. If cause and effect are wiped out, there will be no Buddha. However, he saw the perfect material appearance of the Tathāgata; where did this come from? This doubt was cut off by the Buddha who pointed out that the Tathāgata should not be perceived by means of His perfect material appearance.

'Subhūti, what do you think? Can the Buddha be perceived by His completely perfect physical body (rūpa-kāya)?'

'No, World Honoured One, the Tathāgata should not be so perceived. Why? Because the Buddha says the completely perfect rūpa-kāya is not, but is called the completely perfect rūpa-kāya.'

'Subhūti, what do you think? Can the Tathāgata be perceived by His completely perfect forms?'

'No, World Honoured One, the Tathāgata should not be so perceived, because the Tathāgata says the completely perfect forms are not but are called completely perfect forms.'

[1] If a merit can be estimated and expressed in words, it will not be great. On the other hand, if a merit is not conditioned by the conception of existence and non-existence, it will be really very great.

The above prevents the forms of Sambhoga-kāya being used to reveal the oneness of Dharma-kāya and Sambhoga-kāya. The completely perfect Rūpa-kāya was the Sambhoga-kāya adorned with myriads of perfect virtues. As many aeons have been spent to liberate living beings for the adornment of Buddha lands, this resultant fruit is a reward of the (perfect) cause and is called by the Tathāgata, the completely perfect Rūpa-kāya. Moreover, this Sambhoga-kāya was fundamentally Dharma-kāya and for this reason, He said: 'It is not the completely perfect Rupa-kāya.' Dharma-kāya and Sambhoga-kāya being one, He said: 'It is called the completely perfect Rūpa-kāya.' This was to break up the (view of the reality of) forms which are seen (i.e. the objective). In the next sentence, He wiped out the seeing which was *able to see* (the subjective). As Sambhoga-kāya was identical with Dharma-kāya, there existed no forms which could be seen. Both wisdom and body (or substance) being absolute, the sickness of seeing (or illusory view) was eliminated. The objective seen and the subjective wisdom melting into one, the Dharma-kāya was exposed.[1]

The use of the positive term 'is' or the negative term 'is not' was to protect the disciples against their fall into old ruts by driving away their (false) views. This is why the Tathāgata who taught the Dharma, did not in fact teach anything at all. What He did was to protect living beings against mental sickness by enjoining upon them not to hold (false) views, by eliminating their passionate clinging to the unreal and by urging them to relinquish all attachments. Students should understand that this is (the sole content of His teaching).[2]

Doubt.—Subhūti, who had heard that the Buddha had no forms which could be seen, doubted and thought: 'Who is teaching the Dharma if there are no physical forms?' The Buddha wiped out this (false) view by saying that there is really no Dharma to expound.

'Subhūti, do not say that the Tathāgata thinks: "I must expound the Dharma". Do not have such a thought. Why? Because if someone says so, he will really slander the Buddha and be unable to understand my teaching. Subhūti, when (the Tathāgata) expounds the Dharma, there is really no Dharma to teach: but this is (expediently) called teaching the Dharma.'

This killed the doubt about the Tathāgata's Sambhoga-kāya expounding the Dharma. Since the time of His appearance in this world, the

[1] The elimination of the subjective 'seeing' and objective 'forms' was for the purpose of ensuring the melting of these two extremes into one undivided whole, i.e. the Dharma-kāya or self-natured Buddha.

[2] The Buddha's teaching consisted only of curing His disciples' mental illness by stripping them of feelings and passions so that they could perceive their fundamental nature which was pure and clean. He had no firm Dharma to expound to them.

Tathāgata had no (real) Dharma to expound. He only expediently broke up living beings' feelings (and discernings). He used single words and His 'No' or 'Not' called for a stop to halt (His disciples') wrong thoughts. This was precisely His idea of protecting, and cherishing living beings. Therefore, He said: 'This is called the expounding of Dharma.'

Doubt.—Subhūti had already understood the doctrine of the Dharmakāya which does not speak of and proclaim anything, and is a very profound Dharma, but he did not know whether living beings in future ages would believe and receive it. This doubt arose in his mind and was cut off by (the doctrine of) the non-existence of living beings expounded in the next paragraphs.

Then the wise Subhūti said to the Buddha: 'World Honoured One, will there be in future ages living beings who will believe this Dharma when they hear it?'

The Buddha said: 'Subhūti, the living beings (you just mentioned) are neither living nor not-living beings.[1] Why? Because, Subhūti, the Tathāgata says these living beings are not (really), but they are (expediently), called living beings.'

The above shows the absolute oneness of living beings and Dharma to wipe out the (false) view of the reality of living beings. Subhūti had obtained the wonderful comprehension of the (doctrine of the) Dharmakāya and could believe and receive it. However, this Dharma was very profound and he did not know if there would be in future ages living beings able to believe it. This was due to his view of the reality of birth and death which was still not relinquished, so that he thought of future living beings. The World Honoured One replied that living beings were fundamentally the absolute and are the same as the Dharma. How could there be a future time? The suchness of living beings and the sameness of the three times are the supreme pattern of the ultimate prajñā. When the Buddha said: 'They are neither living beings nor not living beings. Why? Because these living beings are not really, but are expediently called living beings', he meant that they were fundamentally the absolute. For this reason He said: 'They are neither living beings . . .' As the absolute follows circumstantial causes to accomplish actions, He said: '. . . nor not-living beings.' He again explained that the so-called living beings are the absolute that follows circumstantial causes and owe their forms to the combination of various dharmas. Therefore, He said that living beings are falsely called and are not really living beings. They are non-existent but are called living beings (for convenience sake only).

Doubt.—If the Dharma-kāya had no forms and if no Dharma could

[1] Elimination of both 'living beings' and 'not-living beings' which are a pair of opposites.

be acquired, why was it said that the practice of all good virtues (enables) one to attain enlightenment (Bodhi)? This doubt is cut off by the following doctrine of gainlessness in the universal nature.

Subhūti said to the Buddha: 'World Honoured One, does your (own) attainment of Supreme Enlightenment (Anuttara-samyak-saṁbodhi) mean that you have not gained anything whatsoever?'

The Buddha replied: 'Just so, Subhūti, just so, I have not gained even the least Dharma from Supreme Enlightenment, and this is called Supreme Enlightenment. Furthermore, Subhūti, this Dharma is universal and impartial; wherefore it is called Supreme Enlightenment. The practice of all good virtues (Dharmas), free from attachment to an ego, a personality, a being and a life, will result in the attainment of Supreme Enlightenment. Subhūti, the so-called good virtues (Dharmas), the Tathāgata says, are not good but are (expediently) called good virtues.'[1]

This destroys the (false) view of Buddha and Dharma. Subhūti had already understood that the Dharma-kāya was pure and clean, and that there was no Dharma which could be acquired. However, he still doubted and thought there was (an actual) gain when the Buddha said that the practice of all good virtues (Dharmas) would enable one to obtain enlightenment. (He thought:) Was the Tathāgata's Bodhi fruit not acquired? The Buddha replied that nothing was obtained, because the Buddha and living beings are the same and are neither two nor different (entities). Bodhi means this and nothing else. Therefore, there is nothing that can be realized and obtained. When it was said that the practice of good virtues (Dharmas) led to the attainment of Bodhi, this meant that the four forms should be relinquished when practising these good virtues. As practice was tantamount to no-practice, so was attainment to non-attainment. Since there was no acquisition, the Dharma was really a perfect one.

Doubt.—Which Dharma is best if the (concept of) good Dharma is wrong? The next paragraph explains that the Dharma which reaches prajñā is the unsurpassed one.

'Subhūti, if (on the one hand) a man, in his practice of charity (dāna) gives away the seven treasures piled up in a heap as great as all the Mounts Sumeru in the Universe put together, and (on the other hand) another man receives, holds (in mind), reads and recites even a four-line stanza of this Prajñā-pāramitā Sūtra, and expounds it to others, the merit resulting from the former's dāna will not be worth one-hundredth, one-thousandth, one-ten-thousandth and one-hundred-

[1] After speaking of good virtues, the Buddha immediately eradicated all traces thereof, lest Subhūti might grasp the dual concept of the good and evil which are non-existent in the universal and impartial reality of prajñā.

thousandth part of that obtained by the latter, as no conceivable comparison can be made between the two.'

This praises the unsurpassed merit of the form-relinquishing prajñā. Subhūti thought that if the practice of a good Dharma did not ensure the acquisition of Bodhi, the Dharma in question would not be the unsurpassed one. Then, which Dharma was unsurpassable? The Buddha said the one which reached prajñā. In the universe there are 100,000,000 mount Sumerus and if the seven treasures were piled up in a huge heap as great as all the mount Sumerus put together, there would indeed be many treasures to be given away in the practice of dāna. The merit resulting therefrom would (however) not be comparable to the merit derived from a four-line stanza which reached prajñā. The reason is that the former still clings to forms with a desire for his own gain. As prajñā relinquishes all forms, it is incomparable and unsurpassable.

Doubt.—Subhūti had heard that living beings and Buddhas are the same (or one undivided whole). If so, there would be no living beings at all. Then, why is it said that the Tathāgata should liberate living beings? (Thus) Subhūti still clung to the concept of an ego and a personality. In the following text, this doubt was cut off by wiping out both ego and personality.

'Subhūti, what do you think? You should not say the Tathāgata has this thought (in His mind): "I should liberate living beings." Subhūti, you should not think so. Why? Because there are really no living beings whom the Tathāgata can liberate. If there were, the Tathāgata would hold (the concept of) an ego, a personality, a being and a life. Subhūti, (when) the Tathāgata speaks of an ego, there is in reality no ego, although common men think so. Subhūti, the Tathāgata says common men are not, but are (expediently) called, common men.'

This removes the doubt about the Buddha holding the concept of an ego and a personality in order to reveal the Dharma-kāya's real self. It was said: 'The Buddha and living beings are the same' and if this doctrine of sameness holds good, there would be no Buddha and no living beings. Then why was it said: 'I should liberate living beings?' As a living being is a personality, if I liberate him, the I or ego would exist. If ego and personality really exist, the four forms will not be eliminated. This is referred to in Ch'an teaching as attainment of the borderline of Dharma-kāya but not the actual penetration into the 'Transcendental Sentence'[1]

[1] In Ch'an terminology, the 'transcendental sentence' or 'first sentence' is the symbol of the real, or Dharma-kāya. As soon as a thought arises, it will be the second or third sentence, for a discriminating mind always strays from the absolute prajñā.

of Dharma-kāya. For this reason, the Tathāgata spoke words to destroy this idea when He said: 'Do not say that I, the Tathāgata, have this thought of liberating living beings. If "I" had, "I" would be a common man.' Even the common men, mentioned by the Tathāgata, are not really common men. How then could He still hold the view of an 'I'? This wiped out the concept of both the saintly and worldly, resulting in the impartial One Way.[1] This completes the doctrine of prajñā.

Doubt.—If Dharma-kāya is egoless and if the form of Sambhoga-kāya cannot be perceived by form, is the World Honoured One who was endowed with thirty-two physical characteristics not a (real) Buddha?

'Subhūti, what do you think? Can the Tathāgata be recognised by His thirty-two physical characteristics?'

Subhūti reply: 'Yes, yes, He can.'

The Buddha said: 'Subhūti, if the Tathāgata can be recognised by His thirty-two physical characteristics, a world ruler (cakravartī) would be the Tathāgata.'

Subhūti said to the Buddha: 'World Honoured One, as I understand your teaching, the Tathāgata cannot be recognised by His thirty-two phsyical characteristics.'

Thereupon, the World Honoured One recited the following gāthā:

'He who sees me by outward appearance
(And) seeks me in sound,
Treads the heterodox path
(And) cannot perceive the Tathāgata.'

The Buddha pointed out that Nirmāṇa-kāya could not reveal the Dharma-kāya which was beyond all forms. Subhūti had already understood that a Buddha was a true one when His Dharma-kāya was egoless and His Sambhoga-kāya had no characteristics. (But) he still doubted and asked himself who was the Buddha, visible here, with His thirty-two physical characteristics? This was his view of the Buddha.[2] The World Honoured One asked him: 'Is it true that the Tathāgata can be recognized by His thirty-two physical characteristics?' As Subhūti clung to these signs which (seemed to) show the (true) Buddha, the World Honoured One broke up his (false) view by saying that a world ruler also has thirty-two physical characteristics. Now Subhūti understood that the Tathāgata could not be recognized by His thirty-two characteristics, and the World Honoured One read the gāthā on relinquishment of forms, which ran:

[1] One Way, the way of deliverance from mortality, the Supreme Yāna.

[2] By holding the view of the existence of the Buddha, Subhūti still grasped the dual conception of a 'subject', the holder of such a view, and an 'object', the Buddha viewed as existing. This dual view obstructed the attainment of Bodhi.

'He who sees me by outward appearance—and seeks me in sound—treads the heterodox path—and cannot perceive the Tathāgata.'

Doubt.—Subhūti had heard that both Dharma-kāya and Sambhoga-kāya had no forms and that Nirmāṇa-kāya was not real. Now there arose in his mind, in respect of Dharma-kāya, the view of annihilation, because of his inability to reach the real self of Dharma-kāya. The Buddha broke up this view by His doctrine of non-annihilation.

'Subhūti, if you have (in your mind) this thought: "The Tathāgata does not rely on His possession of characteristics to obtain supreme Enlightenment," Subhūti, banish that thought. Subhūti, if you think it while developing the Perfect Enlightenment Mind, you will advocate the annihilation of all Dharmas. Do not have such a thought. Why? Because one who develops the Supreme Enlightenment Mind, does not advocate the annihilation (of things).[1]

'Subhūti, if (on the one hand) a Bodhisattva gave in his practice of dāna, all the seven treasures in quantities sufficient to fill worlds as many as sand-grains in the Ganges, and (on the other hand) another man comprehended that all dharmas were egoless and thereby achieved perfection of patience (kṣānti), the latter's merit would surpass that of the former. Why? Because, Subhūti, all Bodhisattvas do not receive reward for their merits.'

Subhūti asked the Buddha: 'World Honoured One, why do Bodhisattvas not receive reward for their merits?'

'Subhūti, Bodhisattvas should have no longing and no attachment when they practise meritorious virtues; therefore, they do not receive a reward.'

The Buddha broke up the view of annihilation. As Subhūti heard that form should be relinquished in order to perceive the Buddha, the view of annihilation arose in his mind, and he thought that the Tathāgata did not rely on His possession of characteristics to obtain enlightenment. The Buddha taught him this: 'Do not have such a thought, because if you have it (in your mind), you will advocate annihilation (of all dharmas). Those who develop the Bodhi Mind, do not advocate the annihilation of things, but only the non-existence of the ego in all things. If a Bodhisattva knew that all dharmas were egoless and succeeded in his practice of the patience-perfection (pāramitā), his merit would surpass that of a giver of sufficient of the seven treasures to fill worlds as many as sand-grains in the Ganges, because the former did not receive reward for his merit. When it was said that he did not receive any reward, this did not mean that there was no reward at all. It is enough to have no longing for and

[1] Since all forms originally were not created, they should not be annihilated. Creation and annihilation are two opposites and should not be clung to when developing the Bodhi Mind which is free from the duality of things.

no attachment to, any merit. It was said: 'No doer, no doing and no receiver, (but) good and evil karma cannot be wiped out.'

After His appearance in this world, and for forty-nine years, the World Honoured One only said the word NO. All living beings in the nine worlds[1] clung to the concept of an ego in all things but the Tathāgata used (only) the word *no* to destroy it. This was the right Dharma eye which looked straight into the Transcendental Way. For this reason, the Ch'an sect transmits only the direct pointing through which alone one enters (the real).

Doubt.—It had been said that there is no ego and no receiver of merit, but when the Tathāgata was seen walking, standing, sitting or lying, was not this His ego? This was due to attachment to the false conception of unity-with-differentiation[2] of the Three Bodies (Trikāya) and to the non-comprehension of the universalized Dharma-kāya.

'Subhūti, if someone says the Tathāgata comes or goes, sits or lies, he does not understand what I mean. Why? Because the Tathāgata has neither whence (to come) nor whither (to go); therefore, He is called the Tathāgata.'

The above shows the ultimate return to the reality of the Dharma-kāya. Hitherto, Subhūti because of his (false) view of coming and going had thought that the Tathāgata was One whose deportment inspired respect.[3] Did the Tathāgata in fact really come and go? The moment had now come when all clingings disappeared and all feelings ceased, and when the disciple comprehended the sameness of the mutable and immutable. He thus reached the most wonderful reality of the absolute. However, he still held the (false) view of unity-with-differentiation and his mind could not yet grasp the profound meaning of the Trikāya in one body. This (wrong) view is wiped out in the following paragraph about the world and dust.

'Subhūti, what do you think? If a virtuous man or woman reduced to dust all the worlds in the Universe, would those particles of dust be many?'

Subhūti replied: 'Many, World Honoured One. Why? Because if they really existed, the Buddha would not say they were particles of dust. And why? Because when the Buddha speaks of particles of dust, they are not, but are (expediently) called, particles of dust. World Honoured One, when the Tathāgata speaks of worlds, they are not, but are (expediently) called, worlds. Why? Because if they

[1] The nine worlds are those of: (1) Bodhisattvas, (2) Pratyekas, (3) Śrāvakas, (4) devas, (5) men, (6) asuras, (7) animals, (8) hungry ghosts and (9) the denizens of hell.

[2] Unity-with-differentiation: monism and pluralism, Oneness and otherness.

[3] Respect-inspiring deportment: dignity in walking, standing, sitting and lying.

really exist, they are just agglomerations.[1] The Tathāgata speaks of agglomerations which are not, but are (expediently) called, agglomerations.'

'Subhūti, that which is called an agglomeration cannot be spoken of, but the vulgar man has longing for and attachment to this thing.'[2]

This broke up the (false) view of Unity-with-differentiation. As Subhūti's mind had not yet grasped the reality of the Trikāya in One Body, the World Honoured One used the dust and world, as examples, to point out that the one was not monistic nor the other pluralistic. Particles of dust, united together to form a world, seem pluralistic but are not really so. When the world is broken up and reduced to dust, it seems monistic but is not really so. Thus (the so-called) unity-with-differentiation does not obtain anywhere, and therefore is not real. If unity-with-differentiation exists, it would only be an agglomeration (without permanent reality). An agglomeration owes (its seeming existence) to a dual view because monism cannot be pluralistic nor pluralism monistic. If the dust really exists, it cannot agglomerate to make a world, and if a world really exists, it cannot be reduced to dust. The common man takes it for unity but the unity of which the Tathāgata spoke was different. If the two extremes are wiped out, this can be called unity, but when the two extremes have been eliminated, (even) this unity cannot be spoken of.[3] The ordinary man cannot give up the two extremes, such as existence and non-existence, or monism and pluralism, and clings to them. This explains his inability to understand the doctrine of the Trikāya in one body of the universalized Dharma-kāya.

Doubt.—If Dharma-kāya is universal and if all things are unreal and cannot be conceived, why did the Buddha speak of the view of four forms? This doubt is removed in the following paragraph.

'Subhūti, what do you think? If someone says: "The Buddha speaks of the view of an ego, a personality, a being and a life," Subhūti, does that person understand what I mean?'

'No, World Honoured One, that person does not understand. Why? Because (when) the Tathāgata speaks of the view of an ego, a personality, a being and a life, it is not really, (but) is (expediently) called the view of an ego, a personality a being and a life.'[4]

'Subhūti, he who develops the Supreme Enlightenment Mind, should thus know, see, believe and comprehend (all things); he should not set up the percep-

[1] Particles of dust united together to form a world.

[2] The unreal phenomenal.

[3] Because it is the reality and is inexpressible.

[4] The Buddha spoke of these views held by worldly men but He did not hold these views.

tion of things (dharma-lakṣaṇa)[1] in his mind. Subhūti, the so-called form of things (dharma-lakṣaṇa), the Tathāgata says is not but is (expediently) called the form of things.'

This wiped out the (subtle) view of relinquishment of form. Subhūti had already understood the doctrine of the absolute universalized Dharmakāya, but still doubted and thought: If the body or substance of Dharmakāya could not be seen by means of form, why did the Tathāgata speak of the relinquishment of the view of four forms? The Buddha was apprehensive that Subhūti might still have this doubt hidden in his mind and asked him this question: 'Supposing that someone says: "The World Honoured One says there is the view of the four forms," do you think this person understands what I mean?' Thereupon, Subhūti understood and replied: 'No, this person does not understand what the Tathāgata means. Why? Because (when) the World Honoured One speaks of the view of four forms, there is actually no such view that can be pointed out and spoken of.' This was to wipe out attachment to the view about forms. Therefore, He said: *Not*, which differed in meaning from the previous occasions when he used the word. It was used frequently before in a negative sense whereas here it banishes completely the view concerning forms held in the minds of living beings. They, not the Buddha, held this view. Therefore, He said: '(It) is called the view about forms.' (Here) the two words 'is called' also differ in meaning from when they were used before. Students should examine carefully this difference in meaning.

As all living things are deluded and upset by their views of forms and since their grasp is very hard to break, the Buddha used the Diamond-mind wisdom to demolish these views one by one, in order to enable them to perceive the fundamental wisdom of the Dharma-kāya's body.

At first they clung to the forms of the five aggregates (skandhas) of body and mind and to the six sense data. They were attached to these forms while giving alms (dāna) to seek merits in their quest of Buddhahood. The World Honoured One broke up this by the doctrine of non-attachment.

Next, they clung to the form of Bodhi and the Buddha broke it up by the doctrine of gainlessness.

Next, they clung to the form of Buddha lands adorned by almsgiving (dāna) and the Buddha broke it up by declaring that there are no lands which can be adorned.

Next, they clung to merits which would result in the appearance of

[1] Dharma-lakṣaṇa: form, appearance, aspects and characteristics of dharmas, or things.

the Reward body (or Sambhoga-kāya) and the Buddha broke it up by stating that it is not in fact the completely perfect form body (Rūpa-kāya).

Next, they clung to the appearance of the Trikāya which the Tathāgata possessed and the Buddha broke it up by declaring that the Nirmāṇa-kāya is not real and that Sambhoga-kāya is beyond forms.

Next, they clung to the view that the Dharma-kāya must have forms, and the Buddha broke this up by declaring that the Dharma-kāya has none.

Next, they clung to the existence of a true ego in the Dharma-kāya and the Buddha broke it up by declaring that all things are egoless.

Next, they clung to the view that the Tathāgata possessed the forms of the Trikāya and the Buddha broke up this by declaring that the real is neither monistic nor pluralistic.

Thus all their false views were broken up successively one after the other, and with the elimination of all idea of form and appearance, the mind had nowhere to alight. (The moment had come when) the fundamental Law was in its absoluteness after the relinquishment of all feelings, pointing straight to the reality of Dharma-kāya. As all false forms which *were seen* were non-existent, the seeing which *could see* them also vanished. This was the ultimate pattern of true Prajñā which penetrated right into the Transcendental Path of the Dharma-kāya. Therefore, the Buddha gave them this commandment: 'He who develops the Bodhi-mind should, in respect of all things, thus know, see, believe and interpret; he should not give rise (in his mind) to things with form (dharma-lakṣaṇa).' Only then could there be true knowing, seeing, belief and interpretation, and no more (false) knowing and seeing of the forms of things would ever rise again. Thus the two views of the reality of ego and of things (dharmas) would disappear; the conception of the saintly and worldly would be buried in oblivion; and there would be no room for words and speeches as well as for all mental activities. Since it would be wrong to stir the mind and to arouse a thought, He again told them: 'The so-called dharma-lakṣaṇa is not dharma-lakṣaṇa.' This was the true and real dharma lakṣaṇa which was not the same as the falsely viewed one. This is the profound doctrine of Prajñā in its ultimate subtleness.

Doubt.—Subhūti who had been awakened to the whole substance of the Dharma-kāya doubted and thought that if Dharma-kāya could not expound the Dharma, the speaker would be Nirmāṇa-kāya and the Dharma expounded by Nirmāṇa-kāya would not reach the region of Dharma-kāya. How then could those who observed the said Dharma gain merits? The next paragraph explains that the Dharma expounded by Nirmāṇa-kāya was the true Dharma because of the Trikāya in one body.

'Subhūti, if on the one hand, someone gave away in alms (dāna) the seven treasures in quantities sufficient to fill all the worlds in uncountable aeons, and if on the other hand, a virtuous man or woman developed the Bodhi-mind, and received, held (in mind), read and recited even a four-line stanza of this sūtra and expounded it to others, the latter's merit would surpass that of the former. In what manner should it be taught to others? By teaching it without attachment to form with the immutability of the absolute.'[1]

The above points out that the Nirmāṇa-kāya Buddha teaches the absolute Dharma. Subhūti doubted and thought that if the Dharma taught by the Nirmāṇa-kāya Buddha would not reach the region of Dharma-kāya, merits could not be gained. The Buddha said the Dharma taught by the Nirmāṇa-kāya was exactly the same as if taught by the Dharma-kāya because of the oneness of the Trikāya, and if even a four-line stanza of this Dharma could be held (in mind) and taught to others, the resultant merits would be unsurpassable, owing to the detachment from form while abiding in the immutability of the absolute. This was called the widespread explaining of the Dharma by dust and regions.[2]

Doubt.—Since the Dharma-kāya is calm and not liable (to reincarnation), how can one who is calm, expound the Dharma? The following text points out the correct meditation. As Prajñā is immaterial, the phenomenal should be looked into first for the (subsequent) entry into the void which is called absolute voidness, because of the identity of the seeming with the real.

'Why is it? Because:

> 'All phenomena are like
> A dream, an illusion, a bubble and a shadow,
> Like dew and lightning.
> Thus should you meditate upon them'

The above wonderful meditation leads to the entry into the true voidness of Prajñā. As the true voidness is still and unfathomable, the meditation should be made by means of the seeming, and if the meditation on the above six things, namely dream, illusion, bubble, shadow,

[1] Literally the immobility of Bhūtatathatā.

[2] A Buddhist term: Samantabhadra Bodhisattva's ears could hear a straw, a plant and a particle of dust expounding the unsurpassed wonderful Dharma. This meant that in the ten directions of space, each particle of dust had a region and each region had a Buddha who expounded the Avataṁsaka Sūtra. In other words, this Bodhisattva perceived the all pervading reality in each particle of dust, plant and region.

dew and lightning, is successful, the true void appears. Up to this point the Ruling Principle (or Fundamental Law) has been expounded but here is given the method of meditation which students should follow for their entry (into Prajñā). Here the true realm of Dharma-kāya is finally dealt with.

When the Buddha had finished expounding this sūtra, the elder Subhūti, together with bhikṣus, bhikṣuṇīs, upāsakas, upāsikās, and all the worlds of devas, men and asuras who had listened to His teaching, were filled with joy and believed, received and observed it.

The listeners were filled with joy and their minds were wonderfully at one with the doctrine. As a result their beliefs were true, they received the sūtra in earnest, and their observance of it had purpose.

PART IV

A STRAIGHT TALK

ON THE HEART SŪTRA

(*Prajñā-pāramitā-hṛdaya Sūtra*)

By Ch'an Master Han Shan

(*from the Hsin Ching Chih Shuo*)

Foreword

ACCORDING to the T'ien T'ai (Tendai) School, the five periods of the Buddha's teaching are:

1. The Avataṁsaka or first period in three divisions, each of seven days, after His enlightenment, when He expounded this long sūtra.
2. The twelve years in which He expounded the Āgamas in the deer park.
3. The eight years in which He expounded Mahāyāna-with-Hīnayāna doctrines, the Vaipulya period.
4. The twenty-two years in which He expounded the Wisdom (Prajñā) Sūtras.
5. The eight years in which He expounded the Lotus Sūtra and, in a day and night, the Mahāparinirvāna Sūtra.

The Heart (Hṛdaya) Sūtra which is now presented to Western Buddhists, is a short one, being a condensation into a total of only two hundred and sixty-eight Chinese characters including its title, of the whole teaching of the Wisdom Sūtras during a period of twenty-two years, consisting of I do not know how many million characters. The Sūtra itself is, therefore, very difficult to understand, but with a comprehensive commentary by Ch'an Master Han Shan written after his own enlightenment, it is comparatively easy to comprehend for those who are already familiar with the Mahāyāna doctrine. Its aim is to wipe out all traces of illusions of the five aggregates, the six sense organs, the six sense data, the six consciousnesses, the eighteen realms of sense, the twelve links in the chain of existences, the four dogmas and finally even wisdom and gain so as to disentangle the mind from all dualisms which are but one by their very nature and have no room in the absolute Reality. When released from all dual conceptions, the mind itself will also disappear when integrating into its fundamental nature. This is realization of the truth or attainment of enlightenment (Bodhi).

This Sūtra deals with the theory and its mantra gives the method of practice. The mantra is likened to a hua t'ou devised by Ch'an masters to stop the unending chain of thoughts, and if it is held in the mind at all times and in all places, it will enable its holder to disentangle himself from all illusions and to uncover the absolute wisdom inherent in his own self. Wisdom is likened to a sharp sword that cuts down all obstacles on one's path to liberation. As Master Han Shan said, there is no other method surpassing the one taught in this short Sūtra.

In this presentation, I have used English equivalents of Sanskrit terms, followed by the corresponding Sanskrit words in brackets, because the former do not convey the full meaning of the latter. I have also added explanatory notes so that readers can find the meaning of each Sanskrit term.

Throughout this translation, instead of the word 'Mind', I have used the word 'Heart' to be in accord with the title and text, for 'Heart' is the equivalent of what is called 'Mind' in the West.

In China, both the Diamond and Heart Sūtras are bound in one volume, the former preceding the latter, and Chinese Buddhists who recite the one, recite the other also. The Chinese Heart Sūtra differs from the Tibetan Heart Sūtra only in that the latter contains some opening and closing sentences which are not found in the former. In spite of this slight difference, the deep meaning is exactly the same in both Sūtras.

All brackets are mine.

UPĀSAKA LU K'UAN YÜ.

Hongkong, 30th November, 1957.

The Prajñā-Pāramitā-Hrdaya Sūtra

In the title Prajñā means 'Wisdom' and Pāramitā 'Reaching the other shore'.

The world (saṁsāra)[1] of miserable destinies is likened to a great ocean and living beings' feelings and thoughts are shoreless. They are ignorant and do not know that the waves of their consciousness (vijñāna)[2] run high and are the cause of illusion and karmic[3] actions resulting in the (endless) round of births and deaths. Their sufferings are inexhaustible and they are unable to ferry themselves across (the bitter ocean of mortality). Therefore, it is called 'this shore'.

Our Buddha used the brightness of His great wisdom to illumine and break up the passions (kleśa) caused by the six objects of sensation (guṇa) and to put an end to all sufferings for ever. This leads to the complete elimination of the two kinds of death (natural and violent) and to a leap over the ocean of misery for the realization of Nirvāṇa.[4] Therefore it is called 'the other shore'.

The *heart* mentioned (in the title) is the heart of the great wisdom (prajñā) that reaches the other shore. It is not the (human) heart which (worldly men use for) thinking wrongly. The ignorant man does not know that he fundamentally possesses the heart of the bright light of wisdom. He regards as real the lump (of muscle) attached to the flesh and blood, which recognizes (only) the shadows resulting from wrong thinking and grasping stimulated by circumstances. Consequently the body of flesh and blood is (wrongly) considered as his possession and is used to commit all kinds of evil deeds (karma).[3] Thus thoughts succeed one another in their unceasing chain without a (single) one of them turning the light inwards on oneself for self-cognition. With the unending accumulation of nothing but karma and suffering from birth to death and from death to birth, how can one ferry oneself across (the ocean of mortality)? Only the Buddha who was a saint (ārya) was aware of the true fundamental wisdom which can illumine and break up the body and heart of the five aggregates (skandhas)[5] which are fundamentally non-existent and whose substance is entirely void. Therefore, He leaped over (appearance) and reached the other shore instantaneously, thus crossing the bitter ocean. As He took pity on deluded men, He used this Dharma door (to enlightenment) which he had personally experienced to disclose it to them and to guide them, so that every man would be aware that his wisdom was fundamentally self-possessed, that his erroneous thoughts were basically false, that his body and heart were entirely non-existent and that the universe was nothing but a transformation. Then in order to avoid committing evil actions and to escape Saṁsāra, he would rise from the ocean of sufferings and attain the bliss of Nirvāṇa. This is why He expounded this sūtra.

Sūtra is the Saint's words and teaching, and the eternal Law (Dharma).

When Bodhisattva Avalokiteśvara practised the profound Prajñā-pāramitā, he investigated and perceived that the five aggregates (skandhas)[5] were non-existent thus securing his deliverance from all distress and sufferings.

The Bodhisattva was one who *could practise* (the subjective) and the very profound Prajñā (-pāramitā) was the Dharma that *was practised* (the objective). The investigation and perception of the non-existence of the five aggregates were the *method* of practice. The deliverance from all distress and sufferings was the real *efficacy* of the practice.

Upon hearing from the Buddha about this profound Prajñā (-pāramitā), this Bodhisattva thought of it and practised it by using his wisdom to introspect the five aggregates which are void, either internally or externally, resulting in the realization that body, heart and universe do not (in fact) really exist, in a sudden leap over (both the) mundane and supramundane, in the complete destruction of all sufferings and in the acquisition of an absolute independence. Since this Bodhisattva could deliver himself by means of this (Dharma), every man can rely on it and practise it.

For this reason, the World Honoured One purposely addressed Śāriputra to point out Avalokiteśvara's wonderful performance of which He wanted all others to know. If we make the same contemplation, we will in an instant realize that our hearts basically possess the brightness of wisdom, so vast, extensive and pervading that it shines through the five aggregates which fundamentally are void and the four elements[6] which are non-existent.

(After this realization) where were sufferings which could not be annihilated? Where were karma-fetters which shackled? Where was the obstinate argument about ego and personality and about right and wrong? Where was discrimination between failure and success and between gain and loss? And where were entanglements in such things like wealth, honours, poverty and dishonour? This was the true efficacy of this Bodhisattva's study of Prajñā.

The five aggregates are: form (rūpa), reception (vedanā), conception (sañjñā), mental function (saṁskāra) and consciousness (vijñāna).[5] The investigation comes from Prajñā which *can contemplate* (the subjective) and the five aggregates are objects which *are contemplated* (the objective). (The finding that) the five aggregates are void proves the *real efficacy* (of this method).

Śāriputra!

This was the name of a disciple of the Buddha. Śārī is the name of a bird with very bright and sharp eyes. The disciple's mother had the same bright and sharp eyes and was named after the bird. Hence his own name as the son of a woman who had śārī eyes. Among the Buddha's disciples, he was the wisest. This Prajñā-dharma door was the most profound one and only those of great wisdom could apprehend and realize it. Therefore, Śāriputra was purposely addressed to enhance the fact that this talk could only be given to a wise hearer.

Form (rūpa)[5] does not differ from the void (śūnya)[7], nor the void from form. Form is identical with void (and) void is identical with form. So also are reception (vedanā), conception (sañjñā), mental function (saṁskāra) and consciousness (vijñāna) in relation to the void.

This was said to Śāriputra to explain the meaning of the voidness of the five aggregates. Of the five aggregates, the first one, form, was pointed out first. This form is the appearance (lakṣaṇa) of the (human) body which man grasps as his possession. It is produced by the crystallization of his firm and endurable wrong thinking. It is (caused by) holding the concept of an ego, which concept is the most difficult thing to break up.

Now at the beginning of the meditation, attention should be paid to this (physical) body which is a fictitious combination of the four elements[6] and which is fundamentally non-existent.. Since its substance is entirely void both within and without, one is no more confined within this body and has, therefore, no impediment (in regard to) birth and death as well as (to) coming and going. This is the (method of) breaking up the (first) aggregate, form. If form is broken up, the other four aggregates can, in the same manner, be subjected to the (same) profound introspection.

The teaching about *form (rūpa) which does not differ from void (śūnya)*, was for the purpose of breaking up the worldly man's view that (personality) is permanent. Since worldly men hold that the physical body is real and permanent, they plan (ahead) for a century without realizing that the body is unreal and non-existent, is subject to the four changes (of birth, age, sickness and death) from instant to instant without interruption until old age and death, with the ultimate result that it is impermanent and finally returns to the void. This is still the relative void in relation to birth and death and does not reach as yet the limit of the fundamental law (i.e. absolute void). For the illusory form made of the four elements does not basically differ from the absolute void. As worldly men do not know this, the Buddha said: *Form (rūpa) does not differ from void (śūnya)*, meaning that the physical body does not fundamentally differ from the absolute void.

When the Buddha said: *Void (śūnya) does not differ from form (rūpa)*, His intention was to break up the concept of annihilation (ucchedadarśana)[8] held by heretics, Śrāvakas[9] and Pratyeka Buddhas.[10]

In their practice, the heretics did not realize that the physical body was created by Karma and that Karma was produced by the Heart, resulting in an uninterrupted motion of the turning wheel through the three periods (of past, present and future). This was due to their lack of understanding of the principle of the corresponding relation between Cause and Effect in the three periods. They held the view that after death, the clean vapour would return to heaven and the unclean vapour to earth, the real spiritual nature going back to space. If this view held good, there would be absolutely no law of retribution. Thus good actions would be in vain and evil actions would be profitable. If nature went back to space, good and evil actions would have no effect and would disappear completely without leaving any trace behind. If so, what a misfortune indeed! Confucius said: 'The wandering soul being a transformation, the conditions of ghosts and spirits can be known.'[11] This shows that death is not annihilation and that the law of retribution and transmigration is quite clear. Worldly men do not make any investigation in this direction and nothing is more fallacious than their arbitrary idea of annihilation.

As to Śrāvakas and Pratyeka Buddhas, although they practise the Buddha's teaching, they do not realize that the triple world[12] was created by the heart only and that all things were produced by consciousness (vijñāna). They did not see clearly that birth and death were like an illusion and a transformation. For them, the triple world did actually exist. They regarded these worlds of existence as prisons and loathed the four kinds of birth[13] which they took for real shackles. They did not harbour a single thought about the deliverance of living beings and remained immersed in the void and stagnant in stillness. As they were engulfed in calmness and extinction (of incomplete Nirvāṇa), the Buddha said: *Void (śūnya) does not differ from form (rūpa)*. This means that the absolute void is fundamentally not different from the illusory form, but is not that (relative and) annihilating Void in opposition to form. This (sentence) reveals that Prajñā is the absolute Void of Reality. Why? Because the absolute Void of Prajñā is likened to a great mirror and all kinds of form to appearances reflected in that mirror. If one realizes that these reflections are not separate from the mirror, one will readily understand (the meaning of the sentence): *Void (śūnya) does not differ from form (rūpa)*. Its purpose was to break up the (false view held by) Śrāvakas and Pratyeka Buddhas about the (relative and) annihilating void in contrast with form and the (wrong views held by) heretics about the empty void.

As He was apprehensive that worldly men might mistake the two words *form* and *void* for two different things and in view of their sameness, might not have an impartial mind in their contemplation, He identified *form* and *void* with each other in this sentence: *Form (rūpa) is identical with void (śūnya) (and) void (śūnya) is identical with form (rūpa)*.

With the (correct) contemplation made accordingly and with the resultant realization that form does not differ from void, there will be no avidity for sound, form, wealth and gain, and no attachment to the passions of the five desires (arising from the objects of the five senses, things seen, heard, smelt, tasted or touched). The purpose is the instantaneous liberation of worldly men from their sufferings.

If void is realized as identical with form, there will appear respect-inspiring deportment[14] without interference with the condition of Samādhi; there will be acts of liberating living beings without deviation from the (immutable) Reality; there will be dwelling in the void in spite of the effervescence of all modes of salvation and there will be contact with the existing while the One Way (i.e. Buddha Nature) remains pure and clean. All this is the instantaneous leap over all graspings of heretics, Śrāvakas and Pratyeka Buddhas.

If form and void are realized as identical with each other, there will be in the (condition of) universal suchness, no seeing of living beings being delivered in spite of the fact that every thought is devoted to their salvation and no Buddha fruit to attain in spite of the fact that the heart is wholly set on the quest of Buddhahood. This is the complete perfection of the One Heart without (any idea of acquisition of) wisdom and gain. It is a leap over the Bodhisattva stage in the instantaneous ascension to the Buddha stage. This is the other shore.

If the form is contemplated in this successful manner, the other four aggregates (skandhas) fall in line with the correct thought and are also in complete perfection. This is exactly like 'the liberation of all the six sense-organs when one of them has returned to its source (i.e. One Reality)'.[15] Wherefore, the Buddha said: *So also are reception (vedanā), conception (sañjñā), function in process (saṁskāra), and consciousness (vijñāna), in relation to the void (śūnya).*

If the above can be achieved, all sufferings will be cut off instantaneously, the Buddha fruit will be attainable and the other shore not far off. All this depends solely upon the meditator who in the time of a thought, can achieve the (correct) contemplation of the Heart. Is not such a Dharma very profound?

Śāriputra, the void (śūnya) of all things is not created, not annihilated, not impure, not pure, not increasing and not decreasing.

As He was apprehensive that worldly men might use the saṁsāric (or human) heart to interpret wrongly this real Dharma of the true Prajñā of the absolute void as including also the Dharma of birth and death, purity and impurity, and increase and decrease, the Buddha addressed Śāriputra and explained to him that the reality of the absolute void was not the Dharma of birth and death, purity and impurity, and increase and decrease, for that Dharma belongs to the realm of the feeling and seeing of living beings. The substance of the Reality of the true Prajñā of His absolute void, is (fundamentally) thoroughly pure and clean, like space, and is the supramundane Dharma. For this reason, He used the negative *not* to reject (the idea that the void of all things is created or annihilated, impure or pure, and increasing or decreasing) and to reveal that the five aggregates are (fundamentally) nothing but the reality of the absolute void, thus completely wiping out all these errors, one by one.

Therefore, within the void (sunya), there is no form (rupa) and no reception (vedanā), conception (sañjñā), mental function (saṁskāra) and no consciousness (vijñāna); there is no eye, ear, nose, tongue, body and mind; there is no form, sound, smell, taste, touch and idea; there are (no such things as the eighteen realms of sense (dhātus)[16] from) the realm of sight up to that of the faculty of mind (vijñāna); there are (no such things as the twelve links in the chain of existence (nidānas)[17] from) ignorance (avidyā) with also the end of ignorance up to old age and death (jarāmaraṇa) with also the end of old age and death[18]; there are no (such things as) the four noble truths[19] and there is no wisdom and also no gain.

This is an exhaustive explanation of Prajñā to discard all errors. The real void of Prajñā can wipe out all errors for it is pure and clean and does not contain a single thing, (for within it) there are no traces of the five aggregates, (skandhas); not only are there no five aggregates but there are also no six organs; not only are there no six organs, there are also no six objects of sensation (guṇas); and not only are there no six guṇas, there are also no six consciousnesses (vijñānas). For the realm of six organs, objects of sensation and consciousnesses, is the Dharma of worldly men. These things have no room in the absolute void of Prajñā. Wherefore, the Buddha said that all these things are not in the absolute Void. It is, therefore, beyond the Dharma of worldly men. However, within Prajñā, not only is there no Dharma of worldly men, there is also no Dharma of Saints (Ārya).

The four noble truths, the twelve links in the chain of existence and the six perfections (pāramitās) are the supramundane Dharma of the Saints of the Three Vehicles.

The four noble truths, misery (duḥkha), accumulation of misery (samudaya), extinction of passion (nirodha) and path (mārga) (advocate) aversion to misery, destruction of the accumulation of misery, longing for the extinction of passions and practice of the doctrine of the path, and are the Dharma of Śrāvakas.

The twelve links in the chain of existence are: from ignorance, dispositions; from dispositions, consciousness; from consciousness, name and form; from name and form, the six sense organs; from the six sense organs, contact; from contact, sensation; from sensation, desire; from desire, grasping; from grasping, existence; from existence, birth; and from birth, old age and death. These twelve links are identical with the (first) two noble truths, misery (duḥkha) and accumulation of misery (samudaya).

(The ends of the twelve links in the chain of existence), from that of ignorance to that of old age and death, are the doors of extinction and are identical with the (last) two noble truths, extinction of passions (nirodha) and the path (mārga). These are the (whole) method (Dharma) of contemplation by Pratyeka Buddhas.

Within the substance of Prajñā, there are no (such things as) the above two Dharmas, and if pushed to its extreme (profundity), it contains neither the Dharmas of Śrāvakas and Pratyeka Buddhas, nor the Dharma of Bodhisattvas. Why? Because Wisdom is the contemplating wisdom, which is the wisdom of the Six Pāramitās and the Heart that seeks (the subjective). Gain is the Buddha fruit, the object sought (the objective). However, in the Bodhisattva's self-cultivation, the most important thing is that wisdom which consists in converting living beings here below for the sole purpose of acquiring the Buddha fruit from above. As the realm of Buddha is like the void and has nothing to rely upon, if the quest of Buddhahood relies on a heart that seeks after gain, the result will not be a true one, for within the substance of the absolute void of Prajñā, there are fundamentally no such things (as wisdom and gain). Wherefore, the Buddha said: *There is no wisdom and also no gain.* (For actually) gainlessness is the real and ultimate gain.

Because of gainlessness, Bodhisattvas who rely on Prajñā-pāramitā, have no hindrance in their hearts, and since they have no hindrance, they have no fear, are free from contrary and delusive ideas and attain the Final Nirvāṇa.

As the Buddha fruit can (only) be obtained by means of gainlessness, in their self-cultivation Bodhisattvas should rely on Prajñā in their meditation. Since all things are fundamentally in the condition of Nirvāṇa, if the meditation is made while relying on discriminative feeling and thinking, the heart and objects will bind each other and can never be disentangled from the resultant avid graspings which are all hindrances. If the meditation is made by means of the true wisdom of Prajñā, the heart and objects being non-existent, all their contacts result only in liberation. Therefore, the Buddha said that if Prajñā is relied upon, the heart will have no hindrance. Because the heart has no hindrance, there can be no fear about birth and death. Therefore, the Buddha said that they had no fear. Since there is no fear about birth and death, there will also be no Buddha fruit to seek, for both the fear of birth and death and the quest of Nirvāṇa are contrary and delusive ideas.

The Sūtra of Complete Enlightenment (Yuan Chueh Ching) says: 'Sāṁsara and Nirvāṇa are likened to yesterday's dream.' However, without perfect contemplation by means of Prajñā, it is impossible to wipe out these contrary and delusive ideas. If they cannot be wiped out, it is impossible to attain ultimate Nirvāṇa.

'Nirvāṇa' means 'Calmness and the stopping (of all return to reincarnation)' or 'Perfect Calmness,' in other words the perfect elimination of the five fundamental conditions (of passion and delusion)[20] and eternal joy in the calmness and extinction (of misery). It was the Buddha's return to the Supreme Fruit. This means that only by discarding all feeling about saints and sinners, can one experience an entry into Nirvāṇa. A Bodhisattva's self-cultivation made by any other method would not be correct.

All Buddhas of the past, present and future obtained complete vision and perfect enlightenment (anuttara-samyak-saṁbodhi) by relying on Prajñā-pāramitā.

So we know that Prajñā-pāramitā is the great supernatural Mantra,[21] the great bright, unsurpassed and unequalled Mantra[21] which can truly and without fail wipe out all sufferings.

Not only did Bodhisattvas practise according to Prajñā, but also all Buddhas of the three periods exercised it to obtain the fruit of utmost right and perfect enlightenment (anuttara-samyak-saṁbodhi). Therefore, the Buddha said that all Buddhas of the three periods relied on Prajñā-pāramitā to obtain anuttara-samyak-saṁbodhi which means: *a* (*n*), not; *uttara*, surpassed; *samyak*, universally correct, and *saṁbodhi*, perfect enlightenment. It is the final term for the Buddha fruit.

All this shows that Prajñā-pāramitā can drive away the demon of distress (kleśa) in the world (saṁsāra) hence the great supernatural Mantra. As it can break up the darkness of ignorance, the cause of birth and death, it is called the great bright Mantra. Since there is no mundane and supramundane Dharma which can surpass it, it is called the unsurpassable Mantra. As Prajñā enables all Buddha mothers to produce all boundless merits and since no mundane and supramundane thing can be equal to it, whereas it is equal to all these, it is called the unequalled Mantra.

What is called Mantra is not a different and separate thing but just this Prajñā. It has already been called Prajñā, why is it also called Mantra? This is only to show the speed of its supernatural efficacy, like a secret order in the army which can assure victory if it is silently executed. Prajñā can break up the army of demons in the world (saṁsāra), and is likened to nectar (amṛta) which enables the drinker to obtain immortality. Those who taste Prajñā can dispel the greatest disaster caused by birth and death. Therefore, the Buddha said: *It can eliminate all sufferings.* When He said that it is true and without fail, He meant that the Buddha's words are not deceitful and that worldly men should harbour no suspicion about it and should resolve to practise it accordingly.

Therefore, He uttered the Prajñā-pāramitā mantra which reads:

As Prajñā really has the power of eliminating sufferings and bringing bliss, the Mantra was taught so that living beings could hold it in silence in order to obtain the power.

Gate, gate, pāragate, pārasaṁgate Bodhi Svāhā![22]

This is Sanskrit. Before the Mantra was taught, Prajñā had been taught exoterically, and now it was expounded esoterically. Here there is no room for thinking and interpreting, but the silent repetition of the

Mantra which ensures speedy efficacy made possible by the inconceivable power through the discarding of all feeling and elimination of all interpretation. This Prajñā which makes possible this speedy achievement is the light of the heart which every man possesses, and is realized by all Buddhas for their supernatural powers and wonderful deeds. Living beings who are deluded about it, use it for creating trouble (kleśa) by their wrong thinking. Although they use it daily, they are not aware of it. Thus ignorant of their own fundamental reality, they go on enduring uselessly all kinds of suffering. Is it not a pity? If they can be instantaneously awakened to their own selves, they will immediately turn the light inwards on themselves. In a moment's thought, by means of their accordant self-cultivation, all barriers of feeling in the world (saṁsāra) will be broken as the light of a lamp illumines a room where darkness has existed for a thousand years. Therefore, there is no need to have recourse to any other method.

If in our determination to get out of Saṁsāra we do not use Prajñā, there will be no other means. For this reason it is said that in the middle of the ocean of sufferings, Prajñā is the ferry and in the darkness of ignorance Prajñā is the light.

Worldly men are treading a dangerous path and are drifting about in a bitter ocean, but they are still not willing to look for Prajñā. Really their intentions cannot be guessed! Prajñā is like a (sharp) sword that cuts all things which touch it so sharply that they do not know they are cut. Who but sages and saints can make use of it? Certainly not the ignorant.

NOTES

1 Saṁsāra: The world of birth and death; rebirth and a second death; life and death.
2 The waves of particularized discernment.
3 Karmic: adjective derived from karma: deeds and effects in relation to forms of transmigration.
4 Nirvāṇa: extinction or end of all return to reincarnation with its concomitant suffering, and entry into the transcendental realm of true permanence, bliss, personality and purity.
5 The five skandhas, or aggregates. The components of an intelligent being, especially a human being, are:
(1) Rūpa: form, matter, the physical form related to the five sense organs;
(2) Vedanā: reception, sensation, feeling, the functioning of mind and senses in connection with affairs and things;
(3) Sañjñā: conception or discerning; the functioning of mind in discerning.
(4) Saṁskāra: functioning of mind in its process regarding like and dislike, good and evil, etc.; discrimination.
(5) Vijñāna: mental faculty in regard to perception and cognition, discriminative of affairs and things. Consciousness.
6 The four elements: earth, water, fire and air.
7 Śūnya: void, empty, vacuity, non-existent.
8 Ucchedadarśana: the view that death ends life, in contrast with the view that personality is permanent—both views being heterodox; the heretics' view of world extinction and end of causation.
9 Śrāvaka: a hearer, disciple of Buddha who understands the four dogmas, rids himself of the unreality of the phenomenal, and enters the incomplete Nirvāṇa.
10 Pratyeka Buddha: one who lives apart from others and attains enlightenment alone, or for himself, in contrast with the altruism of the Bodhisattva principle.
11 A quotation from Confucius. Master Han Shan used it to teach his followers who were all Confucian.
12 Triple world: world of desire, world of form and formless world.
13 The four kinds of birth: from eggs, from wombs, from humidity and by transformation.
14 Dignity in walking, standing, sitting and lying.

15 Quotation from the Śūraṅgama Sutra; excerpt from Mañjuśrī's instruction given to Ānanda by order and in the presence of the Buddha.

16 The eighteen dhātus: realms of sense, i.e. the six organs, their objects or conditions and their perceptions.

17 The twelve nidānas, or links in the chain of existence, are:
(1) Avidyā: ignorance, or unenlightenment;
(2) Saṁskāra: action, activity, conception, dispositions;
(3) Vijñāna: consciousness;
(4) Nāmarūpa: name and form;
(5) Ṣaḍāyatana: the six sense organs, i.e. eye, ear, nose, tongue, body and mind;
(6) Sparśa: contact, touch;
(7) Vedanā: sensation, feeling;
(8) Tṛṣṇā: thirst, desire, craving;
(9) Upādāna: laying hold of, grasping;
(10) Bhāva: being, existing;
(11) Jāti: birth;
(12) Jarāmaraṇa: old age, death.

18 The twelve nidānas and their ends: from ignorance and the end of ignorance to old age/death and end of old age/death, are twelve pairs of opposites which are non-existent and have no room in the absolute Prajñā. These pairs of extremes should be wiped out before enlightenment can be attained.

19 The Four Noble Truths, or dogmas, the primary and fundamental doctrines of the Buddha, said to approximate to the form of medical diagnosis, are:
(1) Duḥkha: misery, being a necessary attribute of sentient existence;
(2) Samudaya: accumulation of misery caused by passions;
(3) Nirodha: extinction of passion, being possible;
(4) Mārga: doctrine of the Path leading to extinction of passions.

20 The five fundamental conditions of passion and delusion are:
(1) wrong views which are common to the Triloka, or triple world;
(2) clinging or attachment, in the desire realm;
(3) clinging or attachment, in the form realm;
(4) clinging or attachment, in the formless realm which is still mortal;
(5) the state of unenlightenment or ignorance in the Triloka which is the root-cause of all distressful delusions.

21 Mantra, or Dhāraṇi: an incantation, spell, oath. Mystical formulae employed in Yoga.

22 Indian masters who came to China where they translated Sanskrit

sūtras into Chinese, did not give the meaning of mantras. The above mantra means:

> 'O Wisdom which has gone, gone, gone to the other shore, gone beyond the other shore—Svāhā!'

As '*this shore*' and '*the other shore*' are two extremes or opposites, this pair of extremes is wiped out by the last part of the mantra, '*Gone beyond the other shore*' which exposes the absolute condition of Prajñā.

CHINESE APPENDIX
OF PERSONS, PLACES AND TERMS

	Chinese transliteration	*Japanese transliteration*
禪	Ch'an	Zen
荆溪湛然	Chan Jan (of) Ching Ch'i	Tanzen (of) Keikei
趙州從諗	Chao Chou, Ts'ung Shen (of)	Jōshū, Jūshin (of)
照顧話頭	Chao Ku Hua T'ou	Shōko Watō
真言宗	Chen Yen Tsung	Shingonshū
夾山善會	Chia Shan, Shan Hui (of)	Kyōsan, Zen-e (of)
香嚴智閑	Chi Hsien (of) Hsiang Yen	Kyōgen (of) Chikan
智顗智者	Chih I (alias) Chih Che	Chigi (alias) Chisha
指月錄	Chih Yueh Lu	Shigetsuroku
青龍疏鈔	Ch'ing Lung Shu Ch'ao (commentary)	Seiryūshōshō
景德傳燈錄	Ching Te Ch'uan Teng Lu	Keitoku Dentōroku
居士傳	Ch'u Shih Ch'uan	Kojiden
金華俱胝	Chu Ti (of) Chin Hua	Gutei (of) Kinka
中峯廣錄	Chung Feng Kuang Lu	Chūhō Kōroku
大梅法常	Fa Ch'ang (of) Ta Mei	Hōjō (of) Daibai
法相宗	Fa Hsiang Tsung	Hossōshu
法華	Fa Hua	Hōkke
法眼	Fa Yen (Sect)	Hōgen

	Chinese transliteration	*Japanese transliteration*
傅大士	Fu Ta Shih	Fudaishi
寒山	Han Shan (Cold Mountain)	Kanzan
憨山	Han Shan (Silly Mountain	Kansan
青原行思	Hsing Szu (of) Ch'ing Yuan	Seigen (of) Gyōshi
虚雲	Hsu Yun	Kyoun
玄奘	Hsuan Tsang	Genjō
雪峯義存	Hsueh Feng, I Ts'uan (of)	Seppō Gizon (of)
話頭	Hua T'ou	Watō
話尾	Hua Wei	Wabi
南嶽懷讓	Huai Jang (of) Nan Yo	Ejō (of) Nangaku
黄龍普覺	Huang Lung, P'u Chueh (of)	Ōryō, Fukaku (of)
黄梅	Huang Mei	Ōbai
黄檗希運	Huang Po, Hsi Yun (of)	Ōbaku, Kiun (of)
瑯琊慧覺	Hui Chueh (of) Lang Yeh	Ekaku (of) Rōya
南陽慧忠	Hui Chung (of) Nan Yang	Echu (of) Nanyō
慧可	Hui K'o	Eka
惠能	Hui Neng	Enō
石鞏慧藏	Hui Ts'ang (of) Shih Kung	Ezō (of) Sekikyō
南嶽慧思	Hui Ssu (of) Nan Yo	Eshi (of) Nangaku
天台慧文	Hui Wen (of) T'ien T'ai	Emon (of) Tendai
慧遠	Hui Yuan	Eon

	Chinese transliteration	*Japanese transliteration*
一行	I Hsing	Ichigyō
高僧傳	Kao Seng Ch'uan	Kōsōden
古尊宿語錄	Ku Tsun Su Yu Lu	Kosonshuku Goroku
古巖	Ku Yen	Kogan
灌溪志閑	Kuan Ch'i, Chih Hsien (of)	Kankei, Shikan (of)
觀本	Kuan Pen	Kambon
章安灌頂	Kuan Ting (of) Chang An	Kanjō (of) Shōan
溈山靈祐	Kuei Shan, Lin Yu (of)	Isan, Reiyu (of)
溈仰宗	Kuei Yang Tsung (Sect)	Ikyōshū
公案	Kung An	Kōan
楞嚴經	Leng Yen Ching	Ryōgonkyō
梁武帝	Liang Wu Ti	Ryōbutei
雲棲蓮池	Lien Ch'ih (alias) Yun Hsi	Unsei (alias) Renchi
臨濟義玄	Lin Chi, I Hsuan (of)	Rinzai, Gigen (of)
靈照	Ling Chao	Reishō
呂洞賓	Lu Tung Ping	Ryotōhin
龍潭崇信	Lung T'an, Ch'ung Hsin (of)	Ryōtan Soshin (of)
馬祖道一	Ma Tsu (alias) Tao I	Baso (alias) Dōitsu
末山了然	Mo Shan, Liao Jan (of)	Massan, Ryōnen (of)
南泉普願	Nan Chuan, P'u Yuan (of)	Nansen, Fugan (of)
百丈懷海	Pai Chang, Huai Hai (of)	Hyakujō, Ekai (of)

	Chinese transliteration	*Japanese transliteration*
龐蘊道玄	P'ang Yun (alias) Tao Hsuan	Rōun (alias) Dōgen
寶林寺	Pao Lin (monastery)	Hōrinji
彭祖	Peng Tsu	Hōso
普陀	P'u T'o	Fuda
神秀	Shen Hsiu	Jinshū
神讚	Shen Tsan	Shinsan
石頭希遷	Shih T'ou, Hsi Ch'ien (of)	Sekitō, Kisen (of)
達觀	Ta Kuan	Takkan
丹霞天然	Tan Hsia, T'ien Jan (of)	Tanka, Tennen (of)
天台道邃	Tao Sui (of) T'ien T'ai	Dōsui (of) Tendai
德清	Te Ch'ing (Han Shan and Hsu Yun)	Tokusei
華亭德誠	Teh Ch'eng (of) Hua Ting	Katei (of) Tokusei
德韶	Teh Shao	Tokushō
德山宣鑒	Teh Shan, Hsuan Chien (of)	Tokusan, Senkan (of)
天慧徹祖	T'ien Hui Ch'e (ancestor)	Ten-etetsu
天宮	T'ien Kung	Tengu
杭州天龍	T'ien Lung (of) Hang Chou	Tenryū (of) Kōshū
天台宗	T'ien T'ai Tsung (school)	Tendaishū
曹溪	Ts'ao Ch'i	Sōkei
左溪	Tso Ch'i	Sakei
紫陽真人	Tzu Yang (Taoist)	Shiyō

	Chinese transliteration	*Japanese transliteration*
韋陀	Wei To	Ida
文殊	Wen Shu	Monju
無	Wu (no, not)	Mu
悞	Wu	Satori
無著文喜	Wu Chu (alias) Wen Hsi	Mujaku (alias) Monki
五台山	Wu T'ai Shan	Godaisan
五燈會元	Wu Teng Hui Yuan	Gotō Egen
無為	Wu Wei	Mu
仰山慧寂	Yang Shan, Hui Chi (of)	Kyōzan, Ejaku (of)
演徹	Yen Ch'e	Entetsu
鹽官齊安	Yen Kuan, Chi An (of)	Enkan, Saian (of)
永明延壽	Yen Shou (of) Yung Ming	Enjū (of) Yōmyō
巖頭全豁	Yen T'ou, Ch'uan Huo (of)	Ganjō, Zenkatsu (of)
藥山惟儼	Yo Shan, Wei Yen (of)	Yakuzan, Igen (of)
御選語錄	Yu Hsuan Yu Lu	Gosen Goroku
高峯原妙	Yuan Miao (of) Kao Feng	Gemmyō (of) Kōhō
雲門文偃	Yun Men, Wen Yen (of)	Ummon, Bunen (of)
雍正	Yung Cheng	Yōsei
永嘉玄覺	Yung Chia, Hsuan Chueh (of)	Yoka, Genkaku (of)
有為	Yu Wei	Ui

Japanese transliteration by Dr. Carmen Blacker.

GLOSSARY OF CHINESE AND SANSKRIT NAMES, TERMS AND PLACES

ADBHUTA-DHARMA: Miracles; one of the twelve divisions of the Mahāyāna canon.

ĀGAMAS: A collection of Hīnayāna doctrines. The Four Āgamas are: Dīrghāgama, or 'Long' treatises, Madhyamāgama, or 'Middle' treatises, Saṁyuktāgama, or 'Miscellaneous' treatises and Ekottarāgama, or 'Numerical' treatises.

ĀGANTU-KLÉSA: Foreign atom, or intruding element, which enters the mind and causes distress and delusion.

AJĀTAŚATRU: A king of Magadha, who killed his father to ascend the throne. At first inimical to the Buddha, later he was converted and became noted for liberality.

ĀJÑĀTA-KAUṆḌINYA: A prince of Magadha, first disciple of the Buddha.

AKANIṢṬHA: The highest heaven of the form-realm.

ALAKṢAṆA: Without form, appearance, aspects, marks and characteristics.

ĀLAYA-VIJÑĀNA: Basic or store consciousness; the last of the eight consciousnesses, usually called the eighth consciousness.

AMITĀBHA-BUDDHA: Buddha of boundless light of the Western Pure Land, with Avalokiteśvara Bodhisattva on his left and Mahāsthāmaprāpta Bodhisattva on his right.

AMOGHAVAJRA: The famous head of the Yogācāra school in China (True Word Sect). A Singhalese of Northern brahmanic descent, he came at the age of fifteen to China where in 718 he became a disciple of Vajrabodhi. Died in 774 in his seventieth year.

AMṚTA: Ambrosial drink which gives immortality.

ANĀGĀMIN: A no-coming or non-returning arhat who will not be reborn, the third stage of the path.

ĀNANDA: Young brother of Devadatta and cousin of the Buddha. He was noted as the most learned disciple of the Buddha, and famed for hearing and remembering His teaching. He was the compiler of sūtras and second Patriarch of the Ch'an Sect.

ANĀSRAVA: No leak; outside the passion-stream as contrasted with Āsrava, 'leaking' or worldly cause.

ANUBODHI: Abbreviation for Anuttara-samyak-saṁbodhi.

ANUTTARA-SAMYAK-SAṀBODHI: Unexcelled complete enlightenment, an attribute of every Buddha. Translated into Chinese: the highest, correct and complete, or universal knowledge or awareness, the perfect wisdom of a Buddha, Omniscience.

APARAGO-DĀNĪYA: One of the four inhabited continents, west of the central Mount Sumeru.

ARHAT: A saintly man, the highest type or ideal saint in Hīnayāna in contrast with a Bodhisattva as the saint in Mahāyāna.

ĀRYA: Saints who are noted for wisdom or insight and transcend the Bhadra in wisdom and character. (See Bhadra.)

AŚAIKṢA: No longer learning, beyond study, the state of arhatship, the fourth of the śrāvaka stages; the preceding three stages requiring study. When an arhat is free from all illusions, he has nothing more to study.

ASAṀSKṚTA: Wu wei in Chinese, anything not subject to cause, condition or dependence; out of time, eternal, inactive, transcendental.

ASAṄKHYA: Innumerable kalpas or aeons.

ASIPATTRA HELL: The hell of swords, or sword-leaf-trees hell, one of the sixteen hells.

ĀSRAVA: Worldly or 'leaking' cause; inside the passion-stream as contrasted with anāsrava, outside the passion-stream.

ASURA: Titanic demons, enemies of the gods, with whom, especially Indra, they wage constant war.

AŚVAGHOṢA: A Brahmin converted to Buddhism; settled at Benares and became the twelfth Patriarch of the Ch'an Sect. Author of 'The Awakening of Faith'.

ĀTMAGRĀHA: Holding to the concept of the ego.

AVADĀNA: Parables, metaphors, stories, illustrations; one of the twelve divisions of the Mahāyāna canon.

AVALOKITEŚVARA: Goddess of Mercy in China, so called because of his appearing as a benevolent lady. He attained enlightenment by means of the faculty of hearing. (See Śūraṅgama Sūtra.)

AVATAṀSAKA SŪTRA: The first long sūtra expounded by the Buddha after His enlightenment.

AVIDYĀ: Ignorance, or unenlightenment; the first of the twelve links in the chain of existence.

AVĪCI: The last and deepest of the eight hells, where sinners suffer, die and are instantly reborn to suffer without interruption.

AVYĀKṚTA OR AVYĀKHYĀTA: Unrecordable, either as good or bad; neutral, neither good nor bad, things that are innocent and cannot be classified under moral categories.

BHADRA: Those who are noted for goodness but are still of ordinary human standard. (See ārya.)

BHĀVA: Being, existing; the tenth of the twelve links in the chain of existence. Bhāva and abhāva are 'existence' and 'non-existence'.

BHIKṢU: A Buddhist monk.

BHIKṢUṆĪ: A Buddhist nun.

BHŪTATATHATĀ: Bhūta is substance, that which exists; tathatā is suchness, thusness, i.e. such is its nature. It means the real, thus always, or eternally so; i.e. reality as contrasted with unreality, or appearance, and the unchanging or immutable as contrasted with form and phenomena.

BODHI: Enlightenment.

BODHIDHARMA: The 28th Patriarch who came to China in 520 to teach Ch'an; he was the first Patriarch of China and died in 528.

BODHIMAṆḌALA: Truth-plot, holy site, place of enlightenment; the place where the Buddha attained enlightenment.

BODHISATTVA: A Mahāyānist seeking enlightenment to enlighten others; he is devoid of egoism and devoted to helping all living beings.

BRAHMALOKA: The eighteen heavens of the realm of form, divided into four dhyāna regions.

BUDDHA: The Enlightened One; the first of the triple gem, the second being Dharma and the third, Saṅgha.

BUDDHA-DHARMA: Doctrine of the Buddha.

CAKRAVARTĪ: A god over a universe; a world ruler.

CH'AN: Name of mind; Ch'an being name and mind being substance; wrongly interpreted as meditation, abstraction, or dhyāna in Sanskrit. (Jap. Zen.)

CHAN JAN OF CHING CH'I: Ninth Patriarch of the T'ien T'ai (Tendai) school.

CHAO CHOU: Master Ts'ung Shen of Chao Chou, successor of Nan Chuan and noted for his kung an 'Wu' (no, not). Died in 897 in his 120th year.

CHAO KU HUA T'OU: Take care of your hua t'ou; look into your mind.

CHEN YEN TSUNG: *see* True Word School.

CHIA SHAN: Eminent Ch'an master, disciple of the Boat Monk. Died in 881.

CHI HSIEN OF HSIANG YEN: Eminent Ch'an master, disciple of Kuei Shan. Died in 914 in his 96th year.

CHIH I (CHIH CHE): Fourth Patriarch of the T'ien T'ai (Tendai) School.

CHIH YUEH LU: Full title is 'Shui Yueh Chai Chih Yueh Lu', or 'Finger Pointing at the Moon', a collection of Ch'an texts, compiled in 1602. 10 vols.

CH'ING LUNG'S COMMENTARY: A Commentary on the Diamond Sūtra by Tao Yin of Ch'ing Lung monastery.

CHING TE CH'UAN TENG LU: The Transmission of the Lamp, a collection of Ch'an texts compiled in Ching Te reign (1004–1007). 14 vols.

CH'U SHIH CH'UAN: Stories of eminent upāsakas, a collection compiled in Ch'ien Lung reign (1770–75). 4 vols.

CHU TI OF CHIN HUA: Eminent Ch'an master, disciple of T'ien Lung in the 9th century.

CHUNG FENG KUANG LU: Sayings of Chung Feng, a collection of the sayings of state-master Chung Feng who was a disciple of master Yuan Miao of Kao Feng mountain. Died in 1337. 6 vols.

CLOTH-BAG MONK: In the Liang dynasty (907–21), there was an erratic monk who carried a cloth bag everywhere he went, hence his name of Cloth-bag Monk. Said to be an avatar of Maitreya.

CREEPERS: Unnecessary things which do not concern the real.

DĀNA: The first pāramitā; charity, almsgiving, i.e. of money, goods or doctrine.

DEVA: The highest incarnations of the six worlds of existence.

DEVADATTA: Cousin of the Buddha, of whom he was an enemy and rival.

DHĀRAṆĪ: See Mantra.

DHARMA: Law, truth, religion, thing, anything Buddhist. It connotes Buddhism as the perfect religion; it has the second place in the triratna or Triple Gem.

DHARMA-AGE: Number of summers or discipline years since the ordination of a monk or nun.

DHARMA-CAKRA: The Wheel of the Doctrine; Buddha truth which is able to crush all evil and all opposition, like Indra's wheel, and which rolls from man to man, place to place, age to age.

DHARMADHĀTU: Dharma realm; the unifying underlying spiritual reality, regarded as the ground or cause of all things, the absolute from which all proceeds.

DHARMA-DOOR: The doctrines of Buddha regarded as the door to enlightenment; a method; any school.

DHARMAKĀYA: Body in its essential nature, or that of Buddha as such. Only Buddhas can see it.

DHARMAKĀYA-BUDDHA: The Buddha in his essential body which is perceptible only to other Buddhas.

DHARMALAKṢAṆA: Fa Hsiang school (Jap. Hossō); established in China on the return of Hsuan Tsang, consequent on his translation of the Yogācārya works. Its aim is to understand the principle underlying the nature and characteristics of all things.

DHARMA-MASTER: A master of the Law who is qualified to explain and comment on the sūtras in the Dharma hall.

DHARMA-RĀJA: King of the Law, i.e. the Buddha.

DHARMATĀ: Dharma nature; the nature underlying all things, the Bhūtatathatā.

DHARMA VOIDNESS: The emptiness or unreality of things; the illusory nature of all things as being composed of elements and not possessing reality.

DHĀTU. THE EIGHTEEN DHĀTUS: Realms of sense, i.e. the six organs, their objects and their perceptions.

DHŪTA: An ascetic; a monk engaged in austerities.

DHYĀNA: Meditation, abstract contemplation.

DHYĀNA-PĀRAMITĀ: Method of attaining enlightenment by means of meditation or contemplation.

DHYĀNA-SAMĀDHI: The Ch'an's samādhi, or state of imperturbability reached in the successful practice of Ch'an.

DIAMOND-CUTTER OF DOUBTS: A Commentary on the Diamond Sūtra by Ch'an master Han Shan (1546–1623).

DIAMOND-PRAJÑĀ: Diamond wisdom, the wisdom inherent in man's nature which is indestructible, like a diamond.

DĪPAṀKARA BUDDHA: The twenty-fourth predecessor of Śākyamuni, who predicted the latter's attainment of Buddhahood.

DUḤKHA: Suffering, misery, being a necessary attribute of sentient existence; the first of the Four Noble Truths.

DUST-WHISK: A Chinese duster.

EGO AND DHARMA: Ego and things, the most subtle dualism which must be wiped out before enlightenment can be attained.

ELEMENTS. THE FOUR: Earth, water, fire and wind or air; the four basic elements constituting the physical body.

ENLIGHTENMENT. PROFOUND: Self-enlightenment to enlighten others, the 52nd stage in the enlightenment of a Bodhisattva.

ENLIGHTENMENT. UNIVERSAL: Omniscience, the 51st stage in the enlightenment of a Bodhisattva.

FA CH'ANG OF TA MEI MOUNTAIN: Dharma-successor of Ma Tsu and teacher of T'ien Lung. Died at the age of eighty-eight in the eighth century.

FA HSIANG TSUNG: See Dharmalakṣaṇa.

FA HUA: Sixth Patriarch of T'ien T'ai (Tendai) school.

FA YEN SECT: One of the five Ch'an sects of China (Jap. Hōgen Zen).

FOREIGN DUST: See guṇas.

FOUR INFINITE MINDS: Catvāri apramāṇāni, the four immeasurables, or universals: Kindness (maitrī), pity (karuṇā), joy (muditā) and indifference (upekṣā).

FOUR NOBLE TRUTHS: Catvāriārya-satyāni, the four dogmas which are: suffering (duḥkha), its cause (samudāya), its ending (nirodha) and the way thereto (mārga). They are the doctrines first preached by the Buddha to his five former ascetic companions, and those who accepted them were in the śrāvaka stage.

FU TA SHIH: An eniment Ch'an upāsaka (497–569).

FUNDAMENTAL FACE: The eternal self-nature.

GĀTHĀ: Poems or chants; one of the twelve divisions of the Mahāyāna canon.

GEYA: Metrical pieces; one of the twelve divisions of the Mahāyāna canon.

GHOSTS. HUNGRY: They inhabit the fifth of the six realms of existence.

GOLDEN GRAIN TATHĀGATA: A Buddha who appeared as upāsaka Vimalakīrti.

GREAT MIRROR WISDOM: Perfect all-reflecting Buddha-wisdom.

GUEST, HOST: The phenomenal and the fundamental.

GUṆA: Dust; small particles; molecules, atoms, exhalations; element or matter, which is considered as defilement; an active conditioned principle in nature, minute, subtle and defiling to pure mind; impurities. The six guṇas are the six sense-data: sight, sound, smell, taste, touch and dharma.

HAN SHAN: 'Cold Mountain', said to be an avatar of Mañjuśrī, appearing as a mad monk living in a cold grotto on T'ien T'ai mountain in Chen Kuan reign (627–649).

HAN SHAN: 'Silly Mountain', a name adopted by Ch'an master Te Ch'ing who was responsible for the revival of the Ch'an Sect in China in the Ming dynasty. Born in 1546 and died in 1623.

HEART SŪTRA. A STRAIGHT TALK ON: A Commentary on the Heart Sūtra by Han Shan (Silly Mountain).

HELL. The lowest of the six worlds of existence.

HETU: A cause.

HĪNAYĀNA: 'Small Vehicle', also called 'Half-word', preliminary teaching given by the Buddha to his disciples who were still not qualified for receiving His Mahāyāna doctrines, called 'Whole-word'.

HOST, GUEST: The fundamental and the phenomenal.

HSING SZU: Famous Ch'an master of Ch'ing Yuan mountain; Dharma-successor of the Sixth Patriarch and teacher of Hsi Ch'ien of Shih T'ou Rock. Died in 741.

HSU YUN: Master Hsu Yun, alias Te Ch'ing, was regarded as the right Dharma eye of the present generation. Born in 1840, died at Chen Ju monastery on Yun C'hu mountain in Kiangsi province in October, 1959.

HSUAN TSANG: A famous Chinese monk who went to India and translated seventy-five works (660–64).

HSUEH FENG: Master I Tsun of Hsueh Feng Peak, teacher of Yun Men. Died in 909 in his 87th year.

HUA T'OU: Literally, a word's or thought's head, ante-word or ante-thought; the mind before it is stirred by a thought. A technique devised by enlightened masters who taught their disciples to concentrate their attention on the mind for the purpose of stopping all thoughts to attain singleness of mind and thereby realize it for the perception of their self-nature.

HUA WEI: A term used by master Hsu Yun to explain the meaning of hua t'ou; hua wei is word's tail, the mind already disturbed by the discriminatory thought of hua t'ou.

HUAI JANG: A Dharma-successor of the Sixth Patriarch and teacher of Ma Tsu. Died in 744 in his 64th year.

HUANG LUNG: Ch'an master P'u Chueh of Huang Lung mountain. Died in 1069 in his 68th year.

HUANG MEI: The Fifth Patriarch of the Ch'an Sect of China.

HUANG PO: Master Hsi Yun of Huang Po mountain; Dharma successor of Pai Chang and teacher of Lin Chi (Rinzai). Died in Ta Chung reign (847–59).

HUI CHUEH OF LANG YEH: A Ch'an master in the Sung dynasty (960–1279).

HUI CHUNG OF NAN YANG: A famous Ch'an master, Dharma-successor of the Sixth Patriarch. Died in 776.

HUI K'O: The second Chinese Patriarch of the Ch'an Sect; Dharma-successor of Bodhidharma. Died at the end of the sixth century.

HUI NENG: The Sixth Chinese Patriarch of the Ch'an Sect. Died in 713 in his 76th year.

HUI TS'ANG OF SHIH KUNG: The hunter monk, an eminent Ch'an master, disciple of Ma Tsu. Died in the eighth century.

HUI SSU OF NAN YO: Third Patriarch of the T'ien T'ai (Tendai) school.

HUI WEN OF T'IEN T'AI: The second Patriarch of the T'ien T'ai (Tendai) school.

HUI YUAN: Founder of the Pure Land School in China in the Chin dynasty (317–419).

I HSING: An eminent Ch'an master who established the True Word School (Chen Yen Tsung) in China (672–717).

ITIVṚTTAKA: Narratives; one of the twelve divisions of the Mahāyāna canon.

JAMBUDVĪPA: One of the four inhabited continents, East of the central mount Sumeru; our world.

JARĀMARAṆA: Old age and death; the last of the twelve links in the chain of existence.

JĀTAKA: Stories of former lives of Buddha; one of the twelve divisions of the Mahāyāna canon.

JĀTI: Birth; the eleventh of the twelve links in the chain of existence.

JETAVANA PARK: A park near Śrāvastī, said to have been obtained from Prince Jetā by the elder Anāthapiṇḍada, in which monastic buildings were erected. It was the favourite resort of the Buddha.

JÑĀNABHAIṢAJYA: An Indian Tripiṭaka-master who planted a bodhi-tree by the side of the altar of Pao Lin monastery and predicted that the Sixth Patriarch would come there some 170 years later to expound the Supreme Vehicle.

KALIRĀJA: A king of Magadha noted for his violence; it is said that in a former incarnation he cut off the ears, nose and hands of the Buddha, who bore it unmoved.

KALPA: The period of time between the creation, destruction and recreation of a world or universe. Aeon.

KAO SENG CH'UAN: Stories of eminent monks, in four collections: Liang dynasty collection, 4 vols. (67–519), T'ang collection, 10 vols. (520–645), Sung collection, 8 vols. (up to 988) and Ming collection, 2 vols. (1127–1617).

KARMA: Moral action causing future retribution, and either good or evil transmigration.

KARMADĀNA: A duty-distributor, arranger of duties, second in command of a monastery.

KARUṆĀ: Pity, compassion; the second of the Four Immeasurables, consisting in saving living beings from suffering.

KAṢĀYA. THE FIVE: The five periods of impurity and turbidity: (1) the kalpa of decay, when it suffers deterioration and gives rise to the ensuing form; (2) deterioration of view, egoism, etc., arises; (3) the passions and delusions of desire, anger, stupidity, pride and doubt prevail; (4) in consequence human miseries increase and happiness decreases; (5) the span of human life is gradually reduced to ten years.

KLEŚA: Worry, anxiety, trouble, distress and whatever causes them.

KLIṢṬA-MANO-VIJÑĀNA: The seventh consciousness; it is the discriminating sense.

KṢAṆA: The shortest measure of time; 60 kṣaṇa equal one finger-snap, 90 a thought, 4,500 a minute.

KṢĀNTI: The third pāramitā, or patience, endurance in any circumstance.

KṢĀNTYṚṢI: A ṛṣi, also wrongly called immortal, who patiently suffered insult, i.e. Śākyamuni, in a former life, suffering mutilation to convert Kalirāja.

KṢITIGARBHA BODHISATTVA: Lit. Earth-store; his role is that of saviour of all creatures between the Nirvāṇa of Śākyamuni and the advent of Maitreya.

KU TSUN SU YU LU: 'The Sayings of Ancient Masters,' a collection of ten volumes compiled in the third year of Hsien Ch'un reign (1267).

KU YEN: Dharma-name of master Hsu Yun when he was ordained at Ku Shan monastery in 1859.

KUAN CH'I: Ch'an master Chih Hsien of Kuan Ch'i, Dharma-successor of Lin Chi and Mo Shan; died in 895.

KUAN PEN: A wealthy academician who left home and followed master Hsu Yun as his senior disciple.

KUAN TING OF CHANG AN: The Fifth Patriarch of the T'ien T'ai (Tendai) school.

KUBHĀNA: Kashmir.

KUEI SHAN: Ch'an master Ling Yu of Kuei Shan mountain; Dharma-successor of Pai Chang and teacher of Yang Shan. Co-founder of Kuei Yang Sect (Ikyō Zen). Died in 853 in his 83rd year.

KUEI YANG SECT: Jap. Ikyō Zen. A Ch'an Sect founded by Kuei Shan and his disciple Yang Shan; one of the five Ch'an Sects of China.

KUNG AN: Jap. Kōan; dossier, case-record, public laws and regulations enforced for settling disputes and maintaining law and order. Likewise, all instructions given by enlightened masters to their students are called kung an; or concurrent causes. The meaning of a kung an is irrevocable for it is as valid as the law.

LAKṢAṆA: Form, appearance, indication, sign, aspect and characteristic.

LENG YENG CHING: *see* Śūraṅgama Sūtra.

LIANG WU TI: An emperor of the Nan Liang dynasty (502–56).

LIEN CH'IH: Master Lien Ch'ih, alias Yun Hsi, a Ch'an master of the Ming dynasty who urged his disciples of low spirituality to repeat the Buddha's name. Died in 1615 at the age of 81.

LIN CHI: Master I Hsuan of Lin Chi (Jap. Rinzai), disciple of Huang Po and founder of the Lin Chi Sect, one of the five Ch'an sects of China. Died in 867.

LING CHAO: Daughter of upāsaka P'ang Yun and an adept in the Ch'an Secet. Died in Chen Yuan reign (785–804).

LOTUS SŪTRA: Saddharma-puṇḍarīka-sūtra, expounded by the Buddha, before the Mahāparinirvāṇa-sūtra in the last of the five periods of His teaching.

LOTUS TREASURY: Lotus store, or Lotus world, the Pure Land of all Buddhas in their Sambhogakāyas or Reward bodies.

LU TUNG PING: Alias Shun Yang, one in the famous group of Eight Immortals of the T'ang dynasty (ninth century).

LUNG T'AN: Master Ch'ung Hsin of Lung T'an (Dragon Pond) was Dharma-successor of Tao Wu of T'ien Huang monastery and master of Te Shan (known as Diamond Chāu). Died in the ninth century.

MĀDHYAMIKA ŚASTRA: Work of Nāgārjuna whose doctrine opposes the rigid categories of exsitence and non-existence, in the interests of a middle way.

MAHĀBRAHMĀ DEVARĀJA: King of the eighteen Brahmalokas. Mahābrahman is regarded as ruler over all the heavens of form, these heavens being of threefold form: Brahmā (lord) Brahma-purohitas (ministers) and Brahma-pāriśadyas (people). Mahābrahman vowed to protect the Buddha-Dharma.

MAHĀKĀŚYAPA: A Brahmin of Magadha, disciple of the Buddha, to whom was handed down the Mind-Dharma, outside of Scriptures; the first Patriarch of the Ch'an Sect; accredited with presiding over the first synod and with supervising the first compilation of the Buddha's sermons.

MAHĀPARINIRVĀṆA SŪTRA: A sūtra expounded by the Buddha just before His Nirvāṇa. 10 vols.

MAHĀPRAJÑĀPĀRAMITĀ SŪTRA: Said to have been expounded by the Buddha in four places at sixteen assemblies. It consists of 600 rolls (chuan) bound in 120 volumes, as translated by Hsuan Tsang and is the fundamental work of the Mahāyāna on Wisdom, which is the sixth pāramitā.

MAHĀSATTVA: A perfect Bodhisattva, greater than any other being except a Buddha.

MAHĀYĀNA: The Great Vehicle which indicates Universalism, or Salvation for all, for all are Buddhas and will attain enlightenment.

MAITREYA: The Buddhist Messiah, or next Buddha, now in the Tuṣita heaven, who is to come 5,000 years after the Nirvāṇa of Śākyamuni Buddha.

MAITRĪ: Kindness; the first of the Four Immeasurables, that of bestowing happiness.

MAÑJUŚRĪ: A Bodhisattva who is the symbol of Wisdom and is placed on the Buddha's left with Samantabhadra on the right. His Bodhimaṇḍala is on the Five-Peaked mountain. (*See* Wu T'ai.)

MANO-VIJÑĀNA: The faculty of mind, usually called the sixth consciousness.

MANTRA: Or Dhāraṇī, an incantation, spell, oath; mystical formulae employed in Yoga.

MĀRA: A demon.

MĀRGA: The Path leading to the extinction of suffering; the last of the Four Noble Truths.

MA TSU: Ma Tsu, alias Tao I, of Kiangsi, was Dharma successor of Huai Jang of Nan Yo mountain and teacher of Pai Chang. Died in 788.

MAUDGALAPUTRA: Also called Mahā-maudgalyāyana, one of the ten chief disciples of the Buddha, specially noted for his miraculous powers.

MIND DHARMA: Doctrine of the mind.

MIND LAMP: The lamp of the mind; inner light, wisdom.

MIND NATURE: Unchanging mind-corpus, or fundamental pure mind, the Tathāgata-garbha.

MO SHAN: Eminent Ch'an nun, disciple of Ta Yu and teacher of Kuan Ch'i (ninth century).

MṚGADĀVA PARK: A famous park north-east of Vārānaśī, a favourite resort of the Buddha.

MUDITĀ: Joy on seeing others rescued from suffering; the third of the Four Immeasurables.

NĀGĀRJUNA: The Fourteenth Patriarch of the Ch'an Sect; he founded the Mādhyamika or Middle school. Is regarded as the First Patriarch of the T'ien T'ai (Tendai) school.

NAIVASAṀJÑĀNĀSAṀJÑĀNĀYATANA: Living beings who are neither thoughtful nor thoughtless; the heaven or place where there is neither thinking nor not-thinking; the fourth of the four immaterial heavens, known as Akaniṣṭha, the highest heaven of form.

NĀMARŪPA: The fourth of the twelve links in the chain of existence; name and form.

NAN CHUAN: Ch'an master P'u Yuan of Nan Chuan mountain; Dharma-successor of Ma Tsu. Died in 834 at the age of 87.

NATURE-OCEAN: The ocean of the Bhūtatathatā, the all-containing, immaterial nature of the Dharma-kāya.

NAYUTA: A numeral, 100,000 or one million, or ten million.

NIDĀNA: Causes or links in the chain of existence. Also sūtras written by request or in answer to a query, because certain precepts were violated and because of certain events; one of the twelve divisions of the Mahāyāna canon.

NIRMĀṆAKĀYA: Transformation body of a Buddha, that of power to transform himself at will into any form for the omnipresent salvation of those needing Him. It is perceptible to men.

NIRODHA: Extinction of passion; the third of the Four Noble Truths.

NIRVĀṆA: Complete extinction of individual existence; cessation of rebirth and entry into bliss.

NIRVĀṆA, INCOMPLETE: Nirvāṇa, of Hīnayāna.

NIRVAṆA, PERFECT: Final Nirvāṇa, is transcendental or the absolute, as expounded by Mahāyāna.

NIṢĪDANA: A cloth for sitting on, which a monk carries in a pocket inside his large sleeve. Translated as cloth-rug.

NO-BIRTH, LAW OF: Patience or endurance leading to the personal experiencing of the uncreate, or immortality, i.e. the absolute which is beyond birth and death; the patience or endurance being required for subduing the wandering mind.

PAI CHANG: Ch'an master Huai Hai (Ta Chih) of Pai Chang mountain; successor of Ma Tsu and master of Kuei Shan and Huang Po. Died in 814.

PAÑCA KLEŚA: The five stupid vices: desire, anger or resentment, stupidity or foolishness, arrogance and doubt.

P'ANG YUN: (Tao Hsuan). An eminent upāsaka who at the beginning of the Chen Yuan reign (785–804) called on Shih T'ou and was awakened to the truth.

Later he called on Ma Tsu and attained instantaneous enlightenment. His family consisting of a wife, a son and a daughter, realized the absolute reality.

PAO LIN MONASTERY: 'Precious Wood' monastery built by the Indian master Guṇabhadra in the fifth century in anticipation of the advent of the Sixth Patriarch who was born in 638.

PĀRAMITĀS, SIX: The six methods of attaining enlightenment: dāna (charity), śīla (discipline), kṣānti (patience or endurance), vīrya (zeal and progress), dhyāna (meditation) and prajñā (wisdom).

PASSIONLESS SAMĀDHI: A state of Samādhi, or imperturbability, in which there is absence of debate, disputation, or distinction of self and other.

PENG TSU: The Methuselah of China, said to have lived 800 years.

PERFECTING WISDOM: The perfecting wisdom of Amoghasiddhi.

POISONS, THE THREE: Concupiscence or desire, anger or resentment and ignorance or stupidity.

PRAJÑĀ: Fundamental wisdom which is inherent in every man.

PRAJÑĀ-PĀRAMITĀ-HṚDAYA SŪTRA: The Heart Sūtra; a condensation in a short sūtra of 268 Chinese characters, of the Buddha's teaching of wisdom sūtras during a period of twenty-two years.

PRATIRŪPAKA: Symbol or image period, to begin five hundred years after the Nirvāṇa of the Buddha.

PRATYEKA BUDDHA: One who lives apart from others and attains enlightenment alone, or for himself, in contrast with the altruism of the Bodhisattva principle.

PROFOUND OBSERVING WISDOM: The profound observing wisdom of Amitābha Buddha.

P'U T'O: A sacred island, off Ningpo, where the Bodhimaṇḍala, or holy site, of Avalokitésvara Bodhisattva is situated; it is said that devotees occasionally have a glimpse of him in Fan Yin grotto.

PURE LAND: Sukhāvatī, the Paradise of the West, presided over by Amitābha Buddha.

PŪRVAVIDEHA: One of the four inhabited continents, east of Mount Sumeru.

ṚṢI: An immortal, The Śūraṅgama Sūtra lists ten kinds of Ṛṣis.

RŪPA: The first aggregate (skandha); form, matter, the physical form related to the five sense organs.

RŪPAKĀYA: Physical body.

ṢAḌĀYATANA: The six sense-organs, i.e. eye, ear, nose, tongue, body and mind; the fifth of the twelve links in the chain of existence.

SAHĀ: Our world of birth and death.

ŚAIKṢA: Need of study; in Hīnayāna those in the first three śrāvaka stages, require study before attaining the fourth stage, or Arhatship.

SAKṚDĀGĀMIN: Once more to come, or be born; the second stage of the Path involving only one rebirth.

ŚĀKYAMUNI BUDDHA: The saint of the Śākya clan; the human Buddha.

SAMĀDHI: Internal state of imperturbability, exempt from all external sensation.

SAMANTABHADRA: A Bodhisattva, symbol of the fundamental law, dhyāna and the practice of all Buddhas. He is the right-hand assistant of the Buddha and Mañjuśrī is His left-hand assistant. His region is in the East. Mount O Mei in Szechwan, China, is his bodhimaṇḍala, and devotees go there to see myriad Buddha lamps in the sky at night.

SAMBHOGA-KĀYA: Reward body of a Buddha, that of bliss or enjoyment of the fruits of his past saving labours. It is perceptible to Bodhisattvas only.

SAṂSĀRA: The realm of birth and death.

SAṂSKṚTA: The fourth aggregate (skandha); functioning of mind in its process regarding like and dislike, good and evil, etc.; discrimination. Also the second of the twelve links in the chain of existence.

SAṂSKṚTA: Yu wei in Chinese; active, creative, productive, functioning, causative, phenomenal, the process resulting from the law of karma.

SAMUDAYA: Accumulation of misery caused by passions; the second of the Four Noble Truths.

SAṂYUKTĀGAMA: One of the Four Āgamas, a collection of doctrines, general name for the Hīnayāna Scriptures, the other three being: Dīrghāgama, Mādhyamāgama and Ekottara-āgama.

SAṄGHA: The Buddhist Order, the last of the Triple Gem.

SAṄGHĀRĀMA: A Buddhist temple, monastery.

SAÑJÑĀ: The third aggregate (skandha); conception or discerning; the functioning of mind in discerning.

ŚĀRIPUTRA: A disciple of the Buddha, noted for his wisdom.

SARVAJÑA: All wisdom, Buddha wisdom, perfect knowledge, omniscience.

ŚĀSTRA: Treatises; one of the three divisions of the Tripiṭaka.

SEALING OF MIND: Mental impression, intüitive certainty; the mind is the Buddha-mind in all, which can seal or assure the truth; the term indicates the intuitive method of the Ch'an Sect which is independent of the spoken or written word.

SELF-NATURE: The self-substance, or unchanging character.

SHEN HSIU: A disciple of the Fifth Patriarch, who lost the sixth patriarchate to Hui Neng (*See* Altar-sūtra of the Sixth Patriarch).

SHEN TSAN: Dharma successor of Pai Chang: (middle of ninth century).

SHIH T'OU: Ch'an master Hsi Ch'ien of Shih T'ou Peak, Dharma successor of Hsing Szu of Ch'ing Yuan, and master of Yo Shan and Tao Wu. Died in 791 at the age of 91.

ŚĪLA: Precept, prohibition, command, discipline, rule, morality; the second pāramitā.

SIXTH PATRIARCH'S DHARMA TREASURE ALTAR SŪTRA: Sūtra expounded by the Sixth Patriarch Hui Neng.

SKANDHAS, THE FIVE: Pañcaskandha in Sanskrit, the five aggregates: form, feeling, ideation, reaction and consciousness.

SONG OF ENLIGHTENMENT: A song composed by Yung Chia, and later translated into Sanskrit in India.

SONG OF THE BOARD-BEARER: A song composed by Ch'an master Han Shan (Silly Mountain) who urged his disciples not to abide in the stillness of mind but to take a step forward to realize their minds for perceiving their self-nature.

SPARŚA: Contact, touch; the sixth of the twelve links in the chain of existence.

ŚRĀVAKA: A hearer, disciple of Buddha who understands the Four Noble Truths, rids himself of the unreality of the phenomenal and enters the incomplete Nirvāṇa.

ŚRAMAṆA: A Buddhist monk.

ŚRĀVASTĪ: 'The Famous City', near which was Jetavana park, the favourite resort of the Buddha.

ŚROTA-ĀPANNA: One who has entered the stream of holy living, the first stage of the path.

STŪPA: A pagoda, kind of pyramidal tower for the bones, or remains of a dead monk, or for other sacred relics.

SUBHADRA: A Brahmin 120 years old, who was the last convert of the Buddha.

SUBHŪTI: A senior disciple of the Buddha.

SUBJECT, OBJECT: The two terms indicate active and passive ideas, e.g. ability to transform, or transformable, and the object that is transformed.

ŚŪNYA: Void, empty, non-existent.

SUPREME VEHICLE: The Supreme Reality as taught by the Buddha.

ŚŪRAṄGAMA SŪTRA: Leng Yen Ching, a sūtra translated by Paramiti in 705, in which the Buddha revealed the causes of illusion leading to the creation of all worlds of existence and the methods of getting out of them.

SŪTRA: The Buddha's sermons; one of the twelve divisions of the Mahāyāna canon.

TA KUAN: Also called Ārya Tzu Pe, a famous Ch'an master and intimate friend of Han Shan with whom he sat cross-legged face to face for forty days and nights without sleeping. His works were compiled in a collection entitled 'The Works of Tzu Pe' (Tzu Pe Lao Jen Chi), 10 vols. (1543–1604).

TAN HSIA: A Dharma successor of Shih T'ou; became famous for burning a wooden statue of Buddha to enlighten a monk. Died in 824 at the age of 86.

TAO SUI:Tenth Patriarch of the T'ien T'ai (Tendai) school; he is considered a patriarch in Japan because he was the teacher of Dengyo Daishi who brought the Tendai system to that country in the ninth century.

TATHĀGATA: He who came as did all Buddhas; who took the absolute way of cause and effect, and attained to perfect wisdom; one of the highest titles of a Buddha.

TE CH'ING: Dharma name of Han Shan (1546–1623).

TE CH'ING: Another Dharma alias of master Hsu Yun when he was ordained at Ku Shan monastery in 1859.

TEH CH'ENG OF HUA TING: Dharma successor of Yo Shan and teacher of Chia Shan; called the Boat monk—ninth century.

TEH SHAO: State master Teh Shao of T'ien T'ai mountain, Dharma successor of Fa Yen, (founder of the Fa Yen Sect) one of the five Ch'an sects of China. He journeyed to Korea where the only copy of Chih I's works existed, copied it and returned to China to revive the T'ien T'ai (Tendai) school. Died in 972 at the age of 82.

TEH SHAN: (or Te Shan). Name of master Hsuan Chien of Teh Shan mountain, Dharma successor of Lung T'an and teacher of Hsueh Feng. Died in 865 at the age of 84.

T'IEN HUI CH'E: A Ch'an master of Kao Min monastery at Yang Chou in Yung Cheng Reign (1723–35).

T'IEN KUNG: Seventh Patriarch of T'ien T'ai (Tendai) school.

T'IEN LUNG: Ch'an master T'ien Lung of Hang Chou, disciple of Ta Mei and teacher of Chu Ti. Died in the ninth century.

T'IEN T'AI: Jap. Tendai. A Buddhist school which bases its tenets on the Lotus

Sūtra, Mahāparinirvāṇa Sūtra and Mahāprajñāpāramitā Sūtra and maintains the identity of the absolute and the world of phenomena, thus attempting to unlock the secrets of all phenomena by means of meditation.

TRIKĀYA: The threefold body of a Buddha, i.e. Dharma-kāya, or essential body, perceptible only to Buddhas; Sambhoga-kāya, or reward body, perceptible only to Bodhisattvas; and Nirmāṇa-kāya, or transformation body, perceptible to men.

TRIPIṬAKA: The Buddhist canon consisting of three divisions: sūtras (sermons), vinaya (rules of discipline) and śāstras (treatises).

TRI-SAHASRA-MAHĀ-SAHASRA-LOKA-DHĀTU: A great chiliocosm. Mount Sumeru and its seven surrounding continents, eight seas and ring of iron mountains form one small world; 1,000 of these form a small chiliocosm; 1,000 of these small chiliocosms form a medium chiliocosm; 1,000 of these form a great chiliocosm, which consists of 1,000,000,000 small worlds.

TṚṢṆĀ: Thirst, desire, craving; the eighth of the twelve links in the chain of existence.

TRUE WORD SCHOOL: Chen Yen Tsung in Chinese and Shingon in Japanese. This esoteric sect is attributed to Vairocana through Vajrasattva, then through Nāgārjuna to Vajramati and to Amoghavajra.

TS'AO CH'I: Ts'ao Stream, also the name of the district where the Ts'ao Ch'i winds its course, and where the monastery of the Sixth Patriarch was erected.

TS'O CH'I: The eighth Patriarch of T'ien T'ai (Tendai) school.

TZU YANG: An eminent Taoist, well-versed in Ch'an; his works attested his realization of the mind. Emperor Yung Cheng considered him as a real Ch'an Buddhist and included his works in The Imperial Selection of Ch'an Sayings.

UCCHEDADARŚANA: The view that death ends life, in contrast with the view that personality is permanent—both views being heterodox; the heretics' view of world extinction and end of causation.

UDĀNA: Impromptu, unsolicited addresses; one of the twelve divisions of the Mahāyāna canon.

UNITY-WITH-DIFFERENTIATION: Oneness and otherness; monism and pluralism.

UNRECORDABLE: See Avyākṛta.

UPĀDĀNA: Laying hold of, grasping; the ninth of the twelve links in the chain of existence.

UPADEŚA: Discourses and discussions by question and answer; one of the twelve divisions of the Mahāyāna canon.

UPĀDHYĀYA: A general term for a monk.

UPĀSAKA: A male lay disciple who engages to observe the first five rules of morality.

UPĀSIKĀ: A female lay disciple who engages to observe the first five rules of morality.

UPEKṢĀ: Indifference, renunciation, giving up all things or rising above all feelings. The last of the Four Immeasurables.

VAIPULYA: Expanded sūtras; one of the twelve divisions of the Mahāyāna canon.

VAIROCANA: The Dharma-kāya of Śākyamuni Buddha; His Sambhogakāya being called Locana and Nirmāṇa-kāya, Śākyamuni.

VAJRACCHEDIKĀ-PRAJÑĀ-PĀRAMITĀ SŪTRA: The Diamond Sūtra.

VAJRA-KING SWORD: The indestructible sword of wisdom.

VAJRAMATI: An Indian guru who came to China A.D. 619 to introduce the True Word School.

VAJRASATTVA: A form of Samantabhadra, reckoned as the second of the eight Patriarchs of the True Word School.

VARGAS, THE FOUR: Monks, nuns, male and female devotees.

VASUBHANDHU: The twenty-first Patriarch of the Ch'an sect.

VEDANĀ: The second aggregate (skandha); reception, sensation, feeling, the functioning of mind and senses in connection with affairs and things. Also the seventh of the twelve links in the chain of existence.

VIJÑĀNA: The fifth aggregate (skandha); mental faculty in regard to perception and cognition, discriminative of affairs and things. Consciousness. Also the third of the twelve links in the chain of existence.

VIMALAKĪRTI: 'Spotless Reputation', name of a native of Vaiśālī, said to be an avatar of 'The Golden Grain Tathāgata' appearing in the form of a upāsaka to assist Śākyamuni Buddha in converting people to the Mahāyāna doctrine.

VINAYA-PIṬAKA: One of the three divisions of the Mahāyāna canon or Tripiṭaka. It emphasizes the discipline and morality. The other divisions are: sūtras (sermons) and śāstras (treatises).

VIRŪḌHAKA: Crystal King, known as the Evil-Born-King, who killed and supplanted his father, king of Śrāvastī.

VĪRYA: The fourth pāramitā; zeal and progress.

VOID-PATIENCE: Patience or endurance attained by regarding all things as void or unreal.

VOIDNESS, ABSOLUTE: Complete vacuity, reality.

VOIDNESS, RELATIVE: Incomplete vacuity.

VYĀKARAṆA: Prophecies, one of the twelve divisions of the Mahāyāna canon.

WEI TO: One of the generals under the Southern Deva king, guardian in a monastery; his vow was to protect the Buddha-dharma in the eastern, western and southern continents.

WEN SHU: Chinese name of Mañjuśrī.

WISDOM OF EQUALITY: The wisdom of rising above such distinctions as I and Thou, thus being rid of the ego idea, and wisdom in regard to all things equally and universally.

WORLD-DHARMA: The world-law, or law of this world, especially of birth and death.

WU: No. Not. (See Chao Chou for his 'no' kung an.)

WU: Awakening. (Jap. Satori.)

WU CHU (WEN HSI): Eminent Ch'an master, disciple of Yang Shan. Died in 900 at the age of 80.

WU T'AI: The Five-Peaked mountain in China; Bodhimaṇḍala of Mañjuśrī where it is said that he appeared sometimes as a beggar or an old man.

WU TENG HUI YUAN: Five Lamps Meeting at the Source, a collection of Ch'an texts, compiled in the Sung dynasty (960–1279). 20 vols.

WU WEI: Asaṁskṛta, anything not subject to cause, condition or dependence; out of time, eternal, inactive, transcendental.

YĀNA: Vehicle.

YANG SHAN: Dharma-successor of Kuei Shan and co-founder of Kuei Yang Sect (Jap. Ikyō Zen). Died in the ninth century.

YEAR OF THE DONKEY: In China an animal is chosen as a symbol for each lunar year; as a donkey was not chosen, the year of the donkey never comes round.

YEN CH'E: Dharma alias of Master Hsu Yun when he was ordained at Ku Shan monastery in 1859.

YEN KUAN: Master Ch'i An of Yen Kuan, Dharma successor of Ma Tsu. Eighth century.

YEN SHOU OF YUNG MING: Famous Ch'an master, Dharma successor of state-master Teh Shao. Said to be an avatar of Amitābha Buddha; he wrote the extensive collection 'The Sect's Mirror' (Tsung Ching Lu) in which he linked all the seemingly contradictory Buddhist doctrines to one reality. Died in 975 at the age of 72.

YEN T'OU: Master Ch'uan Huo of Yen T'ou, Dharma successor of Teh Shan. Died in 887 at the age of 60.

YO SHAN: Master Wei Yen of Yo Shan mountain, successor of Shih T'ou and teacher of Yun Yen. Died in 834 at the age of 84.

YOGĀCĀRYA: Yogācārya-bhūmi-śāstra, translated by Hsuan Tsang who introduced it into China in 647.

YU HSUAN YU LU: The Imperial Selection of Ch'an Sayings, a collection compiled by emperor Yung Cheng (1723–35), 14 vols.

YUAN MIAO OF KAO FENG: Eminent Ch'an master in the Sung dynasty. Dharma successor of Yun Yen and master of Chung Feng. Died in 1295.

YUN MEN: Master Wen Yen of Yun Men monastery, founder of the Yun Men Sect, one of the five Ch'an sects of China. Died in 949.

YUNG CHENG: Third emperor of the Ch'ing (Manchu) dynasty; was well-versed in Ch'an and used to hold in the imperial palace Ch'an weeks which produced enlightened masters and upāsakas (1723–35).

YUNG CHIA: Ch'an master Hsuan Chueh of Yung Chia attained enlightenment the day he called on the Sixth Patriarch for instruction and was called 'The overnight Enlightened One'. He wrote the 'Yung Chia' collection and composed the famous 'Song of Enlightenment' which was read all over the country and translated into Sanskrit later. Died in 712.

YU WEI: *See* Saṁskṛta.

Index